INVESTMENTS
IN FAILURE

INVESTMENTS IN FAILURE

FIVE GOVERNMENT ENTERPRISES THAT COST THE CANADIAN TAXPAYER BILLIONS

Sandford F. Borins

Associate Professor of Business and Public Policy
Faculty of Administrative Studies
York University

with

Lee Brown

MBA, Faculty of Administrative Studies
York University

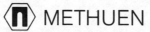 METHUEN

Toronto • New York • London • Sydney • Auckland

Canadian Cataloguing in Publication Data

Borins, Sandford F., 1949–
    Investments in failure

Includes bibliographical references and index.
ISBN 0-458-80340-5

1. Government business enterprises — Canada —
Case studies.   2. Government lending — Canada —
Case studies.   3. Business mortality — Canada —
Case studies.   4. Industry and state — Canada —
Case studies.   I. Brown, Lee.   II. Title.

HD4005.B67 1986   351.009′2′0971   C86-093548-5

Reprinted by permission of the Harvard Business Review.
Excerpt from "Strategies of technology-based business" by
H. Igor Ansoff and John M. Stewart (November-December
1967). Copyright © 1967 by the President and Fellows of
Harvard College. All rights reserved.

Cover design: Susan Hedley

Printed and bound in Canada
1 2 3 4   86   90 89 88 87

ACKNOWLEDGEMENTS

Social science research, today more than ever, is a collective enterprise, and thus it is fitting that we should express our appreciation to those who helped bring this book to fruition. Financial support for the research was provided by the Economic Council of Canada and the Faculty of Administrative Studies of York University. The Max Bell Business-Government Studies Program has invested in the publication itself; it is our hope that the book's sales will allow the investment to be recouped. Our publisher, Methuen of Canada, speeded along in transforming the manuscript into a book. The assistance of Herb Hilderley, Anita Miecz-nikowski, Cathy Munro, and editor Sonia Kuryliw Paine was greatly appreciated.

A number of colleagues have taken the time to read through the entire manuscript and offer a good deal of constructive criticism. Our thanks go to William Stanbury, Bruce Doern, Jeanne Kirk Laux, John Langford, and James Gillies. Participants' comments at a seminar given by Professor Borins to the Faculty of Administration at Ottawa University were also helpful.

Had we confined our research strictly to what was on the public record, our accounts would have lost much of their richness. We owe a great debt to the many people who agreed to be interviewed and who, in some instances, made available to us documents which, for reasons we consider self-serving and illegitimate, were kept from public view. Some interviewees' words are in the text and their name in the footnotes; others requested anonymity. Either way, we are deeply in their debt.

Although our research project was something of a collective enterprise, the actual book is our own, and as such we take full responsibility for the views expressed therein.

CONTENTS

LIST OF TABLES

INDEX OF ABBREVIATIONS

ADA	Area Development Agency
ADL	Arthur D. Little and Co.
AECL	Atomic Energy of Canada Limited
CANDU	Canada Deuterium Uranium Reactor
CCI	Consolidated Computers Incorporated
CDIC	Canada Development Investment Corporation
CFI	Churchill Forest Industries
CGE	Canadian General Electric
DCL	Deuterium of Canada Limited
DND	Department of National Defence
DREE	Department of Regional Economic Expansion
DRIE	Department of Regional Industrial Expansion
EDB	Enterprise Development Board
GAAB	General Adjustment Assistance Board
GAAP	General Adjustment Assistance Program
GATT	General Agreement on Tariffs and Trade
ICL	International Computers Limited
IEL	Industrial Estates Limited
ITC	Industry, Trade and Commerce (Department of)
JBSC	James Bertram and Sons (Canada) Limited
Manfor	Manitoba Forestry Resources Limited
MDA	Manitoba Development Authority
MDF	Manitoba Development Fund
MITI	Ministry of International Trade and Industry
MPI	MP Industrial
NDP	New Democratic Party
ODC	Ontario Development Corporation
OEM	Original Equipment Manufacturer
PAC	Public Accounts Committee
PAIT	Program for the Advancement of Industrial Technology
SYSCO	Sydney Steel Corporation

INVESTMENTS
IN FAILURE

1

Introduction

It has become a tenet of conventional wisdom in Canada that one appropriate role for government is to act as a source of capital. A number of arguments have been made to support this belief. First, it is claimed that certain types of socially desirable investment are too large and/or too risky for the private sector to undertake. Then, both the alleged extreme risk aversion and lack of entrepreneurial ability of the Canadian populace imply that any lone visionary would be unable to entice enough partners to carry his or her project through to fruition. Without the government, where would such visionaries turn? To the banks? Until the last decade or so, Canadian banks took pride in never knowingly taking a risk. To venture capitalists? Venture capital is a very new art in Canada, and still insufficiently developed.

One way to assess the validity of these arguments is to examine the effectiveness of government on several occasions when it did play the role of capitalist. This book examines five cases when government, either federal or provincial, acted as banker by providing funding for major new enterprises, with commercial results that were disastrous. Thus this book casts considerable doubt on the desirability of government serving as banker or venture capitalist. In four of the five cases, the initiators and owners of the enterprises were private-sector firms, and the fifth was a government-owned, but loosely controlled, corporation. Government financing took the form of equity, direct loans, or loan guarantees. The enterprises involved the development of new products that were to be exported or were import-substitutes. The enterprises also had as objectives regional economic development, or "province-building," and job creation. In every case, the projects failed so dismally to achieve their commercial goals that they gained public notoriety. Furthermore, in each case, the commercial failures required the government to take the project over, either by converting it to a Crown corporation, by managing it more closely if it were already government-owned, or by shutting it down.

In order to provide a better sense of the outcomes that we will be explaining, we begin with a brief outline of each of the five cases.

In the early 1960s, Atomic Energy of Canada Limited, a federal Crown corporation, called for bids to supply heavy water for the nuclear reactor program. The contract went to Deuterium of Canada, a com-

pany founded by an American heavy-water expert and backed by the
Nova Scotia government. Deuterium of Canada began to build a heavy-
water plant in Glace Bay, Nova Scotia, but could not complete it. As a
result, the project had to be taken over by Atomic Energy of Canada
Limited. Ultimately, the plant opened almost ten years behind schedule and cost over four times what it cost Canadian General Electric to
build a plant of similar capacity on the other side of Cape Breton Island.
Why was the Glace Bay plant such a disaster?

With financing from the government of New Brunswick, Malcolm
Bricklin attempted to develop an innovative sports car at a time when
barriers to entry into the North American auto market were falling. A
number of foreign firms succeeded in entering. Why did Bricklin fail,
thus causing substantial embarrassment as well as a 25-million-dollar
loss for the government of New Brunswick?

Canadair, a federally owned aircraft manufacturer, attempted to
develop a new executive aircraft, using the work of the famous aircraft
designer Bill Lear. There was a niche in the aircraft market for the
Challenger; had Canadair been more effective and efficient, its product could have been profitable. Why, then, was the ultimate product
millions of dollars over budget, years behind schedule, and unable to
meet its original specifications? Why did the Challenger result in a write-
off of over a billion dollars?

The Manitoba government wanted the private sector to establish an
integrated forestry complex in northern Manitoba. After six years of
offering ever-larger packages of incentives to investors, the government
finally found one. Unfortunately, the forestry complex ended up costing approximately twice what industry experts estimated it should have
cost, with much of the cost attributed to misuse of government funds by
the investors. Why?

Finally, there is the case of Consolidated Computer, a Canadian company that began its life as a glamour stock, since it was one of the first to
develop the interactive computer terminal. The founders of the company began by asking the government to play the role of venture capitalist
and soon lost their company to the government, which put it into
receivership, restructured it, and then ran it unsuccessfully for a decade,
ultimately losing about $120 million. Why did these events occur?

While researching these stories, we became increasingly indignant.
As citizens and taxpayers, we came to resent bitterly these ill-advised
decisions that wasted so many millions of dollars. Though these decisions created some jobs, the jobs were usually temporary and, by virtue
of the failures of the projects themselves, bereft of the self-esteem that
comes from participating in a successful venture. The reader will find
that we have expressed our anger in harsh and sardonic judgements about
the individuals and management systems we believe were jointly responsible for these failures. However, anger is not enough. We have tried to

draw some lessons from these experiences so that similar disasters will not occur.

This study should be of interest to both the business community and the public sector. For many years, the federal and provincial governments have been actively providing support for business, sometimes on a small scale, by means of grant and subsidy programs, and sometimes on a large scale, by playing the role of banker or venture capitalist. The recession of the early 1980s, which led to a number of corporate bailouts, called forth many instances of large-scale support. Furthermore, the present federal government has made it very clear that one of its key objectives is to work together with the private sector. We wish to sound a cautionary note in this new era of relatively good business/government relations and to urge the business community to consider what happened when government played the role of venture capitalist in these five cases and how the government's performance differed from that which might have been expected of other investors. Businesspeople who are aware of these episodes might ask themselves whether they want to approach the government at all. If they decide to, they should at least do so with their eyes open, understanding what the risks are.

This book is also intended for public-sector managers, in particular those responsible for the oversight of Crown corporations, mixed enterprises, or government lending agencies. Hopefully, they will come to understand the lack of monitoring and control that contributed to these sorry outcomes. If goverment wishes to continue playing the role of venture capitalist, which it probably will, awareness of these cases should at least improve its performance.

ORIGINS OF THE BOOK

We cannot claim that the initiative for writing this book was our own. As part of a much larger study of government enterprise, we were commissioned by the Economic Council of Canada to write a report on these five cases of what it called "government enterprise gone awry." The Economic Council chose not to publish the original report, which then became the basis for this book.

The major reason the Economic Council did not publish the report was that its staff and officers differed with us on the appropriate treatment of the historical evidence. The Economic Council expected to receive a report that said that these disasters were due to the incentives affecting the politicians, bureaucrats, and capitalists. The Economic Council evidently accepts the "public choice" model of political economy, according to which all politicians have an incentive to stay in power, all bureaucrats an incentive to maximize their influence with politicians, and all entrepreneurs an incentive to maximize their profits. Furthermore, all behave rationally in accordance with their incentives. Thus,

in the council's view, it was the intrinsic nature of the situations that led
to these disasters. Furthermore, the council would probably claim that
the actual identity of the politicians, bureaucrats, and entrepreneurs
would not have affected the outcomes; anyone facing those incentives
would have done as these individuals did.

We have both been trained in economics and we recognize how such
training could lead to these views. Economists use doctrines of rational-
ity and self-interest to explain events; if one assumes that all actors are
rational, and that individuals have similar objective functions, similar
behaviour should result. Economics has never tried to explain the
behaviour of particular individuals; rather it has attempted to explain
group phenomena based on assumptions about the behaviour of identical,
or at least representative, individuals. Thus we can understand why economists should be uncomfortable with our approach.

However, we reject the economists' view. We have come to feel that it
is too restrictive to produce valid explanations of historical events. We
think that it must be augmented with information about the individuals who were in the key decision-making roles. This conclusion has
emerged from our reading of the literature on public policy, from the
senior author's previous research in public policy, which clearly showed
the importance of individual actors, and from the evidence we have
gathered in this case.[1] Thus, we have emphasized the role of individuals
and we have assessed their responsibility for the outcomes. It is these
assessments which the Economic Council found unacceptable and which
led to its decision not to publish the original report.

Despite refusing to publish the report itself, the Economic Council
did what dedication to the dissemination of knowledge would dictate —
it agreed to release the copyright to us so that we could find a publisher.
We think that this action is magnanimous, in the sense that the council
permitted us to contribute our evidence to the debate about the most
appropriate way to study the evolution of public policy, whether solely
by means of incentive-based models of rational behaviour, or by means
of a more historical approach, which emphasizes the role played by
individuals. Ultimately, our readers must judge for themselves.

STRUCTURE OF THE BOOK

This book looks at the five companies from a life-cycle perspective, comparing them at several phases in their development. Chapter 2 looks at
the governments' initial decisions to invest, attempting to determine
whether they were motivated primarily to maintain their political power.
Chapter 3 looks at what went wrong. We hypothesize four reasons for
failure: adverse changes in the firm's environment, which management
could not have foreseen and over which it had no control; bad political
decisions; management errors; and failures of the governments' system

of monitoring management. These will all be explored in order to determine the importance of each factor in explaining a failure. Chapter 4 looks at the concluding phase of each project, contrasting those projects from which government decided to disinvest to those which, despite the financial problems, it attempted to keep in operation. Finally, Chapter 5 attempts to draw some conclusions and make policy recommendations.

METHODOLOGY

In order to carry out this exercise in comparative history, we had to undertake five detailed corporate histories. We began by using public sources such as books, newspaper and magazine articles, public archive materials, and royal commission reports. In some cases (the Manitoba forestry complex) the public sources were excellent, whereas in others (Consolidated Computer), they were very poor. We supplemented our examination of public sources with interviews and attempts to obtain private documents and files. Although we obtained 37 interviews and some documents, we were unable to do as many interviews and examine as many documents as we would have liked. Some of the people we wanted to interview had died, some could not be located, and some refused to cooperate. Some documents were classified as confidential advice to ministers and thus are excluded from the provisions of the 1983 federal Access to Information Act or comparable provincial statutes. Yet, despite these limitations, we feel that we have captured the essence and much of the detail of the five cases and so have some confidence in the conclusions and recommendations based on this research.

Finally, we wish the reader to recognize that our cases are not a random sample drawn from all instances where the public sector has played the role of venture capitalist or lender of last resort. Some cases (e.g., the loan guarantees to Chrysler) have been successful. If there are public-management scholars (or, for that matter, any of our readers) who feel that we have been unduly critical of the performance of government as venture capitalist or loan guarantor, let them come forward to provide a contrasting study of the success stories, for such a comparison can only contribute to the advancement of knowledge.

2

The Decision to Invest

INTRODUCTION

When the politicians decided to undertake the projects discussed in this book, they knew they were taking risks, but they expected something other than disaster. Indeed, no rational politician would want to invest public money in a project that he/she was almost certain would turn out to be a fiasco. In this chapter, we attempt to analyse the reasons why the politicians decided to make these investments and, insofar as it is possible, to re-create their expectations.

And so we attempt to explain how government got involved in the first place; did the entrepreneurs approach the government or vice versa? Who in the government were the advocates of investment in these projects: the politicians, their advisers, or both? Were alternative ways of achieving the government's objectives examined and compared with these projects? Finally, as a prelude to the following chapter, which examines why disaster occurred, we will consider how the decisions were implemented, that is, the instrument the government used (loans, loan guarantees, or equity participation) and the monitoring system established to oversee the investments.

In examining the investment decisions, we turn for theoretical guidance to the "public choice" paradigm. This paradigm, developed by the conservative American economists Buchanan and Tullock, has gained a great deal of popularity in Canadian academic circles as well. To quote some of the paradigm's most enthusiastic Canadian proponents, Trebilcock, Prichard, Hartle, and Dewees[1]:

> In our framework of analysis, political decision-makers have only one ultimate objective in all policy decisions — promoting their prospects of re-election (vote maximization) and both the choice of interests or values to be advanced and the choice of instrument by which they are to be advanced will be evaluated by them against this benchmark.[2]

Proponents of the public choice paradigm have developed as a corollary to this approach the marginal voter hypothesis, which holds that the policies chosen by governments are designed to confer their benefits on uncommitted or "swing" voters in swing constituencies: those who are most likely to shift from one party to another. The costs of such policies are likely to be spread widely over the electorate, so as not to be noticed, or to be borne by infra-marginal voters, that is, those who are strongly committed either to oppose or support the government. Well-organized interest groups are considered to behave as marginal voters. Regions of high unemployment are also thought to contain many marginal voters, which would impel the government to favour them with job-creation projects. In addition, in order to make voters clearly aware of the benefits they are receiving, vote-maximizing incumbents will enact such policies just before an election and announce them with great fanfare. Stated in this way, the marginal voter hypothesis sounds like a sophisticated version of old-fashioned pork-barrel politics.

Although pork-barrel is much of what politics is about, it isn't the whole story, and, indeed, more reflective analysts would recognize this. When competing for votes in elections, a party cannot promise to concentrate all the benefits of its policies on marginal voters alone, because, as these actual or proposed benefits become visible to the rest of the electorate, they will realize that they are being excluded, thus reducing the probability that the party will win their votes. Furthermore, voters make their decisions based on limited information and often do not care to gain additional information. Under such circumstances, the key factors affecting the election may be one or two major, often symbolic, issues perceived to be of general concern, as well as the perceived qualities ("images") of the party leaders.

In this chapter, therefore, we will examine when in a political mandate the projects were undertaken and who their beneficiaries were likely to be, so as to determine whether they were intended to ingratiate the government to marginal voters or organized interest groups, or whether they were a response to the broadly based sentiments that underlie symbolic or leadership politics.

DEUTERIUM OF CANADA LIMITED

Deuterium of Canada had its origins in the development of the CANDU reactor in the 1950s and 1960s.[3] Unlike other reactors which use enriched uranium, the CANDU reactor uses ordinary uranium, which is in plentiful supply in Canada. In order to control the nuclear reaction in the CANDU reactor, "heavy water" is required. (In enriched uranium reactors, ordinary water can perform the same function.) Heavy water is a compound containing two atoms of deuterium instead of the two atoms of hydrogen in ordinary water. Heavy water behaves chemically the same way as ordinary water, but, because the nucleus of deuterium is heavier than the nucleus of hydrogen, it is 10 percent heavier than ordinary water. A CANDU reactor requires an initial supply of several hundred tons of heavy water, which, assuming proper storage, should be sufficient for its life.

Heavy water occurs naturally as one in every 7000 parts of ordinary water. Heavy water cannot be separated chemically from ordinary water, so physical procedures based on the slight difference in densities between the two must be used. Jerome Spevack, an American atomic scientist who had worked on the Manhattan Project during the Second World War, went into business privately in 1946 as a consulting engineer, and by 1949 had developed (but not patented) a commercially viable procedure for the large-scale separation of heavy water. Spevack's process involves the mixing of natural water with hydrogen sulphide gas in a tower and circulating the mixture through hot and cold zones. The hydrogen and deuterium atoms interchange freely between the water and the hydrogen sulphide, with the deuterium tending to concentrate in cold water and hot hydrogen sulphide. After many hot and cold stages, the deuterium gradually collects together and water containing 30 percent heavy water is obtained at the end of the process. Pure heavy water can then be distilled by electrolysis.

In 1949, Spevack approached the United States Atomic Energy Commission with his proposals for heavy-water production. The following year, the Atomic Energy Commission, as part of its program to develop a hydrogen bomb, contracted with Dupont and the Girdler Corporation to build two heavy-water plants using Spevack's process. Spevack was employed as a consultant. The plants, at Dana, Indiana, and Savannah River, South Carolina, were completed in 1952, and each could produce 200 tons of heavy water per year. The plants met American needs for heavy water for experimental purposes for the next two decades. However, because the Americans developed reactors using enriched uranium, they had little commercial demand for heavy water. Thus they had enough during the 1950s to supply Canada's needs for heavy water, charging U.S. $28.50 per pound. By 1959, the demand for heavy water had diminished sufficiently to close down the Indiana plant.

Jerome Spevack left the Girdler Corporation in 1953 and went back into private business. In 1956, the Atomic Energy Commission proposed to declassify Spevack's unpatented heavy-water production process and publish the details on 1 February 1957. Spevack fought the commission in court to prevent publication. After winning legal sanction from the U.S. Supreme Court in 1958, Spevack obtained his patent in 1959. While the litigation was going on, Spevack was fearful that the material would be published. Thus, on 1 February 1957, he wrote to Lorne Gray, the president of the Crown-owned Atomic Energy of Canada Limited (AECL), advising that there was a possibility heavy water could be produced for a price as low as $10 per pound. Spevack proposed that Canada produce its own heavy water instead of buying from the American Atomic Energy Commission, now Spevack's adversary. Spevack, of course, would be a consultant to AECL. However, Gray wrote back that AECL had no plans to produce heavy water at that time.[4]

By the early 1960s, the situation had changed. AECL's Chalk River reactor was nearing completion and its Douglas Point reactor was under construction. The latter would require 200 tons of heavy water, or an entire year's production at the one American heavy-water plant still in operation. In addition, if there were to be more CANDU reactors, an assured source of supply of heavy water would be a necessity. In 1961, Dupont of Canada (whose parent corporation built the two American heavy-water plants), discussed with the federal and Nova Scotia governments the possibility of building a $50-million heavy-water plant near Sydney, Nova Scotia.[5] Also that year, Spevack obtained a Canadian patent for his process. In June 1962, he incorporated Deuterium of Canada Limited (DCL), a subsidiary of the Deuterium Corporation, of which he was president. The following August, he approached AECL with a proposal to build a 200-ton per-annum heavy-water plant if AECL would guarantee to buy its product at a price slightly less than that being charged by the Atomic Energy Commission.

At that point, AECL decided that there was sufficient interest in constructing a heavy-water plant that it sent a request for preliminary proposals to the following five companies: British American Oil, Union Carbide of Canada, Cominco, Dupont of Canada, and Deuterium of Canada. Based on the preliminary proposals that were submitted, the federal minister of Trade and Commerce, who was responsible for AECL, recommended to Cabinet that it invite proposals from Canadian companies for a 200-ton/year heavy-water plant, and that AECL buy up to 1000 tons of heavy water from the plant at a price not to exceed $22 per pound. The final choice would depend on the extent of Canadian content and financing of the plant, as well as the price for the heavy water. The Diefenbaker Cabinet accepted the recommendation and set a deadline for the proposals of 31 May 1963.[6]

Dupont of Canada did not bid on the grounds that it felt that future demand for heavy water was uncertain. Ultimately, four offers were made to build the plant. The prices for the deuterium ranged from $19 to $22 per pound, and the plants would cost around $30 million. The four bidders were DCL, Dynamic Power Corporation of Calgary, Imperial Oil, and Western Deuterium Company Limited of Victoria, B.C., which was a subsidiary of a major west-coast shipbuilder and heavy-machinery producer.

DCL originally proposed to build the plant in Alberta, using natural gas for fuel and fresh water as raw material. Its asking price for the heavy water was the lowest of the four offers. The plant, designed by the New York engineering firm of Burns and Roe, would cost about $30 million. DCL assured the government that financing would be readily available in Canada.[7]

Initially, the proposals were examined by AECL. DCL had the lowest price, while Western Deuterium had the highest Canadian participation. The Dynamic Power Corporation proposal had the disadvantage of having to ask the federal government to guarantee its first mortgage bonds. Whereas Imperial Oil had the advantage of being able to finance the project internally, it had the disadvantage of being foreign-controlled.

Without a clear winner, AECL proposed that the minister of Defence Production should prepare a supplementary memo considering the proposals further in terms of their location, employment aspects, and the costs of production. This was accepted by the new Pearson Cabinet on 27 June 1963.[8]

At about this time, Spevack and his lawyer, Alex MacIntosh of the prominent Toronto firm of Blake Cassels, realized that the DCL proposal would stand a better chance of winning if it had more Canadian content. MacIntosh, originally from Nova Scotia, told Spevack about Industrial Estates Limited (IEL).[9] A Nova Scotia Crown corporation whose purpose is to stimulate the growth of secondary manufacturing in the province by attracting new industry and encouraging existing industry to expand, IEL was begun in 1957 by the Conservative government of Robert Stanfield, and was the first industrial-development Crown corporation in Canada. By 1963 it had made loans to companies such as Canada Envelope, Oxford Desk, Phillips Cables, and Volvo (Canada). These loans ranged in size from about $30,000 to over $1.5 million, with the average falling in the $100,000 to $800,000 range.[10] Spevack decided to take his proposal to them.

By August 1963, IEL and DCL had reached an agreement whereby the plant would be located in Glace Bay, Nova Scotia, using sea water as raw material and powered by steam produced by burning local coal. The Nova Scotia Power Commission claimed that it could supply steam at the price of $.25 per million BTU. Burns and Roe, the engineering firm that helped Spevack prepare his proposal, had estimated that it would cost $2 million less to use salt water than to draw fresh water from a nearby river. IEL would become a 40-percent shareholder in DCL and it would also lend DCL $12 million after DCL had raised $18 million on its own.[11]

The federal Department of Finance, which was involved in the review of the proposals, taking the nationalist position espoused by its minister, Walter Gordon, still objected to the ownership structure of DCL. Therefore, in October, Spevack signed a new contract with IEL, which conceded that IEL would hold 51 percent of the shares of DCL and appoint a majority of the board of directors. DCL would have to raise $18 million by selling first mortgage bonds in Canada before IEL would provide $12 million in second mortgage bonds, and Spevack would have to make his patents available to DCL. However, Spevack would still be president and chief executive officer of DCL, and Burns and Roe would design and engineer the Glace Bay plant.[12]

With the revised DCL proposal now in place, the bureaucracy considered the four contenders. AECL and the departments of Finance,

Industry, and Trade and Commerce all recommended the Western Deuterium Company proposal. They liked the fact that the company would provide its own financing and had three possible energy sources, all of which were cheaper than DCL's.[13] They had doubts about DCL's proposal to use salt water, which had never before been used to produce heavy water. In addition, the steam price the Nova Scotia Power Corporation quoted DCL depended on a federal government subsidy of $.91 per ton of coal. The Department of Industry calculated that this subsidy would cost the federal government more than $1 million per year for the write-off period of the plant, with the prospect of additional subsidies if the plant were ever expanded. Finally, officials of the Atomic Energy Commission had privately told AECL of their doubts regarding Spevack's capabilities.[14]

The politicians were also considering the proposals. The DCL proposal had their strongest support, with pressure coming from the provincial government, headed by Robert Stanfield, and from Allan MacEachen, minister of Labour and regional minister for Nova Scotia in the Pearson Cabinet. Awarding the contract to DCL was seen as a way of providing jobs in the Cape Breton coal mines and compensating for the nearby Point Edward naval base, which the Department of National Defence was closing down. An example of the pressure occurred in early September, when Premier Stanfield announced publicly, "We believe the Nova Scotia proposal is the best one submitted and we know of no reason why the federal government would not award the contract to a company that would locate here."[15] Linden MacIntyre, who, several years later, wrote a series of fine investigative articles about DCL for the *Halifax Chronicle-Herald*, observed that, "Every chartered group, politicians — anyone whose name had the slightest whiff of prestige — began to bombard the new Liberal federal government with resolutions and pleas."[16]

On 2 December 1963, C.M. Drury, the minister of Industry, announced that the contract for the 1000 tons of heavy water would go to DCL, which had offered the lowest bid, $20.50 per pound.[17] Paul Hellyer, who was a member of the cabinet that made the decision, said later (after having left the Liberal party):

> The discussion raged on for a considerable time. Ultimately, a decision was taken. The decision finally was strictly political. It was a private decision taken by the then Prime Minister and the present President of the Privy Council [Mr. MacEachen]. It defied economics. It was a political decision pure and simple.[18]

Although the DCL proposal was chosen primarily for political reasons, the presence of Jerome Spevack, the acknowledged world expert on deuterium separation technology, undoubtedly gave it technical legitimacy. As Gordon Sims, the author of a thorough dissertation on AECL, suggests, because AECL lacked comparable expertise on the construction of heavy-water plants, it was in a weak position:

> Although the technical staff at AECL had grave misgivings about technical aspects of the proposed DCL process, it would have been very difficult for them to have opposed the DCL proposal on these grounds. If they had, there would inevitably have been a technical wrangle with DCL in which the comparative inexperience of the AECL staff would have been pitted against the experience of Spevack, who had actually made a contribution to building heavy water plants. If AECL had 'won' this argument, it would have found itself in the position of virtually having to guarantee the technical success of whatever other plant was chosen. If it had 'lost,' this would have been an expression of the federal government's lack of faith in its own nuclear technical experts. AECL was in a 'no-win' situation.[19]

Finally, the private comments of the Atomic Energy Commission staff about Spevack would have been discounted because of the history of litigation between Spevack and the commission.

BRICKLIN

The Bricklin story is that of a single-minded promoter who was searching for someone to invest money in his dream of developing a sports car which would bear his name. He ultimately found his investor in Premier Richard Hatfield of New Brunswick.

Malcolm Bricklin got his start franchising hardware stores in the United States in the early 1960s. After being sued by several dissatisfied franchisees in 1964, the chain filed for bankruptcy. Bricklin's next major endeavour was importing and franchising the Subaru automobile in the United States. His pattern of behaviour here was similar to the hardware chain: he promised more than he could deliver, franchisees became angry with poor service, banks were pressing for repayment, and Bricklin was ultimately bought out of the business. Bricklin then attempted to franchise leisure racetracks, on which people would race the small Subarus that he had received in settlement for leaving the Subaru importing business. This idea did not bring success but rather a breach-of-contract suit from a partner.[20]

Dabbling in the automobile industry only served to whet his appetite: Bricklin decided to develop an automobile of his own. He wanted it to have a fibreglass body, which he felt would be cheap, safe, and easily replaceable. The body would look something like that of the Datsun 240Z, which was then becoming very popular, but it would have gull-wing doors, similar to some of the early Mercedes sports cars. In 1971, Bricklin incorporated a Delaware firm, General Vehicle. By late 1972, a custom car designer had succeeded in building a prototype, using parts from many other manufacturers. Because of the availability of some

six-cylinder engines from Chrysler, the car increased in weight from
a planned 1600 pounds to 2200 pounds. With a short film of his prototype, Bricklin searched for investors and succeeded in raising $950,000
from Philadelphia and New York banks. He then rented a building in
Livonia, Michigan, and hired some production personnel to make a
production model of the prototype. Planning to begin production in
March 1973, he looked for a factory. He also hired a sales executive who
had worked for Renault in their St. Bruno, Quebec plant and who found
six dealers willing to place orders for 2000 cars. The sales executive
then suggested he look at the St. Bruno plant, which Renault intended
to close.[21]

Bricklin approached the Quebec government in late 1972, offering a
minority position in the project in exchange for financing of $7 million.
The Quebec government hired Jean de Villers, a former Renault executive, to investigate Bricklin's proposal. De Villers, concluding that
Bricklin's managerial ability was unproven, recommended turning the
proposal down, which the Quebec government did. Bricklin's accountant then contacted a friend in Montreal, who suggested that Bricklin
approach Multiplex Corporation, a federal-provincial economic-develop-
ment corporation based in Saint John, New Brunswick.[22]

After some meetings in March 1973 with Bricklin and his staff, which
now included Jean de Villers as president of Bricklin Canada, the Multiplex Corporation staff quickly prepared a short report to the federal
Department of Regional Economic Expansion (DREE), asking for a grant
of $4 million.[23] The Multiplex report was based primarily on Bricklin's
prospectus and parts of the Quebec government report. It argued that
there was a rapidly growing sports car market, of which the Bricklin
company would be able to get a share. Sales were forecast to increase
from 10,000 in the first year to 32,000 in the fifth. Bricklin claimed to
have presold 2500 cars to U.S. dealers whose bankers would provide
$5.8 million in financing. The cars would be assembled in Saint John,
creating 264 jobs. The cars would be sold to Bricklin's American marketing company for $2172, and then sold to the American consumer
for under $5000. The 20-year return on investment was predicted to
be 18 percent without a DREE grant and 29 percent with it. The Multiplex report contained inflated descriptions of the managerial staff: for
example, Bricklin was described as having "considerable experience
with manufacturing and marketing transportation vehicles." The report
contained no discussion of the car's specifications or technology, particularly on such new developments as the gull-wing doors or the fibreglass-
acrylic body.

After the Multiplex proposal had been submitted to DREE, Richard
Fletcher, the general manager of Multiplex, had a meeting with Harry
Nason, the deputy minister of Economic Growth, and Premier Hatfield.
At the meeting, Bricklin showed them his model and film. Bricklin and

Fletcher did not then ask the New Brunswick government for any financial support; they informed Nason and Hatfield that they would soon be meeting with DREE officials regarding the grant proposal and approaching the Department of Industry, Trade and Commerce (ITC) to have Bricklin included under the Auto Pact. The latter would mean that Bricklin could buy parts duty-free in the U.S. and sell finished autos in the U.S. without having to pay American duties. Bricklin and Fletcher asked for the New Brunswick government's support in their negotiations with Ottawa. At this point, both Nason and Hatfield were relatively neutral towards the project.[24]

Ottawa's initial response was not enthusiastic. ITC was concerned that both the Americans and the Big Three auto manufacturers would object to the inclusion of an auto-maker that was a DREE-grant recipient. Now it came time for Nason and Hatfield to decide whether to give active support to Bricklin's request. Nason and his department found the Bricklin proposal quite perplexing. They had never analysed anything like it; in addition, they could not find an engineering consulting firm to help them, because all auto-industry expertise was under contract to the Big Three. Having checked into Bricklin's staff, they concluded that the staff itself had a good deal of expertise. Finally, they were impressed by the car's marketability. Ultimately, they told Hatfield that it would be a project played at long odds, but for very high stakes.[25]

Hatfield read the Multiplex report, listened to Nason, and talked with Bricklin's bankers (who, of course, were supportive of the proposal). Ultimately relying on his own intuition, he became enthusiastic about the Bricklin proposal. In retrospect, Hatfield himself admitted that, "It's not that I was ever very much interested in cars. It was the sheer sculptured beauty of the Bricklin, with its doors like gulls' wings: the idea that something so revolutionary could be made *here*, in New Brunswick."[26] In May, Hatfield met with Minister of ITC Alastair Gillespie regarding the Auto Pact, but received no support. The next week DREE also was noncommittal. These rebuffs, however, simply strengthened Hatfield's commitment. He saw the response to the Bricklin proposal as another instance in which the economic development of his province was being hindered by the excessive conservatism of a federal government dominated by central Canadian interests.

Hatfield had met with Bricklin a number of times. The chemistry between the two men was good. On discovering that Bricklin and many of his backers were Jewish, Hatfield told one of his close associates that this was reassuring, because in such a closely knit community, young entrepreneurs would have an overwhelming incentive to make good.

Word came from Ottawa that DREE could not give the Bricklin project a grant but that it would provide a loan guarantee, which would take several months to arrange. DREE wanted whatever manufacturing structure that would be established to have majority Canadian ownership. ITC was still noncommittal about including the project under the Auto Pact, but with loan guarantees rather than grants it might be possible.[27]

At this point, Hatfield had decided that the Bricklin project should go ahead. In order to make it happen, the New Brunswick government would provide $3 million in interim loan guarantees until DREE's loans came through. Hatfield gave Nason the task of drawing up a loan-guarantee agreement with Bricklin.

Nothing about the project had yet been announced. Coincidentally, a by-election was being held on June 26 to fill a Saint John seat held by a government member who had died. Hatfield felt that making an announcement on the eve of an election would be reminiscent of old-style pork-barrel politics and he ordered Nason to make sure nothing leaked.[28] However, a question was raised in the Quebec legislature about why Quebec had missed out on such a great investment opportunity.[29] Hatfield's hand thus forced, three days before the by-election, he told a Saint John press conference that Bricklin would establish an auto plant there, and that the government would provide an interim loan guarantee of $2.88 million and purchase the majority of the shares in Bricklin Canada for $500,000. Despite the announcement, the opposition Liberals won the by-election by 86 votes.[30]

The first loan-guarantee agreement with Bricklin was signed on 26 June 1973, giving the New Brunswick government, through Provincial Holdings Ltd. (a holding company for government investments), a 51-percent share in Bricklin Canada in exchange for $500,000. General Vehicle, Bricklin's American company, got the remaining 49 percent in exchange for design and development rights he claimed were worth $1 million. The province of New Brunswick would guarantee $2.88 million in loans to Bricklin. The province's participation would be contingent upon Bricklin's (1) showing that his cars would meet Canadian and U.S. standards, (2) obtaining parts supply contracts at prices comparable to those in his original proposal, and (3) obtaining another $1 million in bank financing for working capital. The agreement left the terms of management contracts with Bricklin personnel to be worked out later. For 1975, the transfer price of the automobiles would be the higher of $2200 or 125 percent of material and component costs; after 1975, it would be set to provide a profit of the greater of $100 or a 20-percent pre-tax return on total assets employed.

The New Brunswick government would have access to all the books and records of the Canadian company and the American parent and would appoint at least two of the five directors of Bricklin Canada. Bricklin Canada could draw on its loan guarantee in amounts of up to $500,000 at any one time, if it provided the government with capital budgets beforehand and evidence of the utilization of the expenditures afterwards.[31]

CANADAIR

In 1968, Canadair was a prosperous, fully integrated aircraft company and airframe component subcontractor. Located in a Montreal suburb, it employed about 9000 people and in that year made a net profit of $2.2 million on sales of $150.9 million.

Until the late 1960s, most of Canadair's activity had been military. As a manufacturer of military aircraft under contract to the Canadian government, Canadair had been a profitable operation for its American parent company, General Dynamics Corporation. However, military activity began to dry up in the late 1960s, and by the early 1970s Canadair had only a few contracts left to complete. The company's sales figures plummetted from $117.5 million in 1970 to $40 million in 1973. General Dynamics had no interest in undertaking a major revitalization of the firm, and instead began looking for a purchaser. Finally, in the midst of the company's worst year, 1975, General Dynamics announced it would close down Canadair if a purchaser could not be found.

The threat of closure created dismay within the Liberal federal government. Canadair was located in the Dollard riding of Supply and Services Minister Jean-Pierre Goyer. Although employment at the plant had decreased considerably since its peak in 1968, Canadair still employed about 2000 people, who could be expected to experience difficulty in finding new jobs in the ailing airframe industry.

In addition, Canadair had been receiving grants from both ITC and the Department of National Defence (DND) since the early 1960s. By 1975, ITC had contributed $68.5 million and DND $4.9 million.[32] These grants were all part of programs aimed at bolstering productivity and technical competence in the industries of the future, with an underlying goal of sustaining or creating employment. To shut down Canadair would therefore have meant losing the technological advances that had been achieved at a cost to taxpayers of nearly $75 million.

Two further reasons for government investment in Canadair have also been suggested.[33] Since Canada is a major consumer of aviation products, the loss of Canadair would have had an unfavourable effect on the country's balance of trade. In addition, it was deemed desirable to maintain the necessary industrial capacity for doing military offsets. However, neither of the above points was mentioned in the House of Commons; the only objective stated at that time by Don Jamieson, the minister of Industry, Trade and Commerce was "to have Canadian control over the aerospace industry."[34] Therefore, on 2 December 1975, the federal government purchased Canadair for US$39 million, or $46 million Canadian.

Jean Chrétien, who as president of the Treasury Board had advocated the purchase of Canadair, became the minister of ITC in September 1976. He asked the new board of directors of Canadair what they thought the government should do,[35] and they outlined three options: to close the company down and sell the land, which would have paid back most or all of the government's $46-million investment in Canadair; to turn the company into an aerospace subcontractor, assembling aircraft designed and developed by other firms; or to move Canadair fully into the aerospace industry by allowing it to design, develop, and manufacture its own product.

The company had not designed a new aircraft since the 1950s, when it developed the turboprop CL-44 transport plane. Despite the management team's years of experience in the aviation industry, they had seldom been involved in the development of a new civilian aircraft and had never developed a civilian jet aircraft. Furthermore, a 1975 report prepared by ITC had concluded that Canadair was not sufficiently staffed to design a new aircraft; for example, its engineering staff numbered a record low of 150.[36]

Early in 1976, Canadair president Frederick Kearns was in contact with Bill Lear, designer of the successful Learjet, who was then trying to interest manufacturers in his latest design for an executive jet. Canadair's managers were impressed with Lear's design, and felt there were profits to be made in this most rapidly growing segment of the aircraft market. Despite their lack of experience and expertise, they decided to attempt to develop Lear's design. The management team presented the project for the new aircraft, named the Challenger, to the board of directors and then to ITC Minister Jean Chrétien, who got Cabinet approval.

In its proposal Canadair told the government that it could develop the Challenger in thirty months at a cost of $106 million. If 136 aircraft could be sold and delivered by mid-1982, all development costs would be recovered. The project's peak financial requirement was forecast to be $128 million. Though senior officials at ITC were divided about whether to support the proposal, Chrétien "felt that the project was worth the gamble."[37] The government decided to finance the project by means of letters of comfort, that is, letters to lending institutions indicating a willingness to give loan guarantees.[38]

In January of 1976, just after the government had purchased Canadair, it replaced the General Dynamics representatives on the board of directors with civil servants: four from ITC and one from the Department of Justice. Among this group was Antoine Guérin, the assistant deputy minister of ITC in charge of industrial development, who had been involved in the decision to buy Canadair. In January, shortly after Cabinet had approved the Challenger project, an interdepartmental review committee was also established, comprised of one member from each of the departments of ITC, Finance, Treasury Board, and Transport, and initially chaired by Guérin.[39] As will be discussed in the next chapter, these monitoring mechanisms proved to be ineffective.

CHURCHILL FOREST INDUSTRIES

Bringing industrialization to Manitoba's forbidding north has been an issue that has concerned that province's politicians since the turn of the century. The area offers many valuable resources: rivers that could be harnessed for hydro-electric power, metals and minerals, and timber, all of which remained untapped for many years because of their inaccessibility.

However, the fervour to develop northern Manitoba did not spring entirely from the attractions of resource wealth. Since Manitoba's entry into Confederation, it never wished to become a prisoner of geography to the eastern provinces. The development of the ocean port of Churchill around the turn of the century was seen as a way of safeguarding the province's autonomy. In addition, there is the long-revered economic view that Manitoba (like the rest of Canada) cannot survive as "a string of beads along the CPR," and thus northern development was necessary to preserve not only the province's independence but its identity as well. Together, these two beliefs formed a powerful northern development ideology which had been widespread in Manitoba for many years.

In 1956, the Liberal government commissioned the U.S.-based consulting firm, Arthur D. Little (ADL), to perform a study on Manitoba's northern resources and techniques for developing them. It was published two years later under the title "Economic Survey of Northern Manitoba 1958." This report provided the first authoritative affirmation that a pulp and paper project based on Manitoba's Precambrian forests could be economically feasible and predicted that plants for the manufacture of wood pulp, newsprint, hardboard, and plywood could be established within the next decade. The report expressed the view that resource development must be carried out by private enterprise with the expectation of a reasonable return on investment, but noted that the many special problems posed by the climate and geography of the area would need to be dealt with. ADL recommended the creation of a Northern Manitoba Development Board and Development Fund.[40]

After defeating the Liberals in the election of 1958, the new Progressive Conservative government under Duff Roblin passed the *Business Development Fund Act*, which created the Manitoba Development Fund (MDF). The fund was to provide loans to help establish new industry anywhere in the province, not solely in the north. Four kinds of undertakings were eligible for loans from the fund: manufacturing, tourist accommodation or facilities, community development corporations, and other businesses that the fund's board of directors designated from time to time, subject to Cabinet approval.

The MDF's board of directors consisted of nine to twelve members appointed by Cabinet for stated terms. The vice-chairman of the fund was also the general manager "responsible for the management, direction, and control of the operations of the corporation and the day to day administration of its affairs."[41] The board of directors was empowered to set the terms under which it would offer loans and stipulate the security to be given and the terms of repayment, as well as prescribing action to be taken against borrowers in default. To protect the fund from political manipulation (and the government from accusations of favouritism), the *Business Development Fund Act* provided that all loans were to be kept confidential and that board members could not be required to give evidence regarding loans to any legislative committee or to the Legislative Assembly as a whole. The fund was capitalized at $5 million, and although it could borrow money from the private sector as well as the government, in practice it was funded solely by the government.

Less than a year after the MDF had been set up, the Manitoba Development Authority (MDA) was created to formulate northern development policy and coordinate the efforts of various government departments in this regard. The MDA consisted of a directorate, which was the policy-making body, and a board, which was the recommendation and implementation group. The directorate was, in effect, a Cabinet committee, consisting of the premier and the ministers of Industry and Commerce, Mines and Natural Resources, and Public Utilities or Public Works. The board consisted of the premier; the deputy ministers of Industry and Commerce, Mines and Natural Resources, and Public Works; the chairman of the Manitoba Hydro-Electric Board; and the general managers of the Manitoba Power Commission, Manitoba Telephone Commission, and the Manitoba Development Fund.[42] As such, Rex Grose, the deputy minister of Industry and Commerce, was to play a multiplicity of roles: in addition to being a deputy minister, he was also the vice-chairman and general manager of the MDF (and thus a member of its executive committee), as well as a member of the MDA board.

The MDA and the MDF together were intended to motivate private industry to develop the north. The MDA had the power to examine different types of incentives, such as grants, subsidies, tax holidays and so on, and to decide whether or not to offer them. The fund's purpose was to provide financing for projects which were deemed by MDF's board members to have a good chance for success. Thus at times, each body undertook projects separately, and at other times they worked in tandem. However, even when the MDA intended to offer incentives to a prospective new business, the MDF still had the responsibility of making its own decision and the authority, at least in theory, to refuse to provide financing despite the MDA's involvement.

In the fall of 1960, the MDA directorate was considering Arthur D. Little's (ADL) report entitled "Recommended Measures to Attract a Forest Products Industry to Northern Manitoba" along with a commentary on it from several deputy ministers. The report noted as obstacles the area's distance from markets and hence high freight costs, the timber's 80-year growth cycle (compared to a 20-year cycle in the southeastern United States), the high cost of townsite development, and the relative lack of experience of major companies in developing northern resources. To counteract these obstacles, ADL recommended lower-than-normal stumpage rates, absorption of fire protection costs by the government, a large timber concession, government financing for townsite planning, and guaranteed low hydro-electric rates for a prolonged period. The report also recommended against government equity participation on the grounds that it would be a detriment rather than an incentive.

The research branch of Treasury commented critically on the ADL report's incentive suggestions. They concluded that, based on the costs cited in the report, a pulp and paper operation in the north was not economically feasible at that time and recommended that attempts to induce a producer to situate there be abandoned. They also recommended:

> If there is some other reason of a nature compelling us to locate a pulp and paper operation in the Province at this time, we suggest that it would have to be a *pilot project*, and that the government *should hold back on any long-term concessions* that it might wish to make, meanwhile *retaining full control or as much of control as it can maintain for the period of the test*.
> What we are recommending in effect is that a pilot project be undertaken, and that any elaborate plans for a townsite be dropped forthwith. . . .
> If the pilot project were to prove successful, there would be plenty of time to go into townsite development at that point. If the project proved to be unsuccessful, we would not have been committed to a highly embarrassing and highly costly experiment of locating three thousand people in a wilderness community with no surviving or alternate economic justification. Of the two embarrassments — low profits on a limited project on the one hand, or the construction of an isolated model town without a purpose on the other — we would think that the latter was even less desirable than the former.[43]

In general, Treasury concluded, ADL presented accurately the main difficulties of a pulp and paper mill located in the north, but failed to present convincing arguments that these could or should be overcome by a program of incentives.

Industry and Commerce Deputy Minister Rex Grose replied in detail on 7 October 1960, stating his belief that Treasury's comments were based on inadequate knowledge of the economics of forest resource development and on undue emphasis on the costs of townsite development.

Grose believed that incentives were necessary only to counteract the disadvantages of a northern location and that the final decision to locate in the north would be a market decision:

> If it was not felt that the northern regions of Manitoba could sustain forest products development, there would be no sense whatever in the preparation of the various documents that have gone into this study. The purpose of the memorandum must be remembered: it was to outline difficulties of operating in the north and recommend various measures to overcome these difficulties. The final proof of the attractiveness of the northern area will be made when the area is developed. It would be senseless for a pulp mill, involving an investment of some $40 to $50 million, to be established if it was not going to be a profitable operation. This does not mean that *maybe it would be a profitable operation*, but that it *must be a profitable operation*. Any company developing new pulp capacities would thoroughly study all the aspects before such an investment would be made.[44]

Grose's rebuttal to Treasury's comments, in other words, was that since no privately owned company would undertake a project they did not believe would operate profitably when complete, the government would be safe in going ahead full steam with the project if a private investor showed an interest. On the one hand, ADL was counselling haste, since opportunities lost at present might never be regained; on the other, Treasury was counselling patience and prudence. In all likelihood, Grose's view prevailed over the Treasury's for two reasons. First of all, it could not have been overlooked that if a full-scale project could be negotiated before the 1962 election, its announcement would impress voters favourably at a critical time; thus Grose's recommendation was in harmony with both the objectives and the desired time-frame of the politicians.[45] Second, Premier Roblin and others in his party subscribed to the popular Manitoba view that northern development was essential to protect the autonomy and identity of the province; under the circumstances, they were probably quite easily convinced that northern development was also feasible. In any event, the MDA directorate met on 11 October 1960 and approved the incentive plan substantially as recommended by ADL. Grose was now free to use the approved incentive program in his efforts to attract a forest products producer. Despite these inducements, however, Grose was thwarted repeatedly between 1960 and 1965. In his 1976 book, former MDF legal counsel Walter C. Newman summarizes:

> Everybody else in Manitoba seemed to oppose this project notwithstanding that it had been sanctioned as a practical dream in the Arthur D. Little report of 1958. The Abitibi Power and Paper Company Ltd. not only strenuously opposed any positive effort to develop the area, but led in opposition to it the leaders of the pulp and paper industry in Canada. In northern Manitoba itself the existing sawmill operators, numbering

some 200 in number, vigorously opposed any large scale development in the north that they rightfully anticipated would affect the future of their own spotty and uncoordinated operations. The New Democratic Party (NDP) then in opposition vehemently attacked it as involving the devotion of Crown resources to exploitation by private interests.[46]

Between 1960 and 1962, Grose negotiated with the Vita-Mayer Company of Italy. Despite the favourable but cautious findings of a joint study with the Department of Industry and Commerce, the company was not convinced. In May 1962, it announced that a pulp development in northern Manitoba was not economically attractive at that time. In the months following, however, the Vita-Mayer company continued to study the feasibility of exporting pulpwood to Europe. The result was a definite proposal to establish a Canadian company to export up to 100,000 cords per year of debarked pulpwood from the Hudson Bay port of Churchill, and to continue to study the feasibility of locating a pulp mill at The Pas. From the company's point of view, a feasibility study was the logical next step. All previous studies had been based on estimated wood costs, which appeared to be (and later proved to be) overly optimistic. Since wood costs accounted at that time for 50 to 75 percent of the cost of manufacturing pulp, Vita-Mayer was anxious to find out if, in fact, the wood costs would be favourable enough to offset locational disadvantages.[47]

The export of resources in unprocessed form, however, was not what the provincial government had in mind in its plan for economic development. In September 1963, the MDA directorate decided to make the establishment of a pulp mill a pre-condition for granting the necessary timber concession. Vita-Mayer declined to make such a promise.

It should be noted that Grose, who in 1960 had stated that the viability of the project would be proven when a developer was willing to make a substantial investment in it, by the fall of 1963 had apparently become convinced that the incentives recommended by ADL would make the project viable to investors and that, in addition, a project was desirable for policy reasons. Thus on 20 April 1964, in a memorandum to his minister (Gurney Evans, minister of Industry and Commerce) Grose wrote:

> In the first place I do not believe the government can afford to wait for the development of the forest resources in [The Pas] area. Extraordinary measures are needed. Private enterprise quite properly is occupied with other matters and in fact should not be expected to accept the responsibility for locating an industry to best serve the needs of the people in that area. After all, the government's main concern in this area must be to find ways and means of providing employment to the Indian and Metis of the area. In other words, government can and must take into consideration factors that private enterprise could not be expected to be concerned with or for that matter afford to become involved with in any project.[48]

In the same memo, he expressed the conviction that the government should create and operate the forestry complex as a Crown corporation. Once its profitability was proven, it could be sold to a private interest.

Another Arthur D. Little report completed in February, 1964, on "The Feasibility of Locating a Pulp Mill at The Pas," was enthusiastic about the prospects of a profitable pulp mill at The Pas, estimating an 18.8 percent return on investment over eleven years (the projected life of the mill). Even in the least favourable circumstances, ADL had estimated a return of 14.8 percent over eleven years.

These rates of return, however, were predicated on wood costs of $14.80 per cord. Costs per cord are affected by such factors as stumpage charges, transportation costs, density of forests, size of trees, and difficulty of terrain. In view of the nature of the northern Manitoba forests, which consist of short, spindly trees, widely spaced on rocky terrain dotted by acidic bogs, a more realistic estimate would have been $20 to $25 per cord.[49] Furthermore, the report estimated the capital costs of building a pulp and paper mill at about $37 million, whereas Sandwell International (the consulting firm ADL had engaged to perform a feasibility study in 1962) had estimated the costs at $43.6 million. Later examination showed that ADL had arrived at its figure by scaling down the 1961 costs of various pieces of equipment by a straight 15 percent without giving any explanation for doing so.[50] Finally, the report still failed to deal with the marketing problem faced by the proposed mill — the problem of where and at what prices the output could be sold. Presumably, any experienced pulp and paper firm would have read the 1964 ADL report with great skepticism because of these inaccuracies.

Beginning in the summer of 1964, the Department of Industry and Commerce began to promote what was referred to as the Arnot project. A letter was sent to a number of companies in the United Kingdom, France, Italy, and Japan describing the proposed project: the establishment of an integrated pulpwood, lumber and groundwood pulp operation at Arnot, where the CNR crosses the Nelson River. The letter (signed by Grose) indicated that about 60 percent of the long-term financing would be provided by the MDF at 6½ percent. The government would agree to build without cost to the company a transmission line to the project and to provide electricity at "extremely favourable rates" for seven years. No realty or business taxes would be levied, and the province would pay $180 for each resident employee toward townsite development. Preferred cutting rights over a large area were offered for twenty years, renewable for another twenty years, and the stumpage charges levied were the lowest in Canada. In spite of these generous inducements, few of the companies contacted were even interested enough to send a reply. However, the incentives offered for the Arnot project came to serve as an important benchmark in later negotiations for the project at The Pas.

Further disappointments occurred in 1964 and early 1965. After Grose reported to Cabinet that the deal he had been negotiating with a consortium appeared to be about to fall through, the Cabinet, realizing that it was now late in its term of office, decided in July 1965 to advertise its interest in backing a pulp and paper company.[51] The widely circulated advertisement brought inquiries from a Swiss firm, Monoca A.G. On 25 September 1965, Monoca's president, Dr. O. Reiser, met with Grose, Premier Roblin, and the ministers of Industry and Commerce, Mines and Natural Resources and the provincial secretary . This preliminary meeting was nothing more than a chance for Dr. Reiser to meet the four ministers and discuss his own and his company's qualifications.[52] A second meeting resulted in a proposal, drafted by Monoca's lawyer, and delivered to Cabinet by Grose on 29 September 1965.[53]

One of the points in the proposal was that the total investment required would be $40.7 million, of which the government would loan (through the MDF) 86 percent, and Monoca, through an operating company it would set up, would invest 14 percent. If more money were required, the loan would be increased to a maximum of another $40.7 million, but the loan would only be 60 percent of such additional requirements, with the operating company required to invest the other 40 percent. Cabinet approved the proposal the same day, and offered Monoca a six-month option on the project.

At the same time, Cabinet decided to reject proposals from Parsons and Whittemore, B.C. Forest Products Ltd., Baragon, and Mayo Holdings Ltd.[54] Mayo had been involved in a consortium arrangement which had not worked out, and Grose had written to R.S. Mayo to see if his firm would be interested in handling the project alone. By the time it submitted a proposal, the option had already been given to Monoca. Parsons and Whittemore, a large New York-based company with broad experience in both the construction and operation of pulp and paper mills, had become interested late in 1965, and despite the rejection of their proposal at that time, they remained interested. Early in 1966, company executives would suggest a three-month feasibility study, but this delay would prove too long for the provincial government.[55] B.C. Forest Products had also expressed an interest at about the time an agreement was reached with Monoca, and they were somewhat surprised to find themselves abruptly out of the running.[56]

Cabinet's involvement in the negotiations had several effects. Because Cabinet had decided to offer Monoca the option, Grose and the MDF assumed that they no longer had the right or the responsibility to interfere in the process and refuse to lend money to Monoca.[57] This in turn meant that the MDF's normal screening procedures were not observed and thus, at the time the option was given, the government had no idea who the owners of the project were, who the managers would be, or how competent Monoca was to undertake the project.

Companies incorporated in Switzerland are not required by law to reveal the identities of their owners, and Monoca had been adamant from the beginning that it would not disclose the names of its principals. On 8 October 1965, after Monoca had been given the option, the MDF requested a credit report on Monoca from the Royal Bank in Winnipeg, which checked with Monoca's bank in Switzerland. The report was singularly uninformative, saying only that the bank's relations with Monoca were satisfactory and that the book value of the company was several million Swiss francs. A Swiss franc at that time was worth about $0.27 Canadian.[58]

Since the option agreement had been signed so rapidly, further negotiation about the specifics of the proposed project continued between October 1965 and March 1966. A week of discussions occurred in January of 1966 in New York. On the way to this meeting, Premier Roblin and Minister of Mines and Natural Resources Sterling Lyon met in Toronto with Abitibi officials in a last attempt to obtain a proposal more favourable than Monoca's. Abitibi's proposal proved to be less favourable than Monoca's and thus was rejected.[59]

Grose and W.D. Fallis, the general manager of Manitoba Hydro, took part in the New York negotiations along with Lyon and Roblin. Reiser had suggested many amendments, and agreement was reached on many points. For instance, the government agreed to set up a Crown chemical company costing no more than $12 million. Monoca would set up an operating company, called Churchill Forest Industries (CFI), which would supervise the chemical plant's construction, manage it for a fee, and purchase all of its output. Once the chemical company's debts had been repaid, CFI would have a one-year option to purchase it for $1,000. Reiser also requested that port facilities at Churchill be improved, that the government take responsibility for organizing, equipping and supervising local Indians and Metis to cut wood, and that Manitoba Hydro supply electricity for twenty years at rates lower than those previously discussed.[60]

All of the above provisions were included in a memorandum which was sent to the government on 4 February 1966. The agreement was referred for comment to James Zeigler of ADL and Stadler Hurter International Ltd., a well-known Montreal firm of engineering consultants. Both consultants declared the agreement to be reasonable. The MDF's legal counsel, Walter C. Newman, also examined the agreement. Newman believed strongly that development of northern Manitoba was critical to preserve the province's identity and autonomy from the east; he, too, declared the agreement to be fair and as favourable to the government as could be expected, given the terms of the agreement made with Monoca the previous September.

Before these opinions were received, however, Roblin decided to make a further check on Monoca. On 15 February 1966, he telephoned Earle

McLaughlin, president of the Royal Bank, with whom he was personally acquainted. McLaughlin, in turn, telephoned a contact in Zurich,
who reported interlocking directorships between Monoca and Technopulp A.G. Technopulp was the engineering firm Monoca had called
in to perform an evaluation of the timber resources of northern Manitoba,
and it would be the project's engineer.

On 1 March 1966, McLaughlin passed along further information
regarding both Monoca and Technopulp. Monoca was described as having a team of financial, technical, and commercial experts as its decision-
makers and a large fund of money at its disposal from shareholders and
associated companies. The only person named in the report, however,
was Dr. Reiser. Technopulp A.G. was described as a subsidiary of the
Technopulp Organization of Montclair N.J., whose principal was Dr.
Alexander Kasser. Reiser was also a director of Technopulp. The report
stated that Kasser was undoubtedly the principal provider of funds to
both Monoca and Technopulp, with which he insisted on remaining at
arm's length.[61] In the next chapter, we shall meet the shadowy Dr. Kasser
and learn more about his unorthodox methods of doing business.

The government was satisfied that Monoca had the financial and
technical resources needed to carry out the project. Rather than to allow
the deal to fall through because of Monoca's non-disclosure of its principals, it was decided to require Monoca to pledge 51 percent of the
voting rights of CFI and to deposit them with the Montreal Trust Company in Winnipeg until the company had invested 14 percent of the
reasonable costs of the project as equity in CFI. With this measure to
safeguard against fraud, the government decided to proceed with the
project.[62]

An order-in-council passed on 25 February 1966 authorized the Cabinet to execute the memorandum of agreement Reiser had submitted.
Premier Roblin, however, did not sign the agreement at that time, but
instead flew to Zurich and signed the agreement at a ceremonial meeting with Reiser and some of his friends on March 4.[63] On March 8,
Gurney Evans announced the project in the legislature in the absence of
the premier, who had not yet returned to Winnipeg. The *Winnipeg
Free Press* that day quoted a government spokesperson as saying the
project would create "4000 new jobs, 2000 directly and 2000 indirectly
. . . Special attention will be given to the people of Indian descent, and
half the workers employed could be Indians and Metis."[64] At the end of
Evans' speech in the legislature, however, when a Liberal member
inquired if the government intended to loan money to Monoca through
the MDF, Evans replied, "The government has no direct commitment
to them financially. They are free to go to the Manitoba Development
Fund as any other industry is."[65]

In April the Roblin government called an election for June 23. On
that day, the provincial Conservatives were re-elected, with economic de-

velopment once again as one of the primary platform planks.[66] The forestry complex at The Pas and a $300-million hydro-electric power project on the Nelson River were offered as proof of the government's ability to bolster the province's lagging economy. The Conservatives went into the election holding 7 out of 9 northern seats by an average of 1000 votes; they retained all their seats, but with a reduced average margin of 600 votes. Province-wide, their strength fell slightly, from 35 to 31 of the seats in the 57-seat legislature.[67]

CONSOLIDATED COMPUTER LIMITED

After six years of leading Honeywell's computer marketing activities in eastern Canada, computer scientist Mers Kutt moved to Queen's University as professor and director of the computer centre. His contract permitted him to establish a company to market a computer innovation he had invented.[68]

Kutt had developed KEY-EDIT, a sophisticated data-entry station that allowed editing of data during preparation, as well as continued entry during processing. It was, in essence, the forerunner of the interactive screen terminal and a substantial improvement over the punched cards then in use. In 1967, Kutt incorporated Consolidated Computer Limited in order to manufacture and market KEY-EDIT. The name of the company changed to Consolidated Computer Incorporated (CCI, henceforth) in 1971.

Kutt faced a formidable obstacle in the marketing strategy of his ultimate competitor, IBM. Rather than selling its equipment, IBM offered one-year leases to its customers. IBM's own cash flow allowed it to finance the leases internally. Furthermore, the arrangement guaranteed that IBM would immediately be informed of any consumer dissatisfaction with its products. The strategy provided flexibility to computer users and allowed them to use their cash elsewhere. All this meant that IBM's competitors would have difficulty financing leases through their own much smaller cash flows. In Canada, bank financing of computer leases was also difficult to arrange at this time. To compete with IBM, equipment had to be offered on a one-year lease, which was not enough time to recover the full cost of production. Financing the production of computers to be leased on less than a payout basis held no attraction for Canada's risk-shy bankers.[69] From 1966 on, Kutt attempted to inform the federal Department of Industry and its deputy minister, Simon Reisman, of this situation and he requested government financing for CCI. Initially, the department was not interested in his proposal. In particular, Reisman was turned off by the nationalist rhetoric with which Kutt embellished the proposal.[70]

CCI took shape slowly, with a few part-time employees and with most of the initial investment ($100,000) made by Kutt himself. However, by

August 1968, Kutt's plans had progressed far enough that he was able to raise $500,000 from the Royal Trust Company, private investors, and his employees. In 1969, the company went public. Perceived as a glamour stock, it raised $8.8 million in convertible shares. By the end of the year, CCI had grown to 200 employees, and sales totalled $650,000.

Kutt was still interested in obtaining government financing, and by this point ITC was also becoming interested. The new minister, Jean-Luc Pépin, displayed great enthusiasm for the department making Canada a world-class competitor in high-technology areas.[71] The public servants in the Electrical and Electronics Branch of ITC, which effectively functioned as an advocate of these industries, urged Kutt to apply for support under the General Adjustment Assistance Program (GAAP).

The GAAP had been established as a result of the Auto Pact in order to allow the government to make loans that would enable Canadian auto-parts manufacturers to adjust to changed competitive conditions. The program had evolved for the purpose of supporting any manufacturer who had to respond to increased foreign competition because of the GATT tariff reductions of the 1967 Kennedy Round. For example, the textile industry became a major client of the GAAP. The program was administered by a seven-person board, of whom three were private-sector representatives and four were civil servants from the departments of Industry, Trade and Commerce; Employment and Immigration; Finance; and Regional Economic Expansion. The chairman at this time was Anthony Hampson, who was also president of Capital Dynamics Management Ltd. of Montreal, a foreign-owned mutual-fund management company. CCI did not fit under the program's definition, but ITC, having been only recently formed by the amalgamation of the departments of Industry and Trade and Commerce, was experiencing considerable turbulence, and could not devote time and resources to setting up a more appropriate program for supporting projects such as CCI. The department decided that the GAAB was the best available funding vehicle.[72]

In January 1970, CCI applied to the GAAB for loan guarantees totalling $72 million for lease financing over the next three years. The Board then commissioned the investment house of Burns Brothers and Denton to do an appraisal of CCI.[73] The report observed that the peripherals market, in which CCI was competing, was the fastest growing segment of the hardware market. CCI had a product that was ahead of the competition, but with a lead of only a year. The analysts noted that there were many small high-tech firms in this market and felt that success would depend on management, marketing, and financial strength, rather than technological expertise. In their opinion, CCI's management team had the necessary depth and experience. The report concluded that CCI was a risky venture, but expected that its shares would appreciate over the next year or two.

CCI presented something of a conundrum to the GAAB. Although the GAAB was an autonomous government board, it had been directed to consider CCI's application by the department to which it was most closely linked. As a result of this, the decision to get involved with CCI became a *fait accompli* apparently without the GAAB ever making a firm, formal decision. None of the people we interviewed who were connected with the GAAB at this time could recall when or how it was decided that CCI should receive support; instead, the decision revolved around *how much* support to give — a contentious issue. The company had requested $72 million over three years; the GAAB was authorized to provide a total of $100 million a year in loan insurance. If CCI were granted the total amount of its request in three equal portions, it would consume nearly one-quarter of the GAAB's total budget each year for the next three years. Rather than making such a sizeable commitment all at once, the GAAB agreed to a trial amount of loan insurance for the first year.

In July 1970, the GAAB approved in principle the provision of up to $12 million in loan guarantees for the first year of CCI's plan provided certain conditions were met. CCI would have to raise $2 million in equity immediately, which CCI did by issuing stock at a depressed price of $3.50 per share, compared to the price of the first issue, which was $8 per share. The loan guarantees were for only 90 percent of the value of the loan. As a result, Canada's ever-cautious banks were not willing to lend to CCI. After considerable legwork, the GAAB found that the Ford Motor Credit Corporation in the United States would finance the loan. The company would not receive its loans when the KEY-EDIT machines were manufactured, but only as the equipment was actually leased out. Ford also placed restrictions on CCI, such as requiring it to maintain a working capital of $2 million and a debt-equity ratio of no more than 3:1.[74] Finally, by accepting loan guarantees from the GAAB, CCI agreed to submit itself to normal GAAB monitoring procedures, which included the latter's right to examine financial statements and sales performance, as well as seek third-party opinions.[75]

SUMMARY

Before continuing on with the story, it is useful to compare the five cases to look for common characteristics so that we can develop a composite portrait, as it were, of disastrous government investment. If, by the end of the book, we have drawn such a portrait, we could use it to predict other instances of disastrous government investments and thus warn against undertaking them.

The easiest way to summarize and compare the cases is in tabular form. Table 1 compares the cases in terms of their major characteristics: the decision-making process, including the objectives of the government's involvement, the source of the initiative for the project, the alternatives rejected, the depth of the analysis of the project, and the bureaucratic and political preferences; the likely political impact of the project, which includes its timing in the political cycle, the expected beneficiaries of the project, the local and national unemployment rates, and the estimated number of jobs created; and the implementation of the project (its financial terms and the monitoring regime established).

Considering, first, the objectives of these projects, the one most frequently present was regional economic development, which figured prominently in four of five cases. Regional economic development meant a number of different things: the maintenance and creation of jobs in high-unemployment regions (Deuterium, Bricklin), the expansion of employment into the north (CFI), or the maintenance of jobs in a particular industry within a metropolis (Canadair). In two cases, the investment was undertaken to develop (CCI) or maintain (Canadair) a Canadian position in a high-technology industry. The CCI decision had the additional aspect that the government was responding to what it perceived as a weakness in the Canadian capital market, namely a shortage of venture capital for small firms in the computer industry. Notice that the local unemployment rates in Montreal, when Canadair was bought by the government, and in Ottawa, when CCI was acquired, were lower than the national average.

Were the investments undertaken in the expectation of making a profit? In the cases of Canadair, CCI, and Bricklin, the governments expected that the investments would be profitable. Deuterium and Churchill Forest Industries were also expected to be profitable once certain concessions were made: in the former, subsidization of energy prices to make them comparable to those in western Canada, and in the latter, substantial government largesse concerning stumpage, cutting rights, and infrastructure. Of course, the profitability expectations were only as valid as the studies upon which they were based. Here, we note that in one case (Bricklin), the study was quite cursory; in another (Canadair), the studies gave conflicting advice, and in a third (CFI) the studies were seriously biased. In short, it appears that in each of these cases, the primary objective was regional economic development: having a report that claimed the project could be profitable lent an air of economic justification to a political decision already made. In such circumstances, we can imagine that the decision-makers would not want to slow the decision process down enough to commission a more definitive economic analysis. The politicians' approach was thus characterized by a willingness to take risk with public money, supported by a good dose of wishful thinking.

The clearest common factor in the five cases is the strong political support for the alternative that was ultimately chosen: in two cases it was a provincial premier's pet project (Bricklin for Hatfield, CFI for Roblin), and in two others it was championed by a strong regional

Table 1. CHARACTERISTICS OF INITIAL INVESTMENT DECISIONS

Characteristics	Deuterium	Bricklin	Canadair	Consolidated Computer	Churchill Forest Industries
1. date of decision	Dec. 1963	June 1973	Jan., Nov. 1976	July 1970	Sept. 1965
2. financial terms	IEL lends $12 million, owns 51% of DCL	N.B. invests $0.5 million, owns 51%; $2.9 million loan guarantee	fed. gov't. buys Canadair for $46 million, letters of comfort for Challenger costs	GAAB provides $12 million in loan guarantees	Manitoba to lend CFI up to ($40.7 × .86) + ($40.7 × .6) = $59.4 million
3. objectives of government intervention	i) regional economic development ii) low-cost heavy water	i) regional economic development ii) profitability	i) regional economic development ii) hi-tech participation iii) profitability	i) correct capital market failure ii) hi-tech participation iii) profitability	i) regional economic development ii) profitability given concessions
4. source of initiative	entrepreneurs (Spevack, Dupont) approach gov't. (AECL)	entrepreneur (Bricklin) approaches N.B. gov't. (Multiplex) after Quebec turns him down	Canadair and entrepreneur (Lear) both interested in developing business jet	entrepreneur (Kutt) approaches gov't. (ITC)	government approaches entrepreneurs
5. alternatives rejected	three bids: CGE, Dynamic Power, Western Deuterium	none	liquidation, aerospace job shop	none	three bids: Parsons & Whittemore, Mayo Holdings, Abitibi
6. nature and depth of analysis	federal bureaucracy conducted detailed interdepartmental review of bids	cursory Multiplex study	ITC examination of capabilities of firm	thorough Burns Brothers and Denton report	very cursory examination

Characteristics	Deuterium	Bricklin	Canadair	Consolidated Computer	Churchill Forest Industries
7. bureaucratic preference	fed. bureaucracy prefers Western Deuterium	some bureaucratic skepticism re: Bricklin dominated by political enthusiasm	ITC supports Canadair acquisition, Challenger development	ITC supports loan guarantees	MDF supports project
8. political preference	strong support for Deuterium (N.S. gov't., N.S. federal liberals)	strong support from Premier Hatfield	strong support from Quebec ministers and caucus	decision consistent with Pépin's preferences	strong support from Premier Roblin
9. local and (national) unemployment rates	10% (5.1%)	8% (5.3%)	6.3% (6.9%)	5.1% (6.2%)	N.A. (2.3%)
10. gov't. estimate of jobs created (annual)	700 in construction	600 when car in production	3000	500	2000 direct, 2000 indirect
11. political timing	right after election	mid-cycle	mid-cycle	mid-cycle	just before provincial election
12. beneficiaries	Cape Breton Island	Saint John, spillovers to rest of province	Montreal aerospace workers	Ottawa computer industry	northern Manitoba, spillovers to rest of province
13. nature of monitoring regime established	gov't. board members	board members, access to books, loan approval	gov't board members, inter-depart. review committee	monitoring through GAAB	monitoring by MDF

minister and caucus (DCL: MacEachen and Stanfield; Canadair Challenger: Chrétien and the Quebec caucus). Comparing the political with the bureaucratic preferences, we find agreement between politicians and public servants in the CFI case, politicians overriding their advisers in the DCL case, and in the Bricklin and Canadair Challenger cases, politicians willing to take risks about which at least some of their advisers were skeptical.

The only exception to this pattern was CCI. Here, there were good economic arguments to support an initial loan guarantee, as shown by the thorough analysis in the Burns Brothers and Denton report. Although this initiative was consistent with the minister's preferences, the decision appears to have been one that emerged from ITC and was endorsed by the minister, rather than having the strong ministerial input of the other four cases.

A number of different types of monitoring regimes were established: government members of the board of directors in three cases (Deuterium, Bricklin, Canadair), monitoring by the bureaucracy in two cases (Canadair, Bricklin) and monitoring by a government lending agency in two cases (CCI, CFI). The next chapter will discuss the difficulties encountered by all of these different monitoring regimes.

Finally, we return to the public choice paradigm with which we began this chapter. The purest pork-barrel investment would be one (1) whose benefits were conferred on marginal voters alone; (2) which had little economic justification; (3) in which the politicians overruled the bureaucrats; and (4) which was announced with great fanfare immediately before an election. Judged by these criteria, the cases that fit the model most closely are Deuterium of Canada and Churchill Forest Industries. Deuterium was chosen by federal politicians who were responding to the pressure of both federal and provincial politicians and who overruled the bureaucracy in order to confer very visible benefits on a high-unemployment swing constituency, Cape Breton Island. The CFI deal was made in great haste right before an election and, as the following chapter will show, with insufficient attention paid to the contract. It departs slightly from the pure pork-barrel paradigm because, whereas its direct economic impact would be on the north, which was a swing area, it would also have substantial indirect impacts throughout the province.

The decisions to buy Canadair and to build the Challenger were aimed at Montreal residents who consistently voted Liberal at the federal level, but whose loyalty to the federal system itself was questionable. This can be seen as consistent with the marginal voter hypothesis, in the sense that Quebec voters are marginal to the federal system. The Bricklin project created jobs in the English-speaking portion of New Brunswick from which Hatfield's Conservatives drew most of their support. But it was clear that Hatfield saw it not just as a mere job-creation project, but rather as a high-technology venture capable of transforming the entire provincial economy. In terms of direct electoral impact, Hatfield did not want his initial decision to invest in Bricklin to influence the St. John by-election. Finally, the CCI decision bears little resemblance to the pork-barrel model. It can be seen as a case in which bureaucrats and politicians, afforded the freedom of being in the middle of a strong mandate, undertook a policy that they felt would contribute to their vision of how the Canadian economy should evolve.

This concludes our discussion of the decision-makers' rationales for undertaking these investments and their hopes regarding their performance. The next chapter discusses the problems that led to a reality which turned out very differently from their hopes.

3

What Went Wrong

INTRODUCTION

This chapter deals with the next phase in the story of these five government enterprises, namely the implementation of the investment decisions. We shall discuss such matters as the construction of facilities, product development, and marketing. In all cases, this is the period when things started to go seriously wrong. The stories will show a variety of problems, such as cost overruns, failure to meet deadlines, and products that were of inferior quality and/or higher price than planned. When we say that these were problems, we mean that the projects, in addition to their objectives of providing political support, also had efficiency objectives or at least were operating under efficiency constraints. When the resource cost of achieving the political objectives became too great, then the projects were seen by the public as failures and thus diminished the political support they were intended to provide.

The emphasis in this chapter will be on explaining, in terms of efficiency objectives, why these failures occurred. There are four possible explanations: adverse changes in the firm's environment, bad political decisions, ineffective monitoring, and management errors. These explanations are not mutually exclusive, and we often find that the failures are a result of some mix of the four.

When discussing adverse changes in a firm's environment, we shall attempt to distinguish between problems that no manager could have been expected to have foreseen and therefore responded to and those that a good manager would have anticipated.

As indicated in the previous chapter, politicians generally played a major role in the decisions to support these enterprises. They were responsible for choosing the managers to run the projects, as well as for delegating authority to a board of directors and/or public servants for monitoring the projects. In so doing, the politicians chose the individuals who would be doing the monitoring and, either through a formal decision or their informal relationship with the monitors, established their powers and communicated what would be expected of them. At this point, the old Latin question comes to mind, "Who shall monitor the monitors?" The answer is the media and the politicians themselves. As the problems became worse, it became impossible for the politicians to ignore them, because they would be picked up by normal public management controls, such as the appropriations process, or because they became known to the public.

When looking at the causes of failure, we work with the notion that there was some domain within which each of the actors involved had discretionary power. In the case of managers and monitors, these domains were defined by the politicians; nonetheless, it should be possible to determine whether managers and monitors made intelligent decisions regarding those issues under their control. Consider managers first. In order to identify managerial behaviour as erroneous, it is necessary to have a management theory. Most modern management theory is contextual, in that it argues that there is not one universally applicable theory of management, but rather that appropriate management policies depend on the market and organizational context within which a firm operates.[1] We shall therefore attempt to show how, in many of these situations, management acted in a way which deviated from what modern management theory would prescribe.

In considering monitors' errors, we make the assumption that an effective monitoring system is designed to allow the owners of capital to ensure that the managers of the enterprise are behaving effectively and efficiently. A monitoring system can break down if the monitors have insufficient expertise, if they have been compromised in some way by the managers, or if they simply refuse to pass evaluative information up to the politicians.

One philosophical problem this chapter presents is whether, when an agent to whom authority has been delegated makes errors, the agent, the principal who delegated authority in the first place, or both, are responsible for the agent's errors. In practice, there are differences of opinion about who is responsible. At one extreme, there is the traditional British notion of ministerial responsibility that any errors committed by the bureaucracy are the responsibility of the minister, and thus we see frequent resignations of British ministers; for example, Lord Carrington prior to the Falklands war. In Canada, we have come to accept a more limited doctrine of ministerial responsibility, according to which ministers may choose to delegate authority to public servants; if the latter commit errors about matters within their range of delegated responsibility, they, not the politicians, are at fault. Our preference is to consider that both could be at fault. We will attribute to managers or monitors errors that were within their domain of delegated authority. In addition, we shall attempt to determine whether politicians should also be considered responsible for having made hasty or naive choices regarding whom to delegate authority to and how much authority to delegate.

The reader will notice that the discussion in this chapter often deals with the decisions made by specific individuals, and that we frequently interpret individuals' motives and assess the wisdom of their decisions.

We feel that this individual level of analysis is crucial to our understanding of these cases. In previous studies of policy decisions, the senior author has argued that individuals' personalities — broadly defined as an amalgam of their ideologies and patterns of managerial behaviour (such as willingness to take risk, ability to delegate authority, and negotiating skill) — will affect policy outcomes. Put differently, if we were to perform the thought experiment of assuming that two different individuals were in the same position at the same point in time and thus were handling the same problem, we would often conclude that, because of their different personalities, they would handle it in different ways and therefore make different decisions. In this chapter, we will show a number of instances where personality, thus defined, influences policy. While we do not have the data to allow us to develop psychological explanations of the dynamics of individuals' personalities (and indeed, we think that would be unnecessary), we feel that we have been able in some instances to show how identifiable personality traits have influenced decisions. It is from this standpoint that we then assess the performance of individuals; we believe these judgements are an essential part of our analysis of why the projects failed to meet their efficiency objectives.

This chapter examines what went wrong at the investment stage of each of the five government enterprises. The discussions are both narrative and analytical in their attempt to sort out the relative contributions of adverse changes in the environment, management errors, ineffective monitoring, and bad political decisions. We conclude this chapter once again by comparing the causes of the problems in order to find common patterns.

DEUTERIUM OF CANADA

Design Problems

After Deuterium of Canada (DCL) won the contract for the heavy-water plant in December 1963, its directors, the majority of whom were appointed by the government's economic development corporation, Industrial Estates Limited (IEL), decided to ask the New York engineering firm of Burns and Roe to draw up an interim feasibility report before the final contract with Atomic Energy of Canada Limited (AECL) would be signed. By January, Burns and Roe came up with an optimistic cost estimate of $28.5 million, somewhat less than the $30 million in the original proposal. Of course, since they wanted the final contract, it was in their interest to err on the side of optimism. As a result of this good news, DCL was able to sign a final contract with AECL in February 1964. Confident that the project was going well and politically very committed to it, IEL signed three new contracts with Spevack that were clearly in his favour. These involved:

- changing the original financial agreement so that IEL would invest its $12 million *before*, rather than *after* Spevack raised his $18 million;

- assigning all patents and process knowledge for the Glace Bay plant to DCL, but permitting any improvements or process inventions that came out of the Glace Bay plant to become the property of Deuterium Corporation, Spevack's American company;
- giving Spevack a $25,000 per annum 20-year management contract, which did not require him to devote full time to DCL.[2]

After these contracts were signed, things began to go wrong. Burns and Roe, which had no experience designing heavy-water plants, soon increased the cost estimate by $1 million. Shortly thereafter, they increased their cost estimate again, this time to $32.8 million. Because of its inexperience and a shortage of drafting personnel, the company missed its May 1965 deadline for completion of most of the engineering work; it was not done until the following November. In addition, a total of 2500 revisions were made in the mechanical drawings for the plant in 1965 and 1966.[3]

Financing and Investment Problems

By mid-1964, the IEL-appointed directors of DCL were becoming concerned about the course the project was taking. At their meeting on 28 June 1964, one said, "We are not sufficiently informed on the program to evaluate what is being done and we have no control over the present proceedings." They hired a consulting firm to monitor the project, but with little effect.[4]

DCL was also having difficulty finding someone to invest $18 million in the project. Spevack himself felt that he was only required to make his best effort to find the financing, but that he was not obligated to do so.[5] By late 1964, the IEL-appointed directors were becoming sufficiently dissatisfied with the situation that they themselves set out to find someone either to invest or to take the entire project over. The directors approached Power Corporation, but it backed out when the capital cost estimates increased to $37 million. During 1965, they also approached Imperial Oil, Distillers Corporation, and Canadian General Electric (CGE). In each case, the talks failed because Spevack refused to reveal anything about the technology before the deal was complete, and the would-be investors refused to buy until they knew more about the technology. Spevack's position can be understood in view of his previous experience with the United States Atomic Energy Commission and his fear that these companies, most of which were his competitors, might have been using the negotiations as a ploy to find out his secrets. Because of the lack of investor interest, as well as the heavy political commitment to the project, IEL agreed to loan DCL another $15 million to keep the project going.[6]

By 1966, the province of Nova Scotia had become even more deeply committed to DCL. In early 1965, AECL felt that Canada needed another heavy-water plant, besides DCL's. Bids were then sought for a 400-ton per annum plant, twice the size of DCL's plant, whereupon DCL offered to double its plant capacity. AECL, aware of DCL's problems, did not take up their offer. Ultimately, the contract went to Canadian General Electric, on the strength of their experience in building reactors for AECL in Canada and for the Pakistani government. In December 1965, the government announced that CGE would build a 400 ton/year heavy-water plant in Port Hawkesbury, Nova Scotia, on the southern shore of Cape Breton Island. The plant, expected to cost $60 million, would have a guaranteed market for ten years' production at a price not to exceed $18 per pound.[7]

The Nova Scotia government, hoping that an expansion of the Glace Bay plant would stimulate investor confidence, was bitterly disappointed by this decision. The Nova Scotia press was also highly critical. Premier Stanfield and Allan MacEachen, unwilling to accept defeat, began to pressure the federal government. Primarily as a response to this pressure, rather than to changed market conditions, the federal government agreed to purchase from DCL an additional 400 tons of heavy water per year for ten years at an agreed price of approximately $18 per pound.[8]

Although winning the contract for DCL may have been politically desirable for the Nova Scotia government, it had the economic effect of increasing its exposure in an already risky venture. Throughout 1966, the government had no success in finding other investors for a project whose estimated cost had by then increased to $73 million. By August 1966, the government found it unacceptable that it should have only 51 percent of the equity of DCL when it was providing all the investment funds. The government then proceeded to pay $2.25 million for Spevack's share of DCL, and $750,000 for his patents and unpatented improvements in the Glace Bay plant. (Spevack retained these rights in the rest of the world.) This buy-out thus terminated the March 1964 contracts, including Spevack's commitment to build the original plant for no more than $35 million.[9] By this time, the Nova Scotia government was, indeed, totally committed.

Construction Problems

In order that the planned opening date of summer 1966 be met, construction of the plant began in October 1964. In searching for a principal contractor, the DCL directors first approached Burns and Roe Construction Ltd., a subsidiary of the engineering firm. Aware of the problems that were surfacing, the company asked for a cost-plus contract. But since the directors wanted a contractor who would agree to a fixed fee, they called for bids. The lowest bidder (and winner) was the Texas-based construction firm of Brown and Root, which had just completed a major contract in New Brunswick.[10]

Brown and Root ran into serious difficulties in labour relations. Many skilled workers, who received higher wages than the local construction workers, were imported. Because Cape Breton Island previously had only two construction trade unions, the carpenters' and the general workers' union, new union locals sprung up overnight. There ensued jurisdictional disputes and membership fights among the various unions. The Brown and Root managers had no experience with this labour situation and, according to an industrial inquiry conducted several years later, failed to achieve any kind of healthy relationship with the workers. The report said the managers' "personalities and attitudes greatly affected employee relations" and blamed one particularly insensitive superintendent. The situation led to numerous grievances and work stoppages.[11]

In addition to labour problems, there were technical failures caused by late equipment deliveries and there were many defects and deficiencies in meeting design specifications for pumps, compressors, and controls. Nature also contributed to the problems, as the winter of 1966-67 was extraordinarily cold and stormy.[12]

The plant's official opening ceremony was held on 1 May 1967, with Premier Stanfield, Allan MacEachen, and Jerome Spevack all playing the role of proud parents. However, the plant was still not yet operational.[13] Construction of the expanded plant was to be completed by June 1968, but because of more strikes and delays in equipment deliveries, it was not finished until that autumn. In November, frustrated by the delays, the board of directors fired Spevack as president of DCL. He was replaced by Robert Burns Cameron, a tough construction executive who was appointed president of the Crown corporation, Sydney Steel (SYSCO), when the province took over the Glace Bay steel mill earlier that year. Cameron had turned around the steel mill and was expected to work similar wonders at DCL.[14]

However, the problems Cameron faced at DCL were much greater. Some time before he took over, the equipment had been tested. Sea water had been introduced into the heat exchangers and, even though people knew it was highly corrosive to most metals, it had been left there for several months without being flushed out. Whether or not this was due to negligence, with or without malice, on the part of the plant managers or workers at the time is not known. One group of consultants who examined the plant several years later believed that the problem had been due to a technical failure rather than negligence; they claimed that the inner discs of the the large butterfly valves that were part of the original design became frozen inside their mountings, thereby trapping salt water in the system.

Two weeks after taking over, Cameron decided to have hydrogen sulphide injected into the system in order to start up the plant. Because of the corrosion in the pipes, large quantities of the poisonous gas leaked from the system. Fortunately, winds blew the gas out over the bay, averting a chemical catastrophe.[15]

The Outcome

In January 1969, the province bought the DCL shares from IEL and made it a Crown corporation. By then, the province had spent more than $100 million on the heavy-water plant. Cameron, dismayed by the attempt to start the plant, brought in the Dupont company as consultants. In August the company reported that in order to make the plant operational, it would cost $30 million (to cover a redesign of the entire feed and effluent system, new pumps and valves, and alterations in the production towers) and take two years.[16] The problem faced by the government of G.I. Smith (who in September 1967 replaced Stanfield as Conservative premier) was whether to cut its losses or to invest more in the plant. These decisions will be discussed in the following chapter.

By contrast, the CGE heavy-water plant, which had been started in 1966, began production in early 1971, about one year behind schedule, primarily because of wildcat strikes and other labour problems. The plant cost about $75 million ($15 million more than the original budget). CGE had two important advantages over DCL. The company was able to use its design for the Savannah River plant, simply multiplied several times in size; and the Port Hawkesbury plant was designed to use fresh water, rather than salt water.[17]

BRICKLIN

Shortly after signing the contract with the New Brunswick government in June 1973, Malcolm Bricklin went into gear. He moved to Arizona, hired his relatives to staff the head office, hired others to run his manufacturing operation, and began to fly frantically over the United States promoting his car. He expected that the car, still only a hand-made prototype, would be in production within three months. As it turned out, production did not begin until August 1974, and the car was much more expensive than originally intended. As we shall see, the key problem was terrible management.

The Technology Problem

The two technological question marks in the Bricklin concept were the gull-wing doors and the body of acrylic bonded onto fibreglass. The gull-wing doors weighed 170 pounds and needed a compact hydraulic cylinder to be raised. Designing the cylinder took longer than expected, and it never really worked correctly.[18] Finding out how to bond acrylic to fibreglass was also much more difficult and time-consuming than expected. In May 1974, the company went to the New Brunswick government's Research and Productivity Council, which helped put them in touch with the best industrial expertise to solve their problem. However, before the problem was solved, the company experienced long delays, used enormous amounts of fibreglass and acrylic, substantially increased the weight of car (thus requiring new shock absorbers and springs), and found that the first set of tools and presses it had purchased had to be replaced.[19]

Management Problems

Though the use of an untried technology created difficulties, the burden of blame must fall upon Bricklin himself. Bricklin was basically a conceptualizer and a promoter. Once he had sufficient financial backing, he immediately set to work signing up dealers, working on advertisements, and planning media events to promote the car. He was very successful at this, signing up 200 dealers in less than a year, and staging media events in New York and Las Vegas that attracted a great deal of publicity. Unfortunately, these events created expectations, and indeed Bricklin made binding commitments that could not be fulfilled.[20]

This management style put great pressure on Bricklin's design and engineering staff, who were expected, in record time, to produce a car that would live up to Bricklin's promises. Though Bricklin had little understanding of the technological problems, he refused to modify his concepts in the face of technological constraints.

Another aspect of his management style that alienated his staff was the hiring of his parents, sister, brother-in-law, uncle, and girlfriend to managerial positions.[21] The worst of these appointments was making his father, who was as technically ignorant as Malcolm himself, president of Bricklin Canada following de Villers' departure in October 1973 (see details below).[22] In addition, Bricklin used the funds invested in the company to adopt a flamboyant life-style. As soon as New Brunswick entered the project, he moved to expensive accommodations in Scottsdale, Arizona, and adopted an Old West motif in his plush offices. Although this approach had some promotional value, it undoubtedly aroused the resentment of his staff.[23]

Bricklin and his family refused to set up any coherent organizational structure or even to delegate authority. Bricklin wanted to be the final authority, even on the technological questions he did not at all understand. This led to low morale, as evidenced by a near-rebellion in the Livonia (Michigan) engineering facility and by frequent resignations.[24] Thus the organization was in a continuous state of flux, as Bricklin kept bringing in friends, acquaintances, or contacts to replace executives who had resigned in frustration. Harry Nason, then deputy minister of Economic Growth, described the mood of Bricklin's staff in the following way:

> These people went through an interesting progression. For a number of months they would exhibit great enthusiasm and confidence, to be followed by several months of grim determination. As frustration set in, they would begin to discuss their problems with us. At about the time a crisis was imminent, new faces would appear or the personnel would be shuffled.[25]

Geographically, the firm was decentralized, with the design shop in Livonia, Michigan, the body components plant in Minto, New Brunswick, the assembly plant in Saint John, the accounting office in New York, the executive offices in Scottsdale, Arizona, and Bricklin himself constantly travelling to do promotions. This came about because of Bricklin's haste to market the car as soon as possible. Besides increased communication, travel, and shipping costs, the geographical decentralization combined with a centralized hierarchical management meant that managers were continuously waiting to attract Bricklin's attention long enough for him to make a decision. And the quality of the decisions was poor: not only did Bricklin evidently not understand the issues, but his decisions had an improvised and erratic nature. For example, design and production were greatly influenced by Bricklin's tendency to buy equipment or parts on the basis of whatever deals he could strike at the moment, with no concern as to how these purchases would affect overall production. One area where this approach became very costly was in the procurement of parts. Unable to do any planning, the company could not make large parts orders in advance and thereby take advantage of economies of scale. Often parts were ordered in small lots at retail prices. Shortages of parts meant that frequently assembly workers were being paid for sitting idle.[26] Another consequence of Bricklin's approach was that the company could not formulate or implement any financial or production planning, and managers who were hired in the expectation that they would be doing planning, resigned.[27]

In terms of management theory, one could conclude that Bricklin did everything wrong. Why? Simply to say the man was inexperienced is insufficient. The information we have gathered suggests that Bricklin was behaving pathologically. He seemed to have a tremendous need for instant gratification through fame, financial success, and its concomitant life-style. In all his ventures, he tried to achieve his goals by finding or developing a new product and then using his considerable persuasive powers to franchise it as quickly and as widely as possible. It would appear that his satisfaction came from both selling and consequent instant recognition, in terms of fame and income.

Bricklin had a powerful yet limited understanding of human character: he knew how to get other people excited in a venture, but he failed to understand what was needed to keep their excitement and loyalty. Thus, he did not see why it was important to put into place structures that would ensure the continued success of the venture. He had so little trust in people other than his family that he could not delegate authority to them or respect their expertise. The strength of his desire for instant gratification so dominated any concern he might have had for building lasting structures that he was quite willing to break any contract he made.[28] Bricklin's contracts, it should be remembered, were always of the sort that gave him gratification at the outset in return for the responsibility to provide services in the future.

By investing in Bricklin, therefore, the government of New Brunswick had agreed to commit its resources to underwrite Malcolm Bricklin's pathological behaviour. The questions that need answers are (1) What did the New Brunswick government derive in exchange for this questionable commitment? And (2) what control did it exercise over this commitment?

The Political Utility of Bricklin

During the summer of 1974, Premier Hatfield, who first came to power in November 1970, was planning an autumn election. Two issues he had chosen to promote were economic development and francophone rights. The former involved a decision to build a nuclear reactor near Saint John, the home town of Liberal opposition leader Robert Higgins. The latter issue was designed to win support of the Acadians in northern New Brunswick.

Hatfield was trying to determine how to deal with the Bricklin investment. By then he had considerable knowledge of Bricklin's difficulties, particularly its production delays and escalating financing requirements. Yet, he was also aware of Malcolm Bricklin's promotional genius, particularly after attending some events, such as the New York launching of the car in June 1974. It is quite likely that, in order to minimize cognitive dissonance (that is, the psychological tension created by value-threatening information), Hatfield convinced himself that the good outweighed the bad, and that the car would ultimately be a success. Hatfield also realized that if he took credit for the Bricklin investment in the election campaign, it would place the Liberals in a difficult situation. They would not wish openly to condemn the project because, by August 1974, the car had finally gone into production and was creating jobs. Hatfield thus took the offensive, identifying the car as a symbol of the province's economic progress and portraying the Liberals as doubters and skeptics.

Hatfield decided to test the strategy in two by-elections, which were held on September 30. One was in rural York County, outside Fredericton, a safe Conservative seat; the other was in the urban swing riding of

Campbellton in the north. His speech at the York County nominating meeting developed his major theme:

> [The Liberals] have done all they could to undermine public confidence, to run down Bricklin's prospects all over Canada and to damage its image in the eyes of millions. . . . [Building Bricklin] couldn't be done because we are not supposed to be doing things like that here. Well, I believe we are going to prove them wrong, and it will be a great thing for this province.[29]

Hatfield then drove a bright orange Bricklin, designated a public relations car by the company, to Campbellton. The crowd rushed over to inspect it. In the by-elections, the NDP candidates predicted Bricklin would be a flop, and the Liberals tried to ignore it. The Conservatives won both by-elections by large majorities.

Hatfield then called an election for November 18. The Bricklin played the same role in the election that it had in the by-elections. The Liberals did not condemn the Bricklin project, but called for a full audit of the company, a feasibility study, and consultation with competent business personnel to determine the extent of the province's financial support for the project. Off the record, however, they ridiculed it.[30]

As will be discussed below, there was more bad news coming in about the Bricklin project during the campaign, this time concerning its insatiable appetite for cash. Having committed himself publicly to the project's success, Hatfield, however, could not reverse his course on the basis of this new information. So, almost like a finance minister telling the foreign exchange market about the soundness of his nation's currency, Hatfield gloried in the Bricklin project, even driving a Bricklin around the province for most of the last three weeks of the campaign. As his own statements showed, the Bricklin had moved from a job creation project into the realm of symbolic politics:

> There are always problems in the beginning. Bricklin's main problem at the moment is getting parts. There is nothing technically wrong. There is a market for more Bricklin cars than can be produced in Saint John, and the future of the operation looks very bright indeed. . . . I am proud of the Bricklin because it is a symbol of what can be accomplished in this province and what is being accomplished.[31]

The Bricklin campaign was ultimately a success. The Conservatives won thirty seats to the Liberals' twenty-five. The Conservatives gained four seats from the Liberals in the north, but the Liberals took four of the six seats in Saint John. Voters in Saint John possibly had somewhat better knowledge of Bricklin's difficulties.

Monitoring the Bricklin Investment

In the first year of the Bricklin project, the government's approach to monitoring its investment was (1) to monitor the company's financial transactions to guard against fraud, and (2) to keep an eye on design and production problems to ensure that the project was technologically feasible. As long as progress was being made, the government was willing to commit funds on an incremental basis. In addition, the government had assumed that Malcolm Bricklin was a competent manager and therefore made no attempt to second-guess his managerial style or his decisions. To quote Harry Nason, in his testimony to the Public Accounts Committee of the New Brunswick Legislature:

> All you can do is go in, commit your money, not at once, but commit it on a month-to-month basis, put in a man who monitors from month to month not just the financial aspect, but how the project is coming, because at any given point a technological problem can just overnight suddenly kill the whole thing and, of course, you want a fast way out.[32]

The person assigned to ongoing financial and technical monitoring was G. Stephenson Wheatley, an engineer by background and a junior officer in the Department of Economic Growth.[33] Nason regarded Wheatley as one of his best staff members and therefore received his reports directly. To prevent fraud, Wheatley undertook monthly reviews of the company's expenditures. He checked cancelled cheques against entries in the company's cash records, verified that cheques were drawn in payment for bona fide invoices, checked personal expense accounts, and reconciled expenditures with receipts of funds from the government and the banks. However, a retrospective description of these activities found in the government's Bricklin files concedes that "these checks were in no way intended to be a full-scale audit, and although the following procedures were used fairly consistently, time constraints and other priorities obviously left gaps. Most checks, however, were done on a spot basis."[34] By 1974, Bricklin and General Vehicle did present budgets, so that it was possible to spot variances. For example, the budget variances in January showed under-expenditures on production and over-expenditures on prototype testing and design, indicating that the company was getting bogged down at the design stage.[35]

At one stage, the Multiplex Corporation was also involved in monitoring. In a letter to Premier Hatfield written on 20 December 1973, the general manager, R.K. Fletcher, presented a forecast of long-range sales and cash flow, which told the premier that previous production forecasts were overly optimistic and that production probably would not begin until March or April of 1974. However, the forecasts, based to a great degree on data provided by Bricklin, still predicted that the project would be profitable.[36] In short, the overall impression that this monitoring gave was that the project was behind schedule and over budget, but that progress was slowly being made.

The informal signals concerning the company's management problems were less encouraging, however. For example, Premier Hatfield himself had an early indication of the management problems. Jean de Villers, the first president of Bricklin Canada, resigned in October 1973 because of Albert Bricklin's (Malcolm's father) interference in his running of the company. When de Villers informed the premier, Hatfield's apparent lack of concern was reflected in their conversation.

"Have you told the board about the resignation?" Hatfield asked.

"Yes," said de Villers.

"Okay, goodbye," Hatfield said.[37]

A few months later, there was another important resignation. Eldon Thompson, a former secretary to the New Brunswick Treasury whom Hatfield had named to the board of Bricklin Canada, resigned. Although the ostensible cause for Thompson's resignation was that he was taking a new job in Ottawa as president of the Trans-Canada Telephone System, upon leaving he warned Hatfield about Bricklin's serious management problems.

Given the cost over-runs, it was necessary for Bricklin to raise additional funding early in 1974. At this point DREE made good its promise of a loan guarantee and provided $2.7 million. New Brunswick's commitment by then had increased to $4.5 million (the original $0.5 million in equity, the $2.88 million in bridge financing until DREE made its commitment, plus a newly approved $1.22 million). The Bank of Montreal and the First Pennsylvania Bank also increased their loans by $0.3 million and $5 million, respectively. An indication of how risky the First Pennsylvania considered the project was that its loan was made at 4 percent above prime.[38]

During this period, the Bricklin project had strong support within the government, for several reasons. First and foremost, it was Premier Hatfield's pet project, particularly during the 1974 election campaign. Secondly, by choosing to monitor the company's finances and its technological progress, Wheatley and Nason were overlooking its managerial problems. They assumed that Bricklin would be as effective a manager as he was a salesman. It was only after they gradually accumulated substantial informal evidence, such as conversations with Bricklin Canada executives who had resigned, that they began to question Bricklin's managerial skills. The government initially did not object to the firm's excessive nepotism, excessive geographic decentralization, high management salaries, and Malcolm Bricklin's sybaritic life-style. Thirdly, on the financial side, Joe Rose, Bricklin's treasurer, handled his requests for additional funding very shrewdly. He always asked for small increments in funding; asking for a larger sum of money might have frightened the government into asking some basic questions about the project. Furthermore, he knew the government was most vulnerable to spending requests during the election campaign, when Hatfield was singing the car's praises, and, indeed, he asked for a great deal of money at that time.[39]

On 8 October 1974 the government announced that it was lending another $2 million to Bricklin. The terms of the loan, though not made public at the time, indicate that the government by then was becoming concerned about Bricklin's management. Bricklin had to agree that all his companies were collectively liable for the loan; he was required to offer a personal guarantee for the loan; and he had to agree not to take salary or expense payments from Bricklin Canada.[40]

On October 31, the owners of the Saint John assembly plant that Bricklin was renting threatened to evict the company for non-payment. On November 6, the government decided to buy the plant for $1.5 million and lease it to Bricklin. On November 8, the Cabinet agreed to lend another $1 million to Bricklin. Neither of these loans was announced before the election.[41]

After the election, the situation did not improve. In a radio interview on November 20, Bricklin admitted that he was having production problems, and estimated that he would soon need to borrow another $6 to $8 million. On November 27, Bricklin Canada's lawyers were asking the government for another $3 million.[42]

The government had done its best to minimize public awareness of the company's problems during the election campaign, but after Bricklin's public statement it was impossible to continue doing so. Publication in the New Brunswick *Gazette* of the orders-in-council (an unavoidable statutory requirement) authorizing the loans made during the election campaign dramatized the problem still further. The New Brunswick media, in particular the Saint John *Telegraph-Journal*, began to criticize the government, as did the opposition.[43]

The best time in a government's mandate for enacting politically painful policies is right at the beginning, when its support is greatest. At this point, it was clear that Bricklin's management problems could no longer be ignored. While Stephen Wheatley was still monitoring the cheques and reporting to Joe Rose on defects he found when test-driving the car, Harry Nason was looking for consultants to make a serious examination of the company's problems and prospects.[44]

On December 2, Hatfield's press conference was a classic example of a politician publicly shifting his ground. While expressing confidence in Bricklin and avoiding details regarding the loans already made, so as to put the best possible face on the situation, he discussed the appointment of a consultant. To quote,

> Well, let me make it clear that the government is not employing a consultant to test or assess or judge its decision to invest in this project. But the government is, as it has with other industries, seeking to find . . . experts, if you will, who, who will be able to assist in meeting its production schedule and in getting faster to a production level, which will be . . . which will return a profit to the company. But I want to make it very clear that we are not, we do not have, we do not . . . we are not opening up for questioning the viability of this project. We believe this project is definitely viable.[45]

A few days later Hatfield shuffled his Cabinet, as was his custom after elections. Paul Creaghan, formerly minister of Economic Growth and responsible for Bricklin, was shifted to Justice. Hatfield replaced him with Lawrence Garvie, whom Fredericks and Chambers, the authors of a journalistic study of the Bricklin story, described as "a 40-year old Fredericton lawyer whose cautious, conciliatory manner had earned him the Speaker's chair in Hatfield's first government."[46] Changing ministers is a necessary prerequisite for changing policies.

Shortly thereafter, Hatfield announced that the government was lending Bricklin the $2.5 million it had asked for.[47] By this time the government had become deeply involved in running the company. It hired the management consulting firm of Clarkson Gordon to monitor transfer prices between Bricklin Canada and General Vehicle and to ensure that the Canadian company was receiving the appropriate revenues from the American parent. It also hired Wespac Development Planning Corporation, a Vancouver-based auto-industry consulting firm to advise on Bricklin's operational and production problems. Finally, the government demanded that Malcolm Bricklin appoint an experienced corporate executive to replace his father as president of Bricklin Canada.[48] Early in January 1975, Bricklin announced the appointment of Ralph Henry, a senior vice-president at the First Pennsylvania Bank, to head Bricklin Canada (which satisfied both the government and Bricklin's other major creditor, the bank).[49]

Bricklin's letter to the government on 15 January 1975, concerning Henry's appointment, is fascinating. After introducing Henry, he then went on enthusiastically and optimistically about various promotions, including his claim to have "made contact with Prince Faisal of Saudi Arabia, who has been in Arizona on a number of occasions and I anticipate by the end of January or beginning of February to be invited to a meeting with the Prince and his father either in Paris and/or Saudi Arabia." Bricklin concluded his letter with the following comments on the labour relations situation:

> The union situation is less than desirable and was culminated by an illegal wildcat strike, caused by an insignificant incident. I believe that the method in which it was cured will go a long way to cure the resentment between management and union. I think we will end up having an excellent relationship with our employees when the various pressures of money and time come into normal focus.[50]

One hopes the New Brunswick government gave these fantasies as little credence as they deserved.

By January the $2.5 million loaned in December had already been spent, and the company asked for another $7.5 million. The government agreed and advanced $3 million of this loan.[51] The terms of the agreement signed in March made it clear that the province no longer trusted Bricklin: it required him to assign all patents and trademarks to

Bricklin Canada and forbade him from undertaking any of the new projects he already had in mind (such as research on a new car and a new power train) until the first Bricklin model became profitable.[52]

At this point, Wheatley was monitoring such issues as personal living expenses paid to consultants hired by Bricklin, the allocation to Bricklin Canada rather than General Vehicle of $35,000 in expenses to bring auto dealers to Saint John to visit the plant, management salary increases, and the like. However, he was also working with the various consultants the government had hired.[53] By mid-1975, the results of the consulting studies began arriving. Wespac, the auto industry consultants, reported that the Bricklin plant was still not producing even 20 cars daily, far short of its target of 40. Problems that continued to plague the company were parts supply and achieving acceptable quality. The cost per car was estimated at $13,000.[54]

Financial statements for Bricklin Canada and General Vehicle for the fiscal year ending 30 June 1975 were disastrous. Bricklin lost $16.6 million and General Vehicle $6 million. Bricklin's balance sheet showed such questionable assets as $1 million for development rights to the Bricklin automobile, $6.6 million in tooling (some of which was scheduled to be replaced in several months), inventories of over $5 million, and almost $1 million in receivables for cars that had been shipped to the United States but not paid for. Liabilities included $5 million owing to suppliers, $2 million in short-term debt to the banks, and $20 million in long-term debt to the province of New Brunswick. The most interesting thing about General Vehicle's balance sheet was that the total share equity was a mere $72,000, of which the New Brunswick government had contributed $20,000. Malcolm Bricklin's only other "investment" in the car was a $2-million personal loan he had received from the First Pennsylvania Bank.

The studies done by the Clarkson Gordon management-consulting team contained more bad news. The transfer price for the 1974-model Bricklins was estimated to be $7400 and for the 1975 model to be $7900, far more than the $2200 originally estimated.[55] The company prepared an operating budget which showed that Bricklin Canada would lose only $500 per car by June 1976 and would therefore need additional government investment of only $2 million in the next fiscal year. This optimistic budget assumed that production costs and overhead could be substantially reduced, that the quality of the Bricklin car would improve dramatically, and that the company would therefore be able to sell its total production. Clarkson Gordon made it clear, however, that they did not consider it likely that all these conditions could be met, in which case Bricklin Canada would require up to $14 million in the next fiscal year in order to stay solvent.[56]

One aspect of the report that was cause for continuing concern was the gull-wing doors. The budget included a $400 warranty cost for each car already sold to cover the cost of converting the hydraulic opening mechanism for the gull-wing doors to a screw-type mechanism. The company had decided to produce future cars with the screw-type mechanism, but had not perfected it yet.[57]

In early September, Clarkson Gordon's pessimistic projections were virtually confirmed when Bricklin Canada asked the New Brunswick government for another $10 million.[58] The government's response to this request will be discussed in the next chapter.

CANADAIR

The Sale of a New Machine

By 1975, General Dynamics' disinvestment policy had reduced employment at Canadair to 1250 and had clobbered morale. For this reason, the Challenger program represented a new lease on life for Canadair's management.[59] On the one hand, the Challenger program had the advantages of a design by Bill Lear and an apparent demand in the executive aircraft market for a larger plane employing the latest technology. On the other hand, the company was greatly understaffed; for example, the engineering staff was at a record low of 150. Furthermore, Canadair had never designed and produced a complete aircraft. In terms of their personal stake in the project, the senior managers of Canadair were then in their early fifties — too young to retire but probably too old to move to a new industry. The Challenger program, if successful, would allow them to retire in a blaze of glory; if unsuccessful, it would at least allow them to hold onto their jobs during their peak earning years and retire with good pensions. The managers chose to gamble by adopting an aggressive strategy to develop the Challenger as quickly as possible and sell as many units as possible.

Canadair president Frederick Kearns and his fellow executives realized that their immediate problems would be to convince the market to place orders for a blueprint of a plane that would be developed by a small, relatively unknown firm and to convince someone to lend Canadair the money to develop the plane. Given the federal government's austerity program, Kearns realized funding would have to come from the banks. The banks would lend only if Canadair could show them committed sales and give them government guarantees to back up the loans.[60] Whereas the government was anxious to maintain employment in Montreal, it seemed that it would be more likely to support the Canadair program if it were projected to be profitable. Thus the solution to the problems depended upon lining up sales.

As part of its agreement with Lear to develop his design, Canadair promised to pre-sell fifty aircraft. On 1 April 1976, the day after the agreement was signed, Kearns hired James B. Taylor, an American ex-fighter pilot and business aircraft super-salesman, who at the time was working for Cessna.[61] Taylor was made vice-president in charge of marketing and president of Canadair Inc., the company's American subsidiary and major sales division. Taylor's assignment was to get fifty orders for the Challenger within six months. Given that Canadair had no experience selling business aircraft, Kearns gave Taylor virtual carte blanche to set whatever terms he felt were necessary to clinch the deals. A lesser salesman might have been deterred by the fact that the Challenger existed only as a design and some computer simulations indicating it would be faster and more economical than its competition. Taylor, however, took this as an opportunity, since he could promise that Canadair would make whatever modifications to the basic design that were necessary to land a contract.[62] In response to Taylor's flexibility, the engineering staff began to tinker with Lear's basic design, making the plane even more spacious.[63] In addition, Jean Chrétien, the minister responsible for Canadair at the time, let the company know about his personal preference for a more spacious plane.

A critical issue was the type of engine the aircraft should have. Canadair was inclined to use tried-and-true General Electric engines. Lear, however, who had had disagreements with General Electric in the past, was urging Canadair to use a new quiet, fuel-efficient turbofan engine being developed by Avco Lycoming. The danger in attempting to combine a new airframe with a new engine is that it squares Murphy's law, dramatically increasing the probability that something will go wrong. The engine was chosen when Taylor got an offer from Federal Express to buy twenty-five Challengers, an offer contingent on Canadair's using the Avco engine.[64] At that time, the American airline industry was still regulated: Federal Express was not allowed to fly anything larger than a business jet. Therefore, the company wanted a business jet that was as large and fuel-efficient as possible.

The terms under which Canadair initially sold the Challenger were very generous. The price was US$4.5 million, which was quite low. To quote Kearns' testimony about the pricing strategy:

> It is common in our industry to start off a new airplane at an attractively low price and then, as quickly as possible, get the price up. There are two major factors that help you do that. One, of course, is escalation in actual costs; and two, as the airplane gets more acceptability in the marketplace, as more people buy it and as the airplanes get into service, if you have got a good product then you have room to keep moving the price up.[65]

The other terms of the early contracts were equally generous: purchasers were required to deposit only 5 percent of the price and deposits would earn the current prime rate; prices were fixed; and Canadair made optimistic commitments regarding the performance characteristics of the aircraft. The original specifications called for a 32,500-pound aircraft that would carry five passengers a theoretical 4000 nautical miles and be able to take off from a 5000-foot runway.[66] The range would be attractive to purchasers, since it would allow them to fly non-stop across the Atlantic or from the Middle East to London. Until November 1978, the Challenger was sold on the basis of these specifications.

Taylor brought in orders for 56 planes, thus exceeding his quota. In November, the Canadian Imperial Bank of Commerce and Provincial Bank of Canada agreed to lend Canadair $125 million on the condition that half the loan be underwritten by the federal government.[67] ITC minister Jean Chrétien convinced Cabinet to go along with the guarantee. Thereafter, the marketing department continued to hustle sales, and by June 1977, Canadair was predicting that within six years, it would deliver 236 Challengers, 100 more than the expected break-even on the program.[68]

Murphy Was An Optimist

When Canadair made the commitment to make the Challenger more spacious, the effect on the airplane's performance had not been studied fully.[69] By 1978, it was discovered that the first prototype could not meet Canadair's specifications. The Avco engines did not have enough power. The engineers attempted to extend the aircraft's range by reducing its fuselage weight and adding more fuel tanks, but these increased the runway length required for take-off. By the time the Challenger was certified in Canada in August 1980, its weight had increased to 40,400 pounds, its range had diminished to 3200 miles, and its take-off runway length had increased to 5400 feet.[70]

Constant modification of the aircraft design had a number of serious consequences. At first, it delayed production and the dates when deliveries were promised. Then, in order to keep from falling too far behind its promised delivery schedule, management decided to begin production before the design problems had been fully solved. As a result of this, it was necessary to modify some of the planes after the customers had taken delivery, which was a very costly labour-intensive operation. In addition, some parts had to be scrapped, and suppliers paid for parts that could not be used. The Canada Development Investment Corporation (CDIC) estimates that the direct costs of the modifications totalled $300 million.[71]

Probably the worst consequence of the delays and failure to meet specifications was that many orders were cancelled. The dominance of Canadair's marketing department became very counterproductive when the economy suffered a downturn. Using their considerable powers of persuasion, the Canadair salesforce tailored each contract to the wishes of the customer and frequently gave way to customer demands in order to obtain orders. Normally, when salespeople are paid on commission, constraints are imposed to prevent deals from being signed that are in the best interests of salespeople and the customer but not the company. Apparently, whatever constraints were imposed by James Taylor, or by head office in Montreal, were not stringent enough, and many of the deals signed were later found by the Public Accounts Committee to be too generous. Part of the reason for this was that the salesforce was convinced that making enough sales to establish the jet in the market and lower unit costs was of greater importance initially than high profits.

The concessions made in these contracts might still have worked in the company's best interests if it were not for the combination of the ailing economy and production's inability to deliver on marketing's promises. Many of the companies that had ordered Challengers were facing unexpectedly bleak prospects, and the last thing they needed was to have to take delivery of a shiny new jet while laying off employees and cutting costs. Since they had already signed contracts for the planes and could not cancel their order, some tried to sell their order positions. Before the economic downturn, while the Challenger was in the midst of its first flush of publicity, speculators had been buying up order positions and selling them at a profit to bidders who did not wish to wait two years for delivery. At this time, however, order positions could not even be sold at a loss. It was very much to the benefit of these reluctant purchasers that the Challenger failed to live up to its original promises. When it was discovered that the Challenger could not meet the specifications detailed in the purchase contracts, buyers were no longer obligated to accept delivery, since the plane that was manufactured was not the same as the plane they had ordered.[72]

One key contract that fell through was with Federal Express. In January 1978, as part of the deregulation of the U.S. airline industry, Federal Express received permission to fly larger aircraft. Since there was a good market in used DC-9s at a price of $2 million, the more expensive and then unflown Challenger was no longer very attractive. At that point Federal Express wanted to back out of the deal and threatened Canadair that, if it were forced to accept delivery, it would simply resell the planes. Canadair was thus faced with the choice of potentially destructive competition if Federal Express took the planes, or a shortening of the order book and a serious erosion of buyer and banker confidence if the contract were cancelled completely. The contract was amended so that Canadair would resell twenty of the twenty-five planes and Federal Express buy the remaining five for $22 million. In March 1978, this order was amended further so that Canadair agreed to sell four of the five planes for Federal Express and give them the profit of $2.1 million per plane. When it ultimately took delivery of the one Challenger in March 1983, Federal Express had received $8.4 million in cash, $4 million more than the $4.4 million it paid for the plane.[73] Although these contracts have never been released for public scrutiny, the rather one-sided outcome makes it clear that maintaining the *appearance of a firm contract* with Federal Express must have been very important to Canadair's management.

Charles Rathgeb, a Canadair director appointed when General Dynamics still owned the company, feels in retrospect that the logical thing to have done in early 1978 after the Federal Express contract had fallen apart would have been to cancel the order to buy the Avco Lycoming engines and go back to General Electric. However, the company continued its relationship with Avco, and this caused further problems. As one might have expected, problems were experienced in developing the engine, which forced Canadair to send its staff to Avco's Stanford (Connecticut) plant to provide assistance. In addition, Avco was then giving greater priority to a tank engine procurement for the U.S. Defense Department. As a result, Avco actually delivered only 45 of the 114 engines it had agreed to deliver, many of which were defective. Therefore, in 1983, Canadair sued Avco for $110 million for lost sales and added costs due to the delays.[74]

In March 1980, Canadair's management, with board approval, decided to embark on an aggressive strategy to respond to the performance problems troubling the original model (which was called the Challenger 600). It decided to develop a stretched Challenger, the 610, using General Electric engines, with a maximum take-off weight of 49,000 pounds, which could carry six passengers 3950 nautical miles. Canadair also decided to develop the Challenger 601, which would also use General Electric engines and incorporate a number of aeronautical improvements to deliver the performance first promised for the Challenger 600. Immediately, Canadair Inc. began marketing both the 610 and the 601. However, the engineering difficulties in simultaneously developing two new aircraft, particularly the 610, proved too great for Canadair. By August 1981, the Challenger 610 program was scrapped, after incurring $9 million in development costs.[75] In order to keep its customers, Canadair offered the firms that had signed contracts for the 610 the alternative of purchasing either the 600 or the 601 at $1 million below list price. In addition, General Electric, after losing the order for the Challenger 610 engines, insisted on renegotiating the contract for the 601 engines: Canadair, in a very weak bargaining position, agreed to take 200 engines for the 601, rather than 100, and at a 20-percent price increase.[76] It was estimated that the incremental cost of developing the 601 was approximately $60 million.[77]

Another cause of delay for Canadair was getting its aircraft certified in both Canada and the United States. The company hoped to have certification completed in both countries by March 1979. Certification was delayed by changes in the standards themselves, Canadair's changes in the Challenger design, and finally by the crash of one of the prototypes during flight testing in April 1980.[78] The initial design of the Challenger

600 was certified in Canada in August 1980 and in the United States the following November. These delays meant that Canadair had to bear the cost of holding planes it could not deliver. The modified versions of the original design also required certification, a process that was not completed until April 1982.[79]

Finally, Canadair suffered from two problems not of its own making. First, the major source of funding for the Challenger program was debt, much of it denominated in U.S. currency and much at floating rates. As interest rates increased, the debt burden increased, so that by the end of 1982, $468 million of the $1.9 billion cost of the program was attributed to interest and foreign exchange.[80] The deep recession of 1982 hurt sales dramatically: between May and July of that year, the number of soft sales (that is, those for which the purchaser had decided to postpone delivery) increased from three to fourteen.[81]

Management's Responsibility

Although some of Canadair's problems, such as the rise in interest rates and the 1982 recession, were not Canadair's fault and were difficult to anticipate, management must bear the major brunt of the responsibility because it made three crucial errors. First, it was much too willing to promise whatever was necessary — price, financing, specifications, delivery dates — in order to sell aircraft. From the point of view of the buyer, signing a contract with Canadair represented very little risk. If the company could deliver on its promises, the buyer would have a great aircraft: if not, it might be possible to get out of the deal. If a purchaser were forced to accept delivery of an airplane priced below cost, it would still be possible to resell it at a profit.

Management's second error was that it was invariably over-optimistic about its market. Forecasted sales always exceeded realized sales. Even as the plane experienced substantial development problems, forecasted sales kept increasing. For example, in 1976, Canadair predicted that it would sell 250 Challengers: by June 1981, the figure had risen to 506. However, by March 1984, only 100 had actually been delivered.[82]

Management's third error was that, because of its inexperience as a business-aircraft producer, it underestimated the technical and production difficulties that would be involved in designing both a new airframe and a new engine simultaneously, having the airplane certified, and then putting it into production. This lack of realism meant that management did little to control what the sales force forecasted or offered the market. As a result, because costs were not estimated correctly, prices were unrealistically low. Promising too much to the market and overestimating sales also compounded the production problems: parts were ordered and airplanes were manufactured too soon, which led to substantial waste.

In terms of management theory, Canadair's problem was that it became an inappropriately marketing-dominated firm. In their classic article about strategy-making in technology-based businesses, Ansoff and Stewart discuss the appropriate relationship between functional areas for technology-based businesses with long product life-cycles:

> With adequate time to learn about competitive market developments and to plan to counter them, there is no need for unusual market sensitivity. In the long-cycle, company emphasis is on established procedure and routine. Organization is usually functional. Managerial decisions usually favor economy and efficiency at the expense of rapid response.

> Moreover, planning is usually sequential — that is, detailed R and D is completed before manufacturing and marketing planning is begun. Manufacturing and marketing are seldom deeply involved in technical planning. In fact, the technical staff may include market research specialists to help with long-run R and D planning.[83]

Not only did Canadair's management make the three management errors discussed above, but it also used a liberal interpretation of program accounting, which had the effect of making the company's financial performance appear to be better than it actually was. Program accounting is designed to match expense and revenue flows for a program (such as the development of a new aircraft) that has large start-up costs which are recoverable only after the product is manufactured and sold. In essence, program accounting permits manufacturers to treat development expenses as an investment and spread them out over the life of the program. In addition, the average cost per plane over the entire life of the program is estimated, and that cost is attributed to each aircraft. In actuality, due to the learning curve effect, costs are higher than average at first and decrease later, a situation that also spreads out the accountant's estimate of costs over the life of the program. Thus, an aircraft company's financial statements would show relatively constant gross profits per aircraft over the life of the program.[84]

Canadair differed from other aircraft manufacturers in that it used program accounting aggressively, thus capitalizing costs which other companies would have expensed: general and administrative overhead, interest, marketing costs, commissions, royalties, and product-support costs. Furthermore, Canadair calculated its costs not on the number of planes it could reasonably expect to sell but on the estimated break-even number of sales. As a result of these practices, Canadair appeared to be in a break-even position in 1980 and 1981, whereas more conservative practices would have shown losses of $141 million and $234 million, respectively.[85]

During the hearings of the Public Accounts Committee, Canadair's auditors (the firm of Thorne, Riddell) felt Canadair's forecasts regarding future orders were sufficiently reasonable that they accepted their projections that the company would achieve its break-even point by 1987.[86] However, one wonders if they looked closely at some of Canadair's contracts, an exercise that might have inspired some skepticism. It was only after the recession had dramatically changed Canadair's prospects that the auditors concluded that the forecasts could no longer be realized. This led to the company's writing off over $1 billion in development costs in 1982, when it appeared that these costs would be unrecoverable.

Monitoring Canadair

It is commonly accepted that representatives of the company's shareholders should hold management accountable, and in a situation such as that discussed above, either persuade it to improve its performance, or replace it with more capable people. Given that the government was Canadair's sole shareholder during this period, the questions then become how the government monitored Canadair, and whether there were any significant breakdowns in its monitoring procedures.

We can identify two distinct phases in the monitoring of Canadair: the first we shall call the "business-as-usual" phase, extending from the acquisition of the company by the government in January 1976 until early 1981; the second, crisis monitoring, took place from early 1981 until the acquisition of Canadair by CDIC in November 1982. Before discussing these phases, it would be useful to compare it to General Dynamics' monitoring of Canadair when it was a wholly owned subsidiary. During this period Canadair was subjected to periodic but intensive scrutiny by the senior management of General Dynamics, who were obviously deeply versed in all facets of the aerospace industry. In this context the role of Canadair's board of directors, like that of many boards of wholly owned subsidiaries, was to advise local management on the Canadian situation and provide some marketing support. Thus, there was very strong shareholder control, something which, as the following sections will show, was lost when the government took Canadair over.[87]

"Business-as-Usual" Monitoring: 1976–81

The key question about the monitoring regime in this period is why it failed to send the government signals about Canadair's problems. In our search for clues, we were faced with three problems. Accounts by Canadair directors and others involved in monitoring the company tend to be self-serving; each person attempted to exculpate himself and blame the others. In addition, one key participant, Frederick Kearns, Canadair's CEO at the time, declined to speak with us. Finally, board of directors' minutes are unavailable. Thus, our conclusions are based on our weighing of the evidence that is on the public record and the interviews we have been accorded.

During this period, the government had two means of monitoring Canadair. First, there was the board of directors. When the government purchased Canadair in January 1976, its five directors, who were employed by General Dynamics, resigned and were replaced by the deputy minister of ITC (O.G. Stoner), three assistant deputy ministers (Burns, Lavigueur, and Guérin) and an assistant deputy minister of Justice (Troop). With the establishment of the second review mechanism, an interdepartmental review committee (discussed below), this representation diminished: Burns and Troop left the board in January 1977 and Stoner in March 1977. Lavigueur soon left ITC to become the president of the Federal Business Development Bank, but stayed on the Canadair board until March 1981. As the assistant deputy minister for Industry and Commerce Development, Guérin served on the Canadair board until he left ITC in September 1981.[88] Thus, he was the government's sole representative on the Canadair board for most of this period. The board also included one representative of management, Kearns, and several long-time outside directors, including Charles Rathgeb, chairman of Comstock Construction; Leo Lavoie, then CEO of the Provincial Bank of Canada; former Cabinet minister Jean-Pierre Goyer; David Culver, chairman of the Aluminum Company of Canada; and Walter Ward, then CEO of Canadian General Electric.[89] The board met monthly and most meetings lasted for an entire day.

The second monitoring mechanism, an interdepartmental review committee, had representatives of ITC, Finance, Treasury Board Secretariat, and Transport. It was chaired by the director-general of the transportation industries branch of ITC, who was a subordinate of Guérin's, but Guérin attended most of the meetings.[90] According to Kearns, Canadair made detailed monthly reports to the transportation industries branch; these were discussed by the interdepartmental committee and were used by Guérin as preparation for his role at Canadair board of directors meetings.[91] In addition, the review committee met four times a year with Canadair management in what Guérin claimed were "full-dress meetings going into a great level of detail."[92] These meetings served as the basis for quarterly reports to ministers.[93] Finally, Guérin himself met frequently with Kearns.[94]

As might be expected, when testifying to the Public Accounts Committee, both Kearns and Guérin argued that these were effective monitoring mechanisms. Kearns gave two examples to show that management kept the board informed throughout this period:

> The bottom line in terms of how we satisfied the board that we still could break even boiled down always to our market projections. These two items were always discussed at great length. In fact, once a year during the history of the [Challenger] program, we brought in the senior members

of the marketing department to the board meeting for what generally turned out to be a two-to-three hour session of presentations and questions and answers. . . . the problem of borrowing versus equity was a frequently discussed problem at our board meetings. At every opportunity, I think it fair to say, we made this concern known, and I believe the board minutes would bear out that we were concerned about the lack of equity from a very early stage in the program.[95]

Guérin's story is similar: "At the board meetings the important issues in design and performance were identified and reported on. . . . I think the board was made up of highly independent individuals who saw a government member there as a necessity, but nothing beyond that."[96] Furthermore, Guérin, when asked at which point he began to recognize Canadair's problems, said that in early 1979, both the review committee and the board of directors became aware of the company's major problems, such as the design, the engine, and the certification process. However, "management did not just attempt to identify problems without providing at least some plan to deal with them."[97]

These claims to the contrary, a number of the people we interviewed felt that management had not kept the board of directors sufficiently informed of some of Canadair's key problems. Both Goyer and Rathgeb claimed that the details of Canadair's disastrous relationship with Federal Express were not fully discussed by the board.[98] Contradicting his testimony to the Public Accounts Committee, Guérin told us that management did not communicate the full extent of the Challenger's technical problems to the board.[99]

Rathgeb gave an interesting account of how he learned of the Challenger's performance shortcomings. As an avid flyer, he was planning to use the Challenger to break the record for an around-the-world business jet flight, but "all of a sudden the chief pilot and everybody that I had been dealing with on this exploit became very vague and not ready to talk and postponed the planning and so on." Rathgeb recalls discussing the matter with Kearns, who said that the company was making modifications to the aircraft, which initially satisfied him. ("Well, I'm not an aeronautical engineer, so I went for that for a while.")[100] Ultimately, Rathgeb (rather than Kearns) raised the issue with the board, but to no effect.

Not only was management less than honest with the board, but the board was less than zealous in its overseeing of management. Goyer recounts that the majority of the board, including its chairman, supported management uncritically, with the result that the board rarely had open discussions of the company's prospects.[101] It should be noted that Goyer's attempts to deal with the company's problems were not taken seriously by his colleagues; Goyer wanted to become chairman of the board and so his criticisms were always viewed as motivated by personal ambition.

The composition of the board also became cause for concern. The first group of directors who came in after the government purchased Canadair were brought in by the management team. After a time, however, the board became dominated by lawyers and investment people, and the majority of new board members' most apparent qualification was that they were Liberal party supporters.[102]

Based on what was said in our interviews, as well as conclusions drawn by the Public Accounts Committee, we believe the board adopted an unduly passive role in monitoring management. There are a number of reasons why this occurred. The government never provided the board with a clear statement of objectives.[103] Nonetheless, board members were politically astute enough to know that the government had an implicit objective in its participation in Canadair, which was to provide jobs in Montreal to prove that federalism was preferable to the separatist option. This unspoken but ever-present objective, as well as Chrétien's enthusiasm for Canadair, could have diminished the board's vigour. Finally, to quote Goyer's testimony to the Public Accounts Committee, "We ourselves even tended to look to the government member [Guérin] to see whether or not he approved of a proposal made by management. If he approved, we concluded that the shareholder also approved."[104]

Given his roles as government representative on the board of directors and the *de facto* head of the review committee, Guérin played a pivotal role in monitoring Canadair. Our interpretation of the evidence is that he lacked expertise, was generally supportive of the project, and did not forcefully communicate any concerns he may have had about the Challenger project to his ministers.[105] Guérin's training was in industrial engineering and management and his experience was in textiles, facts that suggest he lacked the knowledge to undertake detailed criticism of the company's technological and marketing assessments.[106] He had been involved in the government's decision to develop the Challenger.[107] In his testimony to the Public Accounts Committee, his description of his relationship to the ministers of ITC, whom he served, is formal, defensive, and qualified:

> We had mechanisms to provide the minister responsible with full information that we had on the progress being made in the Challenger program and on the issues that were raised from time to time. . . we did advise the minister on all aspects that I was aware of with respect to the management of the enterprise. . . (I briefed the minister prior to attending board meetings) to the extent that the minister was available at the time, of course.[108]

In mid-1981, Guérin left his position at ITC to become a vice-president of Canadair in the customer relations area. The fact that he was offered the job by a management which had been less than forthright with the board suggests that management viewed him as a supporter rather than

a critic. The fact that he took the job indicates he felt comfortable with
the company. Indeed, Guérin told us that he knew about customer dissatisfaction with the Challenger, but he was unaware of the magnitude
of the technical problems.[109]

Although Guérin must shoulder a great deal of the blame for the
poor monitoring of the Challenger project, the review committee was
also at fault. To quote Guérin:

> Now there is perhaps where the question may arise as to whether board
> members, or even officials, were fully qualified to probe deeply into some
> of these [technical] areas and to receive all the appropriate responses.
> Obviously, the management provided assumptions . . . I am not convinced,
> at least at the level of officials, that we were fully qualified to probe and
> to second-guess management assumptions.[110]

On this point, Guérin is corroborated by William Teschke, the associate
deputy minister of ITC in 1981, who took a much more vigorous approach
to monitoring Canadair than did Guérin. Nevertheless, Teschke admitted to the Public Accounts Committee that the government, in particular ITC, was lacking in its capacity to monitor Canadair during this
period. He said, "I believe it is quite difficult to hire and retain, within
its public service staff, people who can adequately judge management
of a commercial corporation, except well after the fact."[111]

To sum up, Canadair was not monitored well during this period.
All individuals and organizations involved merit part of the blame.
Management was not frank with the board of directors, and the board
lacked expertise. In addition, the government, which chose the inexpert directors, also failed to give them a clear sense of its objectives for
the company or for the Challenger program. Thus the board was passive and accepting, rather than an active force in managing the company.
Guérin, the key link between the government and the company, lacked
expertise and also tended to be passive and accepting of the project. He
did not communicate vigorously to his ministers any concerns he might
have had. The interdepartmental review committee worked from the
information Canadair and Guérin provided, and it also lacked expertise.
Finally, the Challenger program had the support of the Trudeau government, in particular the Quebec caucus and as influential a minister
as Chrétien.

Furthermore, funding the company by means of letters of comfort
avoided close parliamentary and/or public scrutiny of the program's
progress.

The Year of Monitoring Closely: 1981-82

By early 1981, Canadair was repeatedly exceeding its projected cash
requirements, and the minister of ITC frequently had to sign letters of

comfort. By this time, the Treasury Board Secretariat was requiring Crown corporations to submit long-term plans regarding their capital requirements. The magnitude of Canadair's request impelled the secretariat to establish an interdepartmental task force in April to examine Canadair's problems more deeply. It was composed of representatives of Finance, ITC, the Treasury Board Secretariat, and Transport, and headed by Mark Daniels, an assistant deputy minister in Finance. The original review committee, having proven ineffective, was disbanded. The new task force had people working full-time, as well as the help of outside consultants, in particular Aviation Planning Services, the company that had been optimistic about the Challenger project in 1976.[112] The task force report, which has not been made public, dealt mainly with Canadair's marketing problems. It observed that the company's sales forecasts were not being met and produced a new set of lower forecasts. The task force also examined the Challenger's escalating costs and estimated that Canadair would be able to operate within a new, higher credit ceiling of $1.35 billion.[113] However, the report did not deal with the aircraft's technical problems; nor did it recommend any radical change in the company's management.

At about the time the task force was being established, Jean-Pierre Goyer independently approached both Herb Gray, the minister of ITC, and Donald Johnston, president of the Treasury Board, to discuss Canadair's problems. Dissatisfied with their responses, Goyer told Trudeau of his concern that Canadair was being mismanaged. Indeed, Goyer threatened to resign if nothing were done. Trudeau suggested that Goyer take up the matter with Michael Pitfield, clerk of the Privy Council Office.[114] On 9 June 1981, Goyer sent Pitfield a memo which outlined his dissatisfaction with the company's management based on its inability to plan and its over-optimism. He recommended a strategic analysis of the aeronautics industry in order to determine Canadair's long-term strategy, as well as the replacement of various directors and senior managers of the company.[115] Presumably, Pitfield checked into the matter and discovered that a task force was already working on it; nevertheless, Goyer's intervention alerted Trudeau and Pitfield to Canadair's emerging problems and added a sense of urgency to the task force's work.

In September 1981, William Teschke replaced Guérin on the Canadair board of directors. Teschke had a stronger mandate and more ministerial interest. He testified, "It was made very clear to me by my minister [The Hon. Herb Gray] before I joined the board that he wished to be kept completely informed."[116] When Teschke became secretary to the minister of state for Economic and Regional Development in January 1982, he was replaced on the board by Gordon Ritchie, the new associate deputy minister. Ritchie described his approach to the meetings in more detail: upon receiving the agenda for a meeting, he consulted with both his staff and his minister; at the meeting, he "attempted forcefully and competently to communicate the concerns of the government to the members of the board of directors;" and immediately after the meeting he provided a detailed report for his minister, who had now become very interested in Canadair.[117]

ITC decided to take a much more active approach to managing Canadair than the task force report recommended. ITC minister Herb Gray presented his proposals to Cabinet, incorporating the task force report as a supporting document. He then met with the Canadair board of directors. Shortly thereafter, on February 15, Kearns and Ritchie (acting as the government's representative) signed a formal agreement by which Canadair agreed to live within the credit limit of $1.35 billion, to submit a five-year corporate plan, and to submit monthly analyses of its performance relative to the plan. If Canadair could not live within the credit limit, the government would give "full consideration of all the alternatives open to [it] to protect its interest as shareholder."[118] In addition, Ritchie revamped Canadair's process of reporting to the department, which he found to have been seriously deficient in the past. The corporation was required to make much more detailed monthly reports of its operations, which Ritchie then conveyed to an ad hoc committee of senior officials chaired by the secretary to the Treasury Board.[119] In the following months, the committee and Herb Gray, the minister of ITC and DREE, reviewed Canadair's statement of objectives and major decisions concerning all its programs.

The weakness in sales during 1982 meant that Canadair was no longer able to live within its debt ceiling. Close monitoring convinced senior officials and ministers that there were serious weaknesses in Canadair's management. By November, the government agreed to request parliamentary authorization to increase its equity in the corporation by $200 million. However, the government assumed even greater control of all aspects of the Canadair program, including marketing, production, materials acquisition, and collective bargaining.[120] In addition, Shieldings Investments Ltd. of Toronto was hired to do an independent analysis of Canadair's financial affairs, including an assessment of the market and the nature of the sales and distributorship contracts into which the company had entered. The report was very critical of the situation:

> The successful public relations program recently used to camouflage the $200 million of additional subsidy makes it appropriate for this report to state bluntly the current realities:
> i) there is no chance for recovering the investment in Challenger,
> ii) the aircraft adds little of significance to the repertoire of Canadian manufacturing or technological capabilities,
> iii) the cost per permanent job created is many times too high,
> iv) management failures have provided a pointed demonstration of how ill-equipped the shareholder has been, in the past, to own and monitor a commercial business,

    v) rather than a triumph, the Challenger is simply another executive
        jet the world could do without.[121]

The next chapter will discuss why the government rejected the line of advice implicit in the Shieldings analysis, and opted instead to keep the Challenger program alive, albeit with new management.

CHURCHILL FOREST INDUSTRIES

The Basic Concept

As mentioned in the previous chapter, the economic justification for building a pulp mill in northern Manitoba was highly questionable, even with government assistance. Arthur D. Little had reported enthusiastically on the region's prospects from 1958 on, but also added that special incentives would be needed to counteract the disadvantages of the region. Initially, the incentives suggested were quite reasonable and included reduced stumpage rates, larger than normal timber cutting grants, reduced hydro rates, and free provision of services, such as fire protection, road construction, and power lines. They later came to include more expensive concessions, such as tax holidays, payments by the province to the municipality for townsite development, purchase and leaseback of certain capital assets, and options to purchase land and other assets at extraordinarily low prices.[122] Because of the ideology of the Roblin government, no reassessment of the wisdom of the project was ever undertaken, despite the number of rejections received and the increasingly generous incentives offered.

    Manitoba also found itself in competition with other provinces for pulp and paper developments. In 1962, for example, Saskatchewan succeeded in attracting Parsons and Whittemore to build a plant in Prince Albert at a cost of $65 million. To accomplish this, the Saskatchewan government accepted most of the risk of the project but relinquished most of the ownership.[123] Not only did this competition for projects add to the pressure to offer more and more incentives, it also caused the Department of Industry and Commerce to send out to prospective developers data whose optimism increased until it bordered on fiction. This caused knowledgeable recipient firms to be suspicious of the project.[124]

The Negotiating Position

Between 1959 and 1965, the steadfastness with which the government refused to give away too much during negotiations eroded rapidly. By late 1965, a great deal of time and money had been expended on these fruitless negotiations. Rex Grose, one of the two most respected civil servants in the Manitoba government at that time, would later testify that he had faced a nearly impossible task in trying to find a pulp and paper company to develop the north.[125] Before Monoca came on the scene in the summer of 1965, the only serious lead still being investigated was a proposal by Mayo Holdings, a company that had no experience in the pulp and paper field.

Furthermore, the Roblin government was coming to the end of its mandate. Since the previous election had been held 14 December 1962, the most attractive time for the next election was between the spring and fall of 1966. The Roblin government was thus interested in having some project or projects to support its campaign for re-election. Grose later denied having been pressured by the government to attract a pulp and paper operation to northern Manitoba before the next election, but admitted, "There was a great desire on the part of the government to get going."[126] The eagerness of the government meant that its negotiating position was not as strong as it might otherwise have been.

The Negotiating Process

Two factors complicated the negotiating process and created later problems. One was that Grose was involved in three roles: as the deputy minister of Industry and Commerce, as the vice-chairman of the Manitoba Development Fund, and as a member of the Manitoba Development Authority. This created confusion with regard to whose behalf he was acting on when dealing with Monoca. During the negotiations, he meant to act only for the Department of Industry and Commerce. Roblin and the Cabinet, however, believed he was acting for the Development Fund, and that he was keeping the fund's board of directors informed of all terms under negotiation. The impact of this confusion will be discussed in the section on decision-making and monitoring.

The second factor, related to the first, was that at each step of the negotiation, the government committed itself to more than it realized. The Commission of Inquiry, in reviewing the legal documents, concluded in 1974 that the option given to Monoca in 1965 was legally binding, and that the government would have faced a lawsuit if it had tried to award the project to another developer. However, Duff Roblin told the commission that he and his ministers believed the agreement only obligated the government to negotiate with Monoca either until an agreement was reached or until the option expired.[127] This was not the case. From 29 September 1965, the government was legally committed to award the contract to Monoca, on at least as favourable terms as contained in the option agreement.

The option itself consisted of a letter, which contained the contractual offer to proceed, and two exhibits. Exhibit A was a memorandum of agreement setting forth some of the specific actions Monoca would undertake, such as feasibility studies. Exhibit B was a memorandum setting forth the general principles and a number of specifics of the proposed loan from the MDF. Both exhibits were drafted by Monoca's lawyers; they were not the product of negotiations between Monoca and the government. Cabinet accepted the total proposal a day after receiving it in September 1965, without first seeking a legal opinion. In doing so, it unwittingly committed the fund to providing up to $40.7 million in financing, and it bound itself to abide by the terms of Exhibit B.

Exhibit B had a number of flaws. To begin with, it obligated only Monoca's operating company, CFI, and not Monoca itself. Normally, when dealing with operating companies set up for the purposes of a specific project, the MDF required contractual assurances from the parent company as well as the operating company. Exhibit B also later prevented Grose and the fund's legal counsel, Walter C. Newman, from obtaining amendments which would improve the fund's position. Because Exhibit B was binding, it provided Monoca with a fall-back position; if no other agreement could be reached, the company could insist on the terms of Exhibit B. Thus, Monoca was under no obligation to allow any more onerous conditions to be placed on it than were provided for in Exhibit B, and in further negotiations, Monoca guarded this right assiduously.[128]

The members of Cabinet were not only unaware that they had made binding commitments, they also believed Rex Grose had been acting on behalf of the fund, and that the fund was fully apprised of the situation regarding the loan. For this reason, the Cabinet was at all times under the impression that the MDF could and would carry out its normal duties — that it would gather information about the principals, evaluate the loan, and decide whether or not to make it. This proved not to be the case (see the section on Decision-Making and Monitoring, below).

The Issue of Non-Disclosure

As mentioned in the previous chapter, the government did not know the identities of Monoca's principals at the time the option was given in 1965. In fact, Monoca's position from the outset was that it would not enter into any agreement which required it to disclose its principals, stating as its reason simply that such disclosure was contrary to Swiss corporate practice. Rather than allow the deal to go sour, the government took what it believed to be an appropriate precaution against fraud and proceeded.

It warrants mentioning that not everyone was willing to alter their practices to accommodate Monoca's way of doing business. The federal Area Development Agency had declared The Pas a disadvantaged area and was willing to offer sizeable grants to companies that would bring new development to such regions. However, the agency stood firm in its insistence that the grant would not be remitted until the identity of the beneficial owners of the project was revealed.

The identity of Monoca's principals became an issue once again when it was discovered that Monoca and Technopulp had interlocking directorships. The Manitoba government did not wish to provide 100 percent of the financing for the project and wanted the 14 percent equity Monoca was to furnish to come from sources other than Monoca affiliates. Allowing profits earned by affiliates to be recycled into the project as equity would create an incentive for CFI to award all subcontracts to its affiliates and for the affiliates to overcharge for their services. Exhibit B, however, provided very little protection against this practice, stating in section 9:

> Goods and services may be purchased from shareholders or affiliates of the Operating Company [i.e., CFI], provided that the cost, terms and conditions of such purchases shall be reasonable and provided further that, in the acquisition of material, equipment, goods and services, preference shall first be given to Manitoba and secondly to Canadian suppliers, provided always that the price, quality and services are equal.[129]

Since refusal to disclose principals is not a standard business practice in Canada, the government might have demonstrated a healthy suspicion of Monoca's stance by being somewhat more stringent about allowing Monoca to award subcontracts to affiliates or shareholders. Instead, the clause effectively prevented the government from protecting itself against recycling of profits by setting a weak and non-objective standard of performance. For an objective judgement to be made regarding the equality of two bids, they would have to differ in no more than one aspect. If there were differences in any two or more factors, it would be a matter of professional judgement as to which was the superior bid, and Monoca had far more professional knowledge than the government. Since Monoca later awarded a great many subcontracts to firms in which it held a beneficial interest, it appears Monoca had little difficulty in overcoming the apparent purpose of this clause.

The MDF's normal practice to ensure that equity contributions could not come from recycled profits was to require borrowers to pay their full equity investment before any money was advanced by the fund. Section 2 of Exhibit B, however, required only the first $500,000 of equity to be paid, with the remainder to be paid "as needed for the Program."[130] Once again, the vagueness of this clause made it completely ineffective. After the project was underway, Monoca, when asked when it would pay the remainder of its equity investment, replied that the equity would be invested after construction was completed.

After the initial excitement created by the project's announcement in March 1966 had subsided, pointed questions were raised in the legislature and in the press concerning the identity of the principals of the company to which the government had awarded a contract purportedly worth $100 million.[131] Responding to questions in the legislature, Roblin said that the dealings of the MDF were confidential, and that assurances of confidentiality had been given to the borrowers. Details of transactions could be not divulged without laying the fund open to legal action. Although this was quite true, there was an even more compelling reason why members of the government could not respond to the questions that were raised: they did not know the answers themselves.

The lack of information about the project brought on a flood of criticism and speculation in the press. To try to appease the critics, Grose tried on numerous occasions to get more information about Monoca. On April 25, he wrote to Reiser and outlined the concerns of the press and the investment community. These were (1) that Monoca had claimed to be involved in the development of pulp and paper ventures in Spain, Italy and North America, but had declined to name them or provide evidence of it; (2) that there was no evidence that experienced people in pulp and paper production would be participating or investing in CFI; and (3) that Monoca was a small firm with capitalization of only 50,000 Swiss francs ($12,000 Canadian) and might not be able to live up to its commitments. He went on to suggest five ways of silencing the critics: announce a strong, experienced board of directors for CFI; rent prestige office space in Winnipeg; advertise for top officials in leading newspapers; move forward the schedule for construction of the sawmill; and bring over technical people immediately. Grose apparently received no reply to this letter. Roblin wrote to Reiser on the same topic on 21 June 1966, and Grose wrote to Monoca's lawyer on June 24.[132] In Grose's letter, he insisted that no money would be advanced until several matters had been cleared up, one of which was the problem of non-disclosure of Monoca's principals. Unfortunately, as Grose later testified to the Commission of Inquiry, this demand was largely bluff.[133] Having signed agreements with Monoca with the clear verbal understanding that no disclosure of principals would be required, neither the MDF nor the government had any legal right to insist upon it, as Reiser pointed out on several occasions.

Grose made repeated attempts to persuade Monoca to reveal its owners' identities, but without success. Finally, in November 1966, Alexander Kasser agreed to disclose two of CFI's associates, both paper companies. Only one name was actually revealed, that of Haindl'sche Papierfabriken. Haindl was an old and respected firm and one of the largest newsprint producers in Germany. The government was delighted to have ammunition with which to silence critics of the project — and were themselves reassured.[134] Regrettably, after Gurney Evans had devoted considerable attention to Haindl in a speech in the legislature in April, it was discovered, quite by accident, that Kasser had misrepresented the degree of Haindl's participation. Far from being a major shareholder, Haindl was providing only technical advice on newsprint production and had received an insignificant number of shares in return for its advice.[135]

With the controversy caused by this revelation still raging, *Financial Post* reporter Philip Mathias added more fuel by announcing that Michele Sindona, a mysterious Italian financier, might be the mastermind behind CFI.[136] When questioned by Grose, Reiser refused to either confirm or deny Sindona's involvement. In the end, neither the Commission of Inquiry nor the U.S. Securities and Exchange Commission were able to establish with certainty that Sindona was not involved, but concluded that the most probable reason for Monoca's insistence on non-disclosure was that CFI, Monoca, Technopulp, and a host of other firms who later became involved with the project were beneficially owned by Kasser and his immediate family. After Sindona's death in a Milan jail some years later, Mathias claimed that, at the very least, Sindona was Kasser's mentor in the art of fraud.[137]

The Genius of Alexander Kasser

Alexander Kasser possesses two types of genius: one in building a reputation of technological expertise in the pioneering of solutions for problems in pulp and paper production, the other in the art of making money deviously. Born in Hungary in 1909, Kasser claims to hold degrees from both the Sorbonne and the University of Grenoble. He entered the United States in 1949 and became a citizen in 1955. By all accounts, Kasser is a highly charismatic man and capable of ruthless manipulation.[138] Kasser's plan for the CFI complex was to maximize his profit by becoming anonymously involved in as many aspects of it as possible.

One of the key elements in Kasser's scheme was his technical reputation. Whether or not Kasser was as brilliant in innovating pulp and paper technologies as some sources claim is unclear. What is clear, however, is that he was able to make people *believe* that he was, and this powerful form of legitimacy shielded him well. Once Kasser had created an image of himself as an inventive genius, it was difficult for those who dealt with him to believe that someone so talented could be as crooked as he was creative.

Kasser's technique, which he had perfected in previous projects, was a masterpiece of corporate sleight-of-hand. To begin with, Kasser would find ways of involving well-known and respected firms in some nominal way, so that he could use these companies' reputations as a blind. He would then set up a maze of shell companies that would appear to be unrelated to one another. This was accomplished by incorporating companies in countries that do not require disclosure of beneficial owners, such as Switzerland, Liechtenstein, the Bahamas, and Panama. The ownership structures of Kasser's companies were invariably complex, and transfers of shares between companies were frequent. To further mask the source of control of his companies, he often vested actual ownership in companies or people with whom he had dealings, but retained effective control through the use of options that would allow him to resume majority ownership at a moment's notice. Thus Kasser could have exercised his options in order to gain control of companies he had placed in the hands of others. However, he invariably had other influences over these nominal shareholders, and these were generally sufficient to ensure their cooperation. It was rarely necessary for Kasser to make use of the options he held. Finally, Kasser rarely signed his name to anything, even letters. Most often than not, he dealt with people over the telephone or in person; when a letter was required, it would usually be signed by one of his henchmen. Kasser's presence was pervasive but penumbrous.

Having set up this intricate and mysterious web of companies which existed only on paper, Kasser then arranged for a great deal of intercompany contracting and purchasing to take place. Each of these transactions, which appeared to observers to be occurring at arm's length, contained provisions for profit, the markup sometimes being 25 to 50 percent. Even when it was necessary to obtain three or more tenders before awarding a contract, Kasser circumvented the intent of this procedure by encouraging companies he knew were not interested in obtaining the contract to tender a bid. He sometimes went so far as to suggest a price for them, which would be even higher than the bid of the company under his control to which he wished to award the contract! Kasser had no trouble in getting contracts awarded to the companies he chose, at the prices he chose.

The final touch in Kasser's scheme was his evasion of income taxes. Non-resident companies that are deemed under Canadian law to be carrying on business in Canada are required to file an income tax return. These are companies that have assets in Canada which tax officials can seize in the event of non-payment of taxes. Non-resident companies that have no presence in Canada, but which take profits out of the country, are dealt with by requiring Canadian contractors and purchasers to withhold 15 percent of the contract price to turn over to the federal tax department. The department then keeps whatever portion of it is assessed as the correct tax payment and refunds the rest. Kasser's way around this system was to create a Canadian company (once again, with few assets) to act as a general contractor. As such, the company should have withheld 15 percent of fees paid to non-resident companies to which it subcontracted, but of course it did not. Kasser's non-resident companies were thus paid in full, but remitted no business taxes. In addition, Kasser's Canadian company filed no income tax return, even though it was legally obligated to do so. In this way, he succeeded in building profit upon profit and taking it all out of the country almost completely tax-free.

After Technopulp's feasibility studies were completed, Kasser concluded that the area of CFI's timber grants would sustain a cut of at least 460,000 cords per year. This meant that the complex could be expanded from the moderate size anticipated by the definitive agreements, signed 24 February 1966. In addition, the federal Area Development Agency (ADA) was offering substantial grants to entrepreneurs who established new industry in underdeveloped areas. The maximum grant for any one project was $5 million. Kasser discovered, however, that by splitting the CFI complex into separate entities owned by different companies, the overall project could be eligible for a grant of up to $12 million.

In April of 1968, Grose met in Italy with Kasser and one of the proposed new participants. The agreements then in force were for a minimum 300-ton per-day pulp mill and a 30-million board-feet sawmill. Following discussions, the proposed project was expanded to consist of a 600-ton per-day pulp mill, a 600-ton per-day paper mill, a 100-million board-feet sawmill, and a pulp-and-paper-machinery manufacturing plant. CFI was to own the pulp mill, and three other separate entities would own the remainder of the complex. Grose reported favourably to the government on the new proposal, stating that it would spread the project risk four ways and had the added advantage of being eligible for between $12 and $14 million in ADA grants rather than only $5 million. The total investment needed would be $85 million, of which the MDF would be required to provide about $60 million, rather than $40 million as originally anticipated.[139] Interestingly, there do not appear to have ever been any feasibility studies done for a 600-ton per-day pulp and paper operation.[140]

Because of the size of the anticipated loan, Grose recommended to the government (now under Walter Weir, as Roblin had resigned in 1967 to contest the federal Conservative party leadership) that a Cabinet committee be formed to carry out the negotiations. The Cabinet refused to involve itself, responding that if, after due consideration, the board of directors of the MDF believed the new program should be undertaken, the government would be prepared to provide the necessary funds.[141]

By this time, Kasser had already reached an agreement with James Brown Jr., chairman and CEO of the Pack River Company. Because neither Kasser nor his associates were experienced in sawmill operations, Kasser had sought Brown's advice in October 1967. Brown surveyed the timber in the region and reported that a mill much larger than 30 million board feet per year could be supported. Brown then entered into a contract with Kasser to set up a company or companies to design, build, own, and operate a 60-million board-feet sawmill, contingent upon the MDF agreeing to provide at least 60 percent of the anticipated $3 million cost of construction.[142] This contract was a joint venture between Brown and Kasser, with Kasser holding an option to purchase for $25,000 half of the shares of the construction company Brown was to form. Brown created Blue Construction to design and build the mill, and River Sawmills was created as a subsidiary of Blue to own and operate the mill. The share option, therefore, gave Kasser a beneficial interest in both the construction and the ownership of the sawmill, while maintaining the fiction of an arm's-length relationship between CFI and Brown.

Brown and CFI then entered into an agreement under which CFI assigned its obligation to build a sawmill to Brown, and contingent upon the construction contract being awarded to Blue Construction, Blue would build a 30-million board-feet mill by 1 October 1969 and add another 30 million board feet within a year. River Sawmills, in addition to owning this mill, would also supply CFI with some of its wood chip requirements for making pulp and would take responsibility for harvesting the timber required for the complex.[143]

A few days later, on 9 February 1968, the construction contract for the 30-million board-feet sawmill was awarded to Blue by CFI. (Presumably, since CFI's existing agreement with the government was only for a 30-million board-feet sawmill, this was all CFI was authorized to contract for.) The price of this mill was set at US$3.95 million, or Can.$4.26 million — a figure some 30 percent higher than the price mentioned in the Kasser-Brown joint-venture agreement for a mill of twice the capacity. The Commission of Inquiry's conclusion was that the price was deliberately inflated to ensure that Blue Construction would generate sufficient profit from the contract to finance River's equity in the larger sawmill.[144] Brown then became both swindler and swindled when he agreed to pay compensation to two other companies which Kasser claimed held the concessions to build the sawmill and furnish wood chips to the pulp mill. In fact, CFI still held these rights and was not permitted to transfer or assign anything without the consent of the MDF and/or the government. One of the two companies was incorporated in the tax-sheltered Bahamas and, apparently unknown to Brown, both were nominally owned by Kasser's two children.

A final agreement, under which Pack River would buy 20 million board feet of CFI's lumber for the first five years of operation at the prevailing market price, was signed on February 16.[145]

In Grose's report to the government in early June 1968, he stated that Technopulp's feasibility studies had shown that the most profitable course of action was to increase the size of the sawmill to 100 million board feet at a cost of $10 million. A master financing agreement was drafted on June 20, under which the MDF would loan up to 80 percent of the total investment, up to $9.6 million, to River Sawmills to construct one or more sawmills. This figure could include loans for working capital if necessary. The first 15 million board feet were to be completed by October 1968, an additional 15 million board feet by October 1969, and the entire 100 million by October 1970.

The agreement was not actually signed until 5 September 1968. Grose and his assistant travelled to Montclair, New Jersey (Technopulp's location) to negotiate with Brown and Kasser. For reasons explained in a later section on monitoring, the MDF's legal counsel was not in attendance. In fact, the MDF received no legal advice from any source before signing the final master financing agreement with River. If counsel had been consulted, two errors might have been avoided. The agreement gave Arthur D. Little & Co. the responsibility of certifying that previously advanced money had been properly expended before each new advance of $2 million was made, but because of the wording of the agreement, no certification was required to ensure that the final $1.6 million of the $9.6 million credit line be properly expended. In fact, since the credit line was only intended to cover 80 percent of the $10 million estimated cost of the mill, the final $1.6 million became a virtual gift: once the first four advances of $2 million were shown to be properly spent, according to the agreement the final $1.6 million had to be handed over with no further questions asked. The second error was that Section 4 of the agreement stipulated that ADL was to be employed by River, not by the MDF. In his later testimony to the Commission of Inquiry, Grose said:

> We had retained Arthur D. Little to . . . be the verifying certification agents . . . [ADL] would submit the bills to us and we would send them on to CFI to approve. My staff came to me — and I take full responsibility — and said it was causing them more problems than anything else . . . it would make a lot more sense if the company dealt direct with the consulting firm.[146]

While acting as the consultant to the fund, it was improper for ADL to be employed by River as the certification agent. The effect of this relationship is explored in greater depth in the section on monitoring.

With regard to the proposed paper-machinery manufacturing plant, Kasser called upon James Bertram & Sons of Scotland. Kasser had first dealt with the Bertrams in connection with a project in Sicily and was well acquainted with the company's dire need for cash. James Bertram, the son of the original founder, died in 1952, followed shortly by his two sisters. This left the entire family fortune in the hands of Bertram's four children. Bertram had made no estate duty provision in his will, with the result that his survivors were forced to sell all the family's assets other than the business itself to pay the death duties. By 1968, James Bertram & Sons, a world-renowned manufacturer of paper-making equipment, was on the brink of financial ruin.[147]

Not only were the Bertrams desperate for cash, Kasser also convinced them that new and important contracts might result from an involvement in the CFI complex. Consequently, they agreed to form a company that would become a front for Kasser in the building of the machinery plant.[148] Bertram & Sons formed a Canadian company called

James Bertram & Sons (Canada) Ltd. (JBSC), into which the Bertrams would inject no equity. A Bahamian company, Montgomery Investments, would put up the necessary equity to allow the company to build and control a manufacturing plant at The Pas. Before the Bertrams met with Grose in late June 1968, Kasser instructed them not to mention Montgomery's involvement to Grose. The Bertrams, under behind-the-scenes instructions from Kasser, then conducted financing negotiations with Grose for an MDF loan of $7 million.[149] Kasser's hold over the Bertrams was not limited to their desire for a portion of the ADA and Canadian Export Development Corporation grants for which the company would qualify: one of Kasser's Liechtenstein companies, Nefertiti Anstalt, had loaned money to the Bertrams, which they were unable to repay immediately.

In October 1968 the Bertrams sent Grose a balance sheet for 1967 which showed clearly the precarious financial condition of James Bertram & Sons and should have occasioned some concerned questions on Grose's part. This apparently did not occur, and the master financing agreement between JBSC and the MDF was signed in May 1969, although the date shown on the contract was 7 November 1968. According to it, the fund agreed to allow the turnkey contract to be awarded to Bertram Verkaufs, a company incorporated in Switzerland by the Bertrams and, truc to form, controlled by Kasser.[150]

Kasser followed approximately the same procedure with regard to the kraft paper mill. He convinced Wilhelm Ernst and his son Klaus to allow him to act as their agent in selling two paper plants in Germany. He promised them he could get a better price for them if he were given a free hand to negotiate the sale, and to facilitate this the Ernsts gave Kasser an option on the two plants. Kasser explained that they could avoid paying a considerable amount of taxes by selling the plants for a very low price to a Liechtenstein company, then reselling it to the intended buyer at a higher figure. He convinced the Ernsts to invest the difference between the two figures in the Manitoba project.

At the same time, Kasser created two Liechtenstein companies, naming them Wilhelmstaler Papierfabrik and WEAG — both similar to the name of the Ernsts' company, Wilhelmstal Werke. WEAG was the vehicle for the Ernsts' investment in Canada. The Ernsts protested that WEAG could be mistaken to stand for Wilhelm Ernst A.G. and initially objected to any name which would associate their company with the Canadian project. WEAG was later changed to Hergard A.G., but not before a wholly owned subsidiary named Wilhelmstal Werke Establishment was created without the Ernsts' knowledge. During the time Kasser was negotiating with the MDF for financing for the paper mill, therefore, what little information could be obtained about these companies would give the impression that they were owned and operated by the Ernsts. Furthermore, late in October 1968, a delegation consisting of Grose, Walter

Weir, Jack Carroll (the M.P.P. for The Pas) and James Zeigler of ADL travelled to Germany and were shown the two paper mills now under option to Kasser's company, Wilhelmstaler Papierfabrik. As expected, the delegation came away with the impression that the Ernsts were intending to become significantly involved in building a paper mill at The Pas.[151]

This temporary involvement of the Ernsts was vital to Kasser's plans. The Ernsts' investment in Hergard, which owned M.P. Industrial Mills (MPI), gave the appearance that they, not Kasser, would control MPI. In truth, the Ernsts held voting preferred shares in Hergard, which had a par value of $10,000 each. Throughout the short period during which the Ernsts were the majority shareholders, Kasser's company, Marlboro Manufacturing Ltd. in Drummondville, Quebec, retained an option on the company's common shares, which, like the preferred shares carried one vote each, but unlike the preferred shares had a par value of only $1 each.[152] Thus, Kasser could at any time take over voting control with only a minimal investment. In this way, he maintained the upper hand, and directed the Ernsts to submit a grant application to the ADA for the paper mill.

The kraft paper mill project was shelved for several months when consultant Hector Godfrey submitted a negative report on the project's feasibility to the MDF board of directors. He pointed out that there would be a problem in marketing the product; the Canadian market was too well covered, and the U.S. market was protected by tariffs. Kasser reopened the negotiations by bringing in the name of the Swedish paper manufacturer Korsnas Marma. Korsnas had mastered the use of a drying technique which, when combined with the special properties of the northern Manitoba timber, would produce a very strong, high-quality paper. The special drying machine, the flakt dryer, was not a Korsnas invention; nor did they hold a patent on it. Korsnas had merely been the first mill to install a flakt dryer and thus had the greatest operating experience. Kasser maintained that the so-called "Korsnas process" was a company secret, but that Korsnas might be convinced to share it with the Manitoba government for a price. Kasser arranged for the MDF to pay CFI $5 million to pay to Korsnas; needless to say, Korsnas never received the money.

In March 1969, after hearing about the possible participation of Korsnas, Grose stipulated that if Korsnas would participate, financing for the paper mill would be arranged. Kasser wrote back that Korsnas had agreed to study the project in detail and provide technical expertise and had taken an option to purchase 25 percent of the shares of MPI. In fact, Korsnas had agreed to no such study, and the option, which they had no intention of ever exercising, had been a gift pressed upon them by Kasser.[153] The master financing agreement, providing for a loan of 86 percent of the total investment up to a maximum of $32 million, was signed on 29 May 1969 by the MDF and Wilhelmstaler Papierfabrik for M.P. Industrial Mills.

The above is by no means an exhaustive list of the many applications of Kasser's distinctive way of doing business. When contracts were allocated from one of Kasser's resident companies to a non-resident company, usually located in a tax haven such as the Bahamas, Liechtenstein or Switzerland, most of the expenses of the project were recorded in the books of companies incorporated in Canada or the United States in order to reduce their taxable income as much as possible. In this way Kasser succeeded in collecting over $33 million in fees, of which the Commission of Inquiry estimated $26.3 million was excessive, virtually tax-free.[154]

Because Kasser's scheme allowed him to derive at least 100 percent of the necessary financing from the MDF, there was no need for him to exercise caution in planning the project. Technopulp's feasibility studies contradicted those done by independent consultants, but Grose, believing he was dealing with four separate firms which would not undertake the project unless they believed it would be viable, relied on Technopulp's studies. In retrospect, however, it appears that Kasser realized the design and construction phase of the project would be the most profitable, and also that the larger the complex was to be, the more profit he could make. Consequently, it appears that some parts of the project were built as ends in themselves and had no hope of ever operating profitably. The JBSC machinery-making plant, for example, later proved totally infeasible. In assessing the fair value of the complex, the Commission of Inquiry commented on the JBSC plant as follows:

(1) The decision to locate such a machinery plant at The Pas was absurd. This opinion is supported by the fact that strenuous efforts were made to find an experienced, reputable producer or user and met with no success whatsoever.
(2) The investment in machinery capable of producing 500-inch wide paper-making machinery when no paper manufacturer was interested in installing such a machine even if produced was improvident.
For the above reasons, we are unable to form an opinion as to the fair value of the James Bertram & Sons (Canada) Ltd. plant.[155]

In addition, the sawmill later proved to have been poorly conceived, having too much capacity relative to the pulp mill. Only between 10 and 16 percent of the logs harvested met the minimum length requirement for sawn lumber. The remainder of the wood harvested for the CFI complex had to be made into pulp or else it would be wasted. The sawmill had to produce 280,000 board feet per day in order to be profitable. The amount of wood that would maintain this level of production would require an 800-ton per-day mill to utilize all of the logs that were too short for lumber. The CFI pulp mill, of course, had a capacity of only 600 tons per day.[156]

Since Kasser's expertise in pulp and paper manufacturing has at no time been called into question, it can only be assumed that some parts of the complex were planned solely to increase the project's eligibility for ADA grants and to provide new profit opportunities for Kasser. This view is supported by the RCMP, who purportedly have evidence that Kasser and his associates never intended to operate the complex, but rather planned to bankrupt it once it was completed.[157]

The Commission of Inquiry estimated that $26.3 million were paid to Kasser and his associates in excessive fees and $10 million were spent on the virtually worthless JBSC machinery plant.[158]

Decision-Making and Monitoring

Some of the early conditions that adversely affected decision-making and monitoring with regard to CFI have been detailed in previous sections. They can be summed up as follows:

1. Cabinet hastily signed an option agreement that allocated certain responsibilities to the MDF;
2. The binding option agreement prevented the MDF from later negotiating more favourable terms;
3. Some of the terms of the option agreement (and thus all later agreements between CFI and the MDF) contravened standard MDF lending practices, particularly with regard to the disclosure of principals and payment of borrower's equity;
4. Other terms set weak or subjective standards of performance, rendering them ineffective as control mechanisms.

From the above it is clear that effective monitoring of the project would be a difficult and time-consuming task. The fund retained James Zeigler of Arthur D. Little to certify that expenditures made by CFI were reasonable in view of standard industry practices. Before loan advances were made, CFI had to submit requisitions supported by detailed documentation which included tenders and tender analysis, purchase orders and actual invoices. From November 1966 to July 1968, CFI balked repeatedly at the stringency of the payout procedures, complaining that slow payment was hampering their progress. Nevertheless, the MDF wisely stood its ground and in July 1968 finally coerced CFI into expressly undertaking a commitment to abide by the terms of the fund's payout procedures. The wrangling that took place before this undertaking was given was most instructive to Walter Newman, the fund's counsel, who later wrote: "[I] insisted throughout on the importance of maintaining financial control over the project, however difficult and unpleasant that it may be, because of [my] conviction that the CFI principals would take full advantage, if permitted to do so, of any opportunity to enrich themselves at public expense."[159]

Ironically, it was at about this same time that an incident occurred which precipitated not more control over the project, but less. In late June of 1968, meetings were held in New York to discuss the financing for the River Sawmill. Newman had earlier opposed splitting the complex into four parts, on the grounds that responsibility would be dispersed and secret profits could be made through inter-company transactions. With regard to the River Sawmill, he was insisting that the MDF have access to the books of both Blue Construction and River Sawmill because of the known relationship between these two companies. Newman testified to the Commission of Inquiry that this demand was relayed to Kasser by his lawyer at an informal gathering in the cocktail lounge of the hotel that evening, and that: "He jumped up and said that I was treating him like a thief. My comment was that I wasn't trying to treat him like a thief but if the shoe fit, put it on . . . and at that stage he said 'Get him out!' "[160] After that meeting, Newman claims not to have been consulted or kept informed about broad developments; Grose, on the other hand, denies vehemently that Newman was "phased out" of the discussions.

Newman's version of the story is supported by several incidents. Early in June, when the government indicated to Grose that the board of directors of the MDF had full authority to decide on whether the project should be split into four parts, Grose then submitted a report to the board in which he wrote: "I have submitted this overall plan to the government for approval and have been instructed to proceed."[161] This appears to have been Grose's standard way of dealing with the MDF board. Grose enjoyed a close relationship with the Cabinet and was their senior economic adviser at this time. David Rodgers, secretary of the MDF, later described the relationship between Grose and the board of directors as follows:

> MR. RODGERS: . . . the tactics followed by [Grose] would be to get the authority of the board to negotiate and complete and finalize and report back — and . . . then the agreements that would be entered into would be recorded eventually in the minutes of the Development Fund. He would in consultation with Dr. Kasser and the ADL people — whoever they might be, principally Mr. Zeigler — it would have been resolved at that level, completely without reference to anybody on the staff or the board.
>
> · · ·
>
> MR. SMITH: And the board would say, "Thank you very much for having done that for us"?
> MR. RODGERS: I was never at any meeting that they ever really raised any points.
>
> · · ·
>
> MR. McCAFFREY: Well . . . was it a situation where the board, that this thing was just too complex for them to grasp, and they, in effect,

would say, "Okay, Mr. Grose, if you say so. You're the man who knows that project inside and out."

MR. RODGERS: I would think that they would take that attitude — that Mr. Grose had the approval and the consent and the direction from the government, and he would be handling that; and he had the approval and the direction from the board to go ahead.[162]

In short, at least with regard to the CFI project, the MDF board of directors merely acted as a rubber stamp on decisions made by Grose. Meanwhile, the Cabinet believed that as MDF chairman, Grose was keeping the board of directors informed and that all major decisions were being reviewed and approved by them. Therefore, when they were informed that the MDF board had approved splitting the project in four and increasing its total size, they too ratified the decision. Grose had achieved a degree of status, prestige, and credibility that placed him beyond accountability most of the time, and this decision was no exception.

A second incident that supports Newman's claim that he was phased out of the negotiations was the signing of the River Sawmill master financing agreement. As mentioned earlier, it was signed by Grose on 5 September 1968, without first being approved in its final form by either Newman or the MDF board of directors.[163] Newman continued to act as counsel to the fund, but was involved in only a few isolated instances with regard to CFI.

James Zeigler of Arthur D. Little assisted Grose in monitoring the CFI project by certifying feasibility studies, approving contracts, and supervising the disbursement of loan money. In their review of his performance, the Commission of Inquiry found Zeigler lacking in almost every instance:[164] he did not check and verify invoices, since material amounts were double-billed on at least one occasion;[165] he did not enforce his right to examine books, records, and designs before certifying loan-advance requests; and he appears to have relied almost entirely on Kasser's representations when forming his opinions.[166]

How could Zeigler have failed so dismally to protect the interests of his client, the government of Manitoba? There are several possibilities. Newman suggests that Zeigler simply was not capable of handling the task, describing him as follows:

James Zeigler, as the main representative of Arthur D. Little, Inc. with respect to CFI had established his working offices in the premises used by Dr. Kasser as his headquarters in Montclair, New Jersey. He was a big, soft-spoken, decent, reasonably intelligent man. He liked to see large projects accomplished without fuss or red tape. . . .

Rex Grose left it up to James Zeigler to collect any data that was required and James Zeigler ultimately failed . . . to produce copies of some of the essential documentation . . . [He] moved into a room in Technopulp's head office . . . [and] carried on there without a filing clerk or secretary and was unable to produce equipment lists, flow sheets, engineering studies, [etc.][167]

It was reasonable for Zeigler to set up his office *near* Technopulp, since most of the documents he required were generated by Technopulp. Such close physical proximity, however, strongly suggests that Zeigler became psychologically captured. In fact, considering his dependence on Kasser and Kasser's staff to keep and retrieve records for him, Zeigler appears to have been not merely a captive, but actually a hostage, since he was unable to perform his duties even marginally without Kasser's assistance. If ADL knew of their employee's inappropriately snug relationship with the subject of his monitoring efforts, they were remiss in allowing it to continue.

The wily Dr. Kasser cannot be given complete credit for Zeigler's weak monitoring of the situation; some less charitable sources have suggested that Zeigler lost his objectivity toward the project long before Monoca ever came upon the scene. Zeigler had been involved in the project since 1959, having performed the early feasibility studies and taking part in the search for a company to take on the development project. Through his lengthy involvement and friendship with Grose during this time, Zeigler had become an enthusiast of the project. He, like Grose and others who were in favour of using government incentives to bring a pulp and paper development to northern Manitoba, eventually became so passionately certain of the wisdom of the project that he would brook no criticism of it. For example, on a 1967 trip to visit the CFI site, Zeigler confronted writer Philip Mathias about his allegations of mystery surrounding the identity of Monoca's principals in the *Financial Post*. Mathias recounts:

> In the bus on the way back to the airport, suddenly this fellow [Zeigler] explodes, 'What do you mean, the ownership [of CFI] is not known? What do you mean by writing that this is an anonymous project?' Now this is the representative of the people who were supposed to be protecting the government of Manitoba. The government did not know the true identity of the owners, and all we had said was that the financing was anonymous . . . But Zeigler got totally out of control . . . You'd think a consultant would either wonder where I was getting my information and try to find out if there was any truth in it, or else he'd say, 'Look, fella, we're much closer to this, and you're mistaken.' But instead he went berserk that anyone would dare to criticize this thing in public.[168]

Another suggestion about the reasons for Zeigler's behaviour was that he was a good forester but had no understanding of political nuance and no nose for trickery. Initially, Zeigler seems not to have had any ulterior motive in certifying disbursement claims without proper examination. He seems merely to have been completely deceived by Kasser and his associates. Zeigler's motives cannot be regarded as equally pure after the signing of the MP Industrial contract in May of 1969, however. In this contract, Zeigler was named as the plant's architect, despite the fact that he had no qualifications in this area. Whether this assignment was made because Zeigler perhaps had more knowledge of competent North American architectural firms than Kasser, or whether it was simply a way of further involving Zeigler in Kasser's web of deception is open to conjecture. All investigations eventually cleared Zeigler of any participation in Kasser's schemes, but evidence such as the above makes it difficult to believe he was unaware to the very end that some of Kasser's activities were rather shady. Why, then, did he not act when he began to suspect wrongdoing on Kasser's part? He may have simply believed that since others had the same information that he had and chose not to act on it, perhaps the government's interests were best protected by doing whatever was necessary to allow the project to be completed without further bad publicity. Alternatively, since Zeigler was a forester rather than a businessman, and seems to have known about only the mildest of Kasser's misdeeds, Kasser may have succeeded in convincing him that he was merely doing what any other shrewd businessman would do.

With Zeigler providing no opposition to Kasser whatsoever, this left Grose as the sole possible source of control over the project. Grose, however, had an even greater personal and emotional stake in the project. Grose had long been a great advocate of resource megaprojects as a method of economic development. His views had greatly influenced the government since 1956 because of his stature within the civil service, and thus Grose's personal pride and reputation were very much bound up in the successful completion of the project. In addition, according to David Rodgers, CFI had become Grose's main activity within the fund:

> MR. RODGERS: I'd say it was dedication to a real, large-size project within the Province, that would be to the credit of the architect that brought all of the groups together and finally made it possible for northern Manitoba to have a fully integrated forest industry. He was absolutely dedicated to it [and] worked . . . tremendous hours at it. It was his complete job, really, within [the MDF]. Most of the other matters . . . were attended to by the staff, to the exclusion of Mr. Grose. This was his real pet project, if you want to term it that, and he was completely dedicated to its completion, to the finalization of it.[169]

For these reasons, Grose was in no position to provide objective review and possible restraint of the project.

One final factor which adversely affected the monitoring of the project was the threat posed by the NDP's repeated attempts to discredit the Conservative government through attacks in the press on both CFI and the operations of the MDF.

The Effects of Political Turbulence

From the day construction began, the promised benefits of the project failed to materialize. Disagreements quickly erupted over woodcutting rights when CFI tried to exclude existing woodcutters from its timber reserve area. In granting 40,000 square miles, the government had envisaged CFI awarding cutting contracts to local woodcutters and allowing them access to the reserved area. Instead, CFI claimed it was not satisfied with the unskilled labour available and attempted to bring in a crew of fifty trained Italian woodcutters. CFI also paid low wages and offered few benefits to employees. Almost every action taken by CFI drew further criticism.

The provincial NDP party picked up on the general disaffection for the project and used it toward its own ends. In the months preceding the provincial election on 25 June 1969, party leader Edward Schreyer repeatedly heaped abuse on the MDF in general and on CFI in particular. He made numerous statements to the press, in which he referred to the project as "the blackest moment in Manitoba's economic history" and called for an inquiry into the dealings of the MDF. Threats of expropriation or denial of funds to CFI were also made if CFI did not soon show proof of adequate equity investment.

On July 10, after winning the election but before assuming office, Schreyer stated on a radio hot-line show that "the only way to clear the air is to have a proper enquiry made." Upon assuming office, Schreyer (who was not only the premier but at first also the minister of Industry and Commerce) met briefly with Grose on July 21. He received verbal assurances that the loan advances were being carefully and prudently supervised.[170] At another meeting ten days later, this time with Finance Minister Saul Cherniak, Kasser, Reiser, and several other members of CFI's management in attendance, no material documents were reviewed. Schreyer did not read any of the principal agreements; nor did he request anyone else to do so until some months later.[171] Three points were renegotiated: CFI agreed to ensure that by 1971 at least a third of the capital investment in the project would come from private sources; the right to export unprocessed timber was revoked; and 6,000 square miles of the original (40,000 sq. mi.) land grant reverted to the government. In addition, the company agreed to install anti-pollution gear and to make more information on the project available through a public relations firm. At the close of the meeting, Schreyer told the local press: "Our four hour meeting was almost an investigation in itself and we see no need for any further investigation into this particular transaction unless by the end of 1970 performance does not match assurance."[172]

We surmise that Schreyer and his fellow ministers had much to do in their first few weeks in office and so turned their attention to matters other than the CFI project, which at first glance may have appeared to be in good hands. Furthermore, one might also surmise that the four-hour meeting was primarily an exercise in symbolic politics, rather than the detailed investigation Schreyer claimed it had been.

Far from preventing unwise expenditure of public money, Premier Schreyer's pre-election threats acted as a catalyst in the breakdown of the monitoring system of the project. If the monitoring was poor before July 1969, after that time, it was non-existent: $12 million had been advanced to the four companies before 21 July 1969 compared to $60 million between 1 August 1969 and 21 May 1970.[173] The accelerated payout was the result of a meeting held July 22 in which Grose and Kasser agreed that the best way to safeguard the project against political interference was to move the project past the financial point of no return before the new government could get its bearings.[174]

Another incident which contributed to the breakdown of the monitoring system was that at approximately this time, Grose signed a contract to become president of MPI beginning 1 December 1969. Grose later testified before the Commission of Inquiry that he decided, after the NDP came to power, that he should look elsewhere for employment and suggested to Reiser that he ask the Ernsts (who had by this time been set up to look like the controlling interest in the proposed paper mill) if they would be interested in having him head MPI. He then received word back that he should draw up a contract for himself and submit it. The witness to Grose's employment contract was James Zeigler, who, as mentioned earlier, was named as the architect in the MPI contract.

The free flow of funds after 1 August 1969 was not without its positive aspects. Starting in the summer of 1969, project construction moved ahead much more rapidly than it had previously. In spite of this, however, the press remained critical. Schreyer decided in October that further checking was warranted and he appointed former federal M.P. Alistair Stewart to investigate CFI. This, too, proved to be something of a paper tiger, since Stewart was given almost no resources and apparently did not have the ear of the premier.[175] By the time Stewart submitted his report in February 1970, he had discovered the weaknesses of the contracts but remained oblivious to the over-advances of funds which were taking place. He suggested the premier disclose publicly the terms of the contract they had inherited from the previous government and get what credit they could for cleaning up the mess.[176] Following the submission of Stewart's report, the government called upon Stothert Engineering to do an engineering audit of the project.

One person who was aware that all was not as it should be was *Financial Post* writer Philip Mathias. In August of 1969, Grose had answered Mathias' many questions by telex, including the expected capital cost of the project. Grose quoted $81.7 million. Yet in a memo to Stewart six months later, Grose stated the capital cost of the project would be $142.6 million.[177] The *Financial Post* decided Mathias should point out the dis-

crepancy to the Manitoba government before publishing anything about
it. In March 1970, Mathias tried for several days to see Premier Schreyer,
but without success. Grose had warned the premier that the *Financial
Post* was connected with Abitibi, which had vehemently opposed the
project, and that Mathias' motives should be considered suspect. Schreyer
did refer Mathias to Alistair Stewart, however.

Stewart and two of his colleagues listened to Mathias' story and became
very concerned. They decided that the premier should be told immediately and tried to call Schreyer out of the legislature. Mathias recounts
the events which followed:

> The first emissary came back a little while later saying Premier Schreyer
> wouldn't see him. So Stewart decides to go up and try. Schreyer came to a
> little alcove . . . and said he didn't want to hear anything about it . . .
> Finally, they see Sid Green walking down the corridor and they call him
> in. I told him to read the telex from Grose in which he stated the mill
> would cost $80 million, whereas he had recently said it would cost $140
> million. Green's first reaction, too, was to deny this bad news and he
> dropped the telex in alarm.[178]

However, Green, who was the minister of Mines, Resources and Environmental Management at that time, knew that the matter could no longer
be ignored and he soon picked up the troubling telex. He later testified
before the Commission of Inquiry:

> I immediately — that day, I believe — got in touch with Mr. Schreyer. He
> was anxious that I take the matter up further with Mr. Grose . . . a meet-
> ing was arranged the same day or a day later . . . Mr. Stewart confronted
> Mr. Grose with these figures, and it was obvious to me that Mr. Grose did
> not want to answer Mr. Stewart, and that Mr. Stewart was bearing hard
> on Mr. Grose . . . Mr. Grose said that he wished to report these matters to
> Cabinet at a meeting . . . I said that this was very satisfactory and that
> there was no need to have the information at that point. Subsequently a
> Cabinet meeting was held on Sunday at the Legislative Building.[179]

Grose was unable to provide satisfactory answers to the Cabinet's
questions, and the meeting ended with an agreement that Grose would
submit his answers in writing. A few days later, after being advised that
Stothert Engineering had been asked to audit the project, Grose resigned.
The reason he gave for his resignation was the increasingly active role
the NDP government was taking in all of MDF's transactions.[180]

The *Financial Post* ran Mathias' article revealing the escalation in
cost on March 27, followed by more articles over the next two weeks.
The NDP government found itself in an awkward situation. Just eight
months before, they claimed they had looked over the CFI transactions
thoroughly, and promised to make the borrowers toe the line. Under
this supposed scrutiny, the cost of the project had somehow risen by over
70 percent without being noticed. The government had already taken

the first step toward adequate control of the project by hiring Stothert to do an engineering audit of CFI. Shortly after the unsatisfactory meeting with Grose, the government enlarged Stothert's assignment to include engineering audits of JBSC, River, and MPI as well, and on March 30, the provincial auditor was instructed to make a special audit of all MDF accounts regarding the project. During the investigations, a news blackout was imposed.[181]

On April 2, an informal Cabinet committee composed of the premier, the attorney-general, and the ministers of Finance and Mines, Resources and Environmental Management took over control of the CFI project from the MDF board of directors. Stothert's audit began turning up some unpleasant facts:

> The payout procedures established in the main MDF agreement appeared adequate to us to have been able to prevent the unjustified loan advances that were subsequently made. When Stothert was called in by Premier Schreyer to carry out an engineering audit in February of 1970 there was, understandably, great difficulty in getting a look at any documents on the project in the Technopulp offices or in the office in Montclair occupied by James Ziegler. Stothert was able to establish within a six week period that tens of millions of dollars had gone out of the loan funds improperly. An example would be the purchase of a two million dollar item of machinery where at the time of issue of the purchase order a 10 percent payment would be required by the manufacturer of the machine. Subsequent payments would be made to the manufacturer based normally on appropriate shop inspections, and for an item of this size the manufacturing period might be 12 months or longer. CFI managed to get the necessary authorizations so that they obtained the full amount of the purchase order from the loan fund rather than the 10 percent required at the time. There were also a number of cases found where there had been kick-backs in the order of 10 percent by manufacturers.
>
> Many of the control conditions provided in the MDF agreement were not followed, including project financial status reports monthly. Such reports normally indicate each purchase or contract commitment made, to whom, the date, the full amount, the amount paid against the purchase order or contract to the month end being reported, the balance of the commitment outstanding . . . Stothert was unable to obtain such project cost control statements from Technopulp, Churchill Forest Industries or Arthur D. Little. In fact when Stothert reported to a committee of cabinet headed by Premier Schreyer about the end of March or early April 1970 Stothert had then prepared its own project cost control status report. They had specifically asked that Arthur D. Little provide the latest available one required under the MDF agreement but none was produced by them at that meeting.[182]

The provincial auditor's interim report, based on Stothert's report, concluded that the Fund and its consultants had not exercised proper control over the project, and on May 21, loan advances were stopped.

By that time, the government had discovered that $60 million had been advanced in the past year, $25 million of which was on deposit in bank accounts in Switzerland.

All four participant companies in the complex were in default on two counts: there was good reason to believe the loan money was not being properly spent, and the companies had failed to provide information and documentation requested repeatedly. This gave the MDF the right to appoint a receiver to take over the project, an action which, if taken, would have allowed construction to be completed without interruption. Instead, the government simply stopped all outflow of funds and imposed a news blackout while it reviewed the situation. CFI and its three associates, in turn, stopped paying the contractors working on the site, and construction ground to a halt.[183]

The decision in May 1970 to cut off further loan advances until the improperly advanced money had been put back into the project appears to have been a reasonable one, given that most of Kasser's fraudulent activity was not yet known to the government. It was not, unfortunately, the best decision that could have been made. More money was paid to the borrowers, some because of an error by the MDF. But the adverse publicity resulting from the announced cutoff of funds irreparably damaged the project's credibility with its contractors.

Newman was vociferous in his view that a receiver should be appointed immediately to rectify the defaults and keep the project moving. However, the government was reluctant to make this move for two reasons: a Canadian receiver would be virtually powerless to retrieve the $25 million on deposit in Swiss banks, and in addition, completion and startup of the project were deemed by the government to be too big an undertaking for a receiver. The government hoped that it could either coax or coerce compliance by other means.[184]

The government and its legal, financial, and engineering auditors, however, met with resistance in their attempts to investigate the project and establish how much progress had been made. The four borrowers repeatedly failed to furnish documents requested by Stothert, and even the MDF, now managed by Grose's former assistant, D.M. Rodgers, failed to cooperate fully. Zeigler's superiors at Arthur D. Little had stepped in soon after Mathias' revelation in March 1970, but it became clear from the bland reassurances they gave the government that they had no real idea of what was going on at the site. All of the above appear to have passively resisted the government's attempts to obtain a clear picture of what was happening.[185]

Early in June, Stothert recommended that the government try to negotiate tripartite agreements with the borrowers to ensure that further advances would be properly spent. The fund would pay further advances into a special bank account that would be held in escrow until the borrowers' equity had been deposited in the same account. A representative of the government would review all payments going to suppliers and subcontractors, and general contractors such as Blue Construction and Bertram Sales would receive no further payments until the project was complete. Tripartite agreements were signed with M.P. Industrial on June 8, with JBSC on July 31, and with River on September 10.

Stothert's engineering audit continued through the summer and fall of 1970. Its interim reports told a radically different story than those of ADL during this same period. For example, ADL had certified that the MPI paper mill was close to completion at a time when, in fact, up to 90 percent of the electrical work was still to be done.[186] By the end of the summer, the government no longer accepted ADL's reassurances and relied increasingly on the advice of Stothert Engineering.

In early November, 1970, the government and its advisers decided to see for themselves exactly what was going on at the building site. After Industry and Commerce Minister Leonard Evans visited the site with a group of advisers, Stothert reported on the many inadequacies and irregularities they had discovered. In a memo dated 4 December 1970, Stothert made detailed recommendations for the government's future action, the last of which was as follows:

> In view of the indications of excessively delayed completion of construction, poor start-up performance, lack of planning, lack of recruitment and training, reported lack of financial strength and inability to raise or supply any working capital without government guarantee, lack of ownership interest and representation, extensive mechanic's liens and failure to make payments to contractors who have always enjoyed good reputations, and failure to provide any form of reporting or documentation to the government in many areas of expenditure, it is believed the [MDF] should prepare to take possession of the sawmills, woods operations, pulp and paper mills, i.e. the assets of River, CFI and MPI.[187]

Thus, by early December the possibility of receivership was seriously considered. A memo by J.M. Jopp, an employee of Stothert's, expressed the opinion that Kasser and his associates had no real intention of operating the complex themselves. He believed Kasser was making a token effort to bring the complex into operation because the federal government would not remit the ADA grants until production began. After Kasser received the $12 million in grants, Jopp believed he would "unload the complex on the Manitoba government."[188] To protect themselves against this, the Manitoba government made sure the ADA would not remit the grants before they had seen for themselves that the pulp mill was operating. On 7 January 1971, the final adjustments to the pulp mill were made in preparation for a visit from DREE inspectors on January 14. On January 8, with military efficiency, the government's newly appointed receiver and manager seized the premises. Kasser and his European associates left the country the same day.

The takeover was carefully planned and executed. Leif Hallgrimson, the receiver and manager of the project, flew in on a plane chartered under the name of the Manitoba Hydro, accompanied by auditors from the MDF and the provincial auditor's office, a private trustee in bankruptcy, and consultant W.D. Stothert and his staff. They were joined by RCMP officers at the airport, and at precisely 7:00 p.m. the complex was seized just as Premier Schreyer went on television to announce the deed.[189] On the desk of Lloyd Hale, the general manager of the complex, they found a handwritten page. It showed how MPI could be put into bankruptcy so that CFI could exercise the special agreement which MDF had approved, allowing CFI to purchase MPI for $1.00 under such circumstances and also be entitled to subsequent additional borrowing from MDF.[190] The results of the takeover will be discussed in the next chapter.

CONSOLIDATED COMPUTER INCORPORATED

The Launch

With the GAAB loan guarantees of $12 million providing some security, Mers Kutt and the other executives of CCI threw their energies into marketing their new product as quickly and as widely as possible. Between early 1970 and mid-1971, they expanded the staff from 150 to 543, of whom 94 were engaged in production, 267 in marketing, 140 in research and development, and 42 in management (including clerical staff). The company's head office was in Toronto, its manufacturing facility in Ottawa, its research and development facility in Santa Clara, California, and 23 sales offices and 7 maintenance centres were established in Canada, the United States, Britain, and West Germany. In addition, CCI made a sales agreement potentially worth $50 million with the British computer giant International Computers Ltd. (ICL), which would market KEY-EDIT systems in Britain, Europe, Asia, Australia, and South Africa. As a result of these efforts, placement of KEY-EDIT systems increased dramatically. By 1 July 1970, CCI had installed seven KEY-EDIT systems and had an order backlog of fourteen; a year later the company had installed 124 systems and had an order backlog of 90. The company was also successful in receiving a grant of $1,250,000 from ITC's Program for the Advancement of Industrial Technology (PAIT) to fund up to 50 percent of its research and development work between October 1970 and March 1972.[191]

However, CCI was suffering the problems that accompany growth without maturity. The company expanded seemingly overnight from a small entrepreneurial enterprise that could be controlled in all its aspects by one very clever and energetic man, to a medium-sized business that required professional managers who had learned over time to work as a team. Business failures are most likely to occur either in the first year of a company's life or when the company expands from a small to a medium-sized business. CCI had entered this latter phase very suddenly as a result of the loan insurance it had received. Furthermore, the company was in a young, turbulent and highly competitive industry. The situation called not merely for competent management, but for exceptional management, which CCI, unfortunately, did not have.[192]

In addition, there were significant differences of opinion between Hampson and Kutt as to how the company should be run and what its priorities should be. Hampson, whose background was in banking and finance, believed the company should pay close attention to the lease documents, setting terms that would provide maximum benefit to the company and making sure all the necessary housekeeping details were looked after. The systems being leased out were the security for the loans CCI received, and the lenders were anxious to ensure their security was legally protected. Hampson was supported in his emphasis on adminis-tration by Ford Motor Credit and by Gordon Cowperthwaite, a consul-tant from Peat, Marwick and Mitchell. Hampson had called in Peat Marwick in the summer of 1970 to study CCI and advise the GAAB on the company's status. They were eventually retained on an ongoing basis as monitors and advisers for CCI.

Kutt's career, in contrast, had taken him through technical and sales positions in Philips Electronics, IBM, and Honeywell, and he believed CCI's priorities were market acceptance and growth. He also realized that few customers ever return a computer system after only a year or two because of the confusion and inconvenience involved in changing over from one system to another. His past experience taught him that once the system was inside the customer's door, it would go on generat-ing revenue for years to come. The company's financial statements, however, could only recognize the amount of the one-year leases as revenue, and thus they understated the true long-term value of each lease. Kutt grew increasingly frustrated with the strictures placed on him by Hampson and Ford, whom he believed were being excessively bureaucratic. Their insistence on thorough administration and on renego-tiating lease agreements which they felt were not adequately favourable was tying his hands and keeping him from doing productive work: mak-ing new sales and building better computers.

Ford and the GAAB agreed that Kutt's time was poorly spent on admin-istrative detail, but insisted that it was nevertheless necessary. They sug-gested to Kutt that he give up the presidency of the company and become its chairman instead, in order that he could then devote himself to "marketing, technical affairs and long-range planning." A president with the administrative and leadership skill desired by Ford and the GAAB could then be appointed.[193] Kutt, however, was not going to hand over control of CCI so easily. He had poured work, ideas, initiative, and thou-

sands of dollars of his own and his friends' and employees' money into
the company. He disliked and distrusted Peter Quinn, the GAAB's secretary and the person with whom he had the most contact.

Kutt was also frustrated to have to deal with the GAAB through a
go-between rather than coming face to face with the decision-makers.
Because of GAAB policy for board members never to deal with applicants
in person, but only through the support staff, Kutt and Hampson had
never actually met. Their impressions of one another came from corre-
spondence and from stories told by third parties. In Hampson's opinion,
Kutt was an intractable man with ideas but no follow-through, and because of the appeals to nationalism that were included in Kutt's application, he suspected him of being something of an "Ottawa hustler" as
well. For his part, Kutt was aware that Hampson came from a wealthy
and established family and that he was connected with the Liberal party;
Kutt, in contrast, was the son of Ukrainian immigrants and had always
had to work for what he had. In Kutt's view, the clashes between himself and Hampson were at least partly attributable to the desire of Canada's elite to maintain its privileged position. Hampson never doubted
Kutt's inventive genius, and Kutt never doubted Hampson's skill as a
financier, but through repeated clashes carried out indirectly, each came
to doubt the other's motives. Under the circumstances, there could be
no cooperation between them, and by 1971, neither could make a move
without being blocked by the other.[194]

The considerable strain on Kutt increased enormously when in 1971
his wife of fifteen years died of cancer, leaving him to raise their two
daughters, aged three and seven. The blow failed to stop him, however;
Kutt endured the grief and stress and carried on.

CCI's rapid growth generated incessant demands for cash, and the
company was chronically in cash-flow difficulties. When only CCI's equipment rental fees, rather than its sales of equipment to the leasing corporation that had been established with Ford, are counted as revenue, the
company lost $5.2 million in 1970, and another $2.8 million in the first
five months of 1971. In order to meet its cash needs and maintain the
3:1 debt-equity ratio required by Ford, CCI raised another $2 million in
a private stock placement in March 1971 and increased its line of credit
with the Chemical Bank to $4 million at 4 percent above prime.[195] With
the encouragement of the GAAB, CCI approached the New York under-
writing firm of Shearson, Hammill to begin plans to issue another 600,000
shares on the New York over-the-counter market, which, it hoped, would
bring in over $5 million. Arthur D. Little was commissioned to do an
evaluation of CCI and concluded:

> [CCI] has attractive opportunities in the shared processor market. Given
> their design, markets, and current reputation, they can aggressively expand
> their position in the data entry field. The market for their equipment is
> growing, partly as a result of normal expansion of the electronic data

processing market, and partly as a result of current trends toward cen-
tralization of computing equipment.[196]

Shearson, Hammill agreed to handle a stock offering for CCI, but
indicated that the company would need another $30 million in loan
insurance in order to make the offering viable.[197] With the company's
sales expanding so quickly, Kutt was confident that this could be arranged. He felt the company had lived up to the stipulations set by the
GAAB when they offered the first $12 million in loan insurance, and
another $30 million per year in loan insurance for the next two years
would bring the company up to the amount initially proposed. However,
when Kutt went to the GAAB for the loan insurance, they refused to
provide it. They were not at all happy with the way the company was
being managed, despite its impressive sales growth. There had already
been more than one occasion when there was some question as to how
the payroll would be met. Furthermore, GAAB had hoped that more
equity investment would help decrease the probability that they would
someday have to make good on the insurance that had already been
given; thus, raising their exposure so significantly in order to reduce
their previous exposure made no sense at all. When news of the delay in
the company's stock offering got around, the price of its shares fell from
$12 to $5.

On 25 August 1971, the GAAB, Ford Motor Credit and the Chemical
Bank met with a representative of Peat, Marwick and Mitchell to try to
decide how to proceed. None of the company's lenders wanted to become
more deeply involved with CCI unless an end could be foreseen to the
hand-to-mouth existence the company was leading. But that same day,
CCI received a firm order from International Computers Ltd. for 160
KEY-EDIT systems, which would bring in revenue of almost $7 million.
Kutt had the telegram announcing the order delivered to the GAAB
before the meeting began. The ICL order gave the Chemical Bank
enough confidence to offer $6 million to CCI if the GAAB would insure
lease financing through to the end of 1972 or guarantee the ICL contract.[198] However, the GAAB was not satisfied that the ICL order would
be profitable or that CCI's management had improved its performance.

Late that night, Kutt received a letter from the GAAB stating that
the board decided not to provide further assistance until the proposed
equity offering had been made and had yielded approximately $5 million.
It further stipulated that any new commitment from the GAAB would
be contingent upon (1) the GAAB's being given the right to appoint the
majority of CCI's board of directors; (2) a significant or majority interest in CCI being acquired by "a substantial firm acceptable to the
GAAB" by the end of 1971; and (3) Kutt agreeing to the appointment
of a new president and chief executive officer acceptable to the GAAB.[199]
Shearson, Hammill felt that the U.S. Securities and Exchange Commis-

sion would not allow the stock to be issued under these conditions and backed out. This left CCI teetering on the brink of bankruptcy, with Chemical Bank agreeing to provide money only on a day-to-day basis.

Kutt was frustrated and angered by these events. His belief that the GAAB's decision was deliberate sabotage was fuelled by the fact that he had not been present at the meeting where the fateful decision was taken. Gordon Cowperthwaite's later assessment of the situation was that the bankers' and lenders' patience had simply run out, and the stiff conditions set by the GAAB indicate that they wanted decisive changes made before they became more involved.[200] Kutt, however, felt the bureaucrats surrounding him were to blame. He believed Quinn was not giving accurate information to the GAAB concerning his company, and that Cowperthwaite was playing the classic consultant's role of telling the client — the GAAB — what it wanted to hear. Also, at about this time, Kutt began hearing rumours that caused him to believe the GAAB was intending to put CCI into bankruptcy.[201]

During the discussions over the company's prospects that followed the August 25 meeting, there were substantial differences in opinion between Kutt and Cowperthwaite about such matters as the profitability of sales to ICL and CCI's financial position. Unable to meet with the board that, as the months passed, was constraining his freedom more and more, Kutt's frustration grew. He attempted to pressure the GAAB by presenting his case to the electrical and electronics branch of ITC, to Jean-Luc Pépin and his executive assistant, to various other federal cabinet ministers, to the Ontario government, and, in a desperate moment, by writing long letters to Prime Minister Trudeau and Premier Davis. Of course, this action simply irritated the GAAB members and convinced them that Kutt was totally out of control.[202]

With no equity infusion, Kutt and his senior managers spent the fall negotiating with the GAAB and looking for a merger partner. Approaches made to Digital Equipment, Control Data, Nixdorf, and Fujitsu proved unsuccessful. CCI and the GAAB then approached ICL, which was sufficiently interested to agree to manage CCI for several weeks and undertake a thorough examination of it, the result of which was a possible merger between CCI and ICL's Canadian subsidiary. Shortly after this preliminary agreement, CCI, unable to meet its payments, went into interim receivership. Its creditors agreed not to institute bankruptcy proceedings until ICL had made its decision.[203] Kutt had heard unofficially that ICL, because it was having cash-flow problems of its own, would refuse to take over CCI. Anticipating that the GAAB would use this refusal as proof that CCI was never viable and thus a pretext for completing bankruptcy proceedings, Kutt gave an interview to the *Globe and Mail* in which he blamed the GAAB for CCI's problems, including the shortage of working capital and the failure of its stock issue.[204] This interview quickly led to Kutt's dismissal by the CCI board of directors, which the GAAB controlled. When ICL indicated publicly that it was not interested in taking over CCI, the company went into receivership.

CCI Slides Into Unprofitability

The CCI story might have ended at this point, with the government having lost only $7 million, except that the GAAB decided to keep CCI in business. As a result of the reorganization that occurred in late 1971, CCI entered the second phase of its history. During this period, CCI was transformed from a private-sector enterprise to a government project. The company became dominated by the GAAB and the Ontario Development Corporation (ODC), with the electrical and electronics branch of ITC and Treasury Board playing lesser roles. It was also during this period that political considerations began to have a strong influence on the fate of the company. The first of these was the decision to reorganize the company after its late-1971 receivership rather than to declare it insolvent and shut it down.

The decision is not as inexplicable as it might at first seem. To begin with, in late 1971 and early 1972, in addition to Kutt and his partner, three others also departed from the story. Anthony Hampson, chairman of the GAAB and the most virulent critic of CCI's management, left the GAAB to become president of the Canada Development Corporation. He was replaced by vice-chairman Douglas Kendall. In addition, the GAAB's secretary, Peter Quinn, who also had been critical of CCI, left to go on executive interchange with the government of Nova Scotia. An incidental departure was that of Gordon Cowperthwaite, who became the managing partner of Peat, Marwick and Mitchell, and was no longer personally involved in CCI. (Peat, Marwick and Mitchell's involvement, however, did continue.) The departure of Kutt, Quinn, and Hampson meant that the main sources of conflict were gone.

Thus, the decision to restructure was made in a considerably different atmosphere than had been the decision to call in the receivers. Some of the company's major opponents were now gone, and a new advocate, the Ontario Development Corporation (ODC), had come into play, backing up its enthusiasm with money. In addition, the company was still virtually the sum total of Canada's computer hardware industry, and the GAAB may have felt that it was still too early to give up on Canada's only participant in this field. Possibly the GAAB felt that the large order of KEY-EDIT systems by ICL would give a reorganized company a point of departure.[205] Finally, the government's image would be less damaged by a reorganization than by an outright bankruptcy. A reorganization would indicate that the government believed it was still backing a winner, whereas a bankruptcy would be an admission that the government had invested public funds unwisely. The GAAB hoped that the restructuring would allow them to sell CCI.

By March 1972, Consolidated Computer Limited had been reorganized and renamed Consolidated Computer Incorporated. After paying $7 million in loan insurance, the GAAB received 37.1 percent of the common shares of CCI and convertible debentures worth $3.9 million, becoming the largest single shareholder. The ODC received 14.6 percent of the common stock, and other shareholders held 48.3 percent. Unsecured creditors received 30 cents on each dollar of the first $100,000 of debt and convertible debentures for the rest.[206] William Hutchison, previously vice-president of international marketing, was appointed president and Donald Early, chairman of the ODC, became chairman of the board.

A significant provision of the reorganization was that the company was no longer permitted to market its products directly to end-users, but was to act solely as an original equipment manufacturer (OEM) and sell its equipment to other companies for leasing in the retail market. In this way, the GAAB hoped to bring the company's voracious needs for cash under control and end its dependence on government assistance. This, unfortunately, did not occur. The company was still so weak and so completely without financial resources of its own that it continued to need ad hoc infusions of cash to meet its operating expenses. In addition, the company had three main clients during the 1972–74 period: ICL, Fujitsu, and Cable and Wireless (a Brazilian firm). The large contract with ICL, as predicted by the GAAB back in August of 1971, proved to bc only marginally profitable, a situation which did nothing to help the company's cash-flow difficulties.

The appointment of Hutchison as president of CCI is puzzling. It was Hutchison who had previously headed the marketing group that had been soundly discredited for its inefficiency. He also had less management experience than Mers Kutt, whose lack of administrative ability had so often been criticized by the GAAB. Kutt believes that Hutchison was a skilful corporate politician who knew how to turn the conflict between him (Kutt) and the GAAB to his own advantage.[207] Kendall, who had become the chairman of the GAAB after Hampson's departure, said in a recent interview that Hutchison was chosen because he had the greatest knowledge of the company. It may also be relevant to recall that the GAAB was not hoping to operate the company, but to sell it. Hutchison himself did not return our telephone calls.

During his first six months as president, Hutchison's priority was to retrench his operation. The staff was reduced to 220 people, and the U.K. and German operations were sold for over $1 million. Financial control and planning systems were improved. The company received another PAIT grant for $670,000. CCI reported a profit of $2 million on $12 million in sales during 1972.[208] However, this profit was primarily the result of the sale of the European operations, the PAIT grant, and the fact that CCI's equipment inventory was deemed to be of no value during the restructuring, meaning that the company's cost of sales was artificially low.

In 1973, CCI's performance again began to deteriorate. On the revenue side, ICL agreed to buy 400 new systems worth $20 million by mid-1975, and in early 1973 Fujitsu purchased $2.6 million worth of KEY-EDIT systems. Partly because of the marginal profitability of the ICL contract, however, the company lost $2.6 million on sales of $12.1 million in 1973, and in 1974 it lost $5.5 million on sales of $15.4 million. The company remained a going concern because the GAAB and the ODC provided additional loan guarantees. During this period, the company moved from its retrenchment phase into a new period of growth, as it expanded production dramatically, doubled its marketing expenditures, and developed two new KEY-EDIT systems as well as a minicomputer. However, it was now facing much greater competition, with the more established manufacturers moving into the minicomputer and microcomputer markets.

Although CCI was selling more machines, the prices it was receiving were declining as a result of learning curve advantages being reaped by its competitors.[209] It appears that during the 1972-75 period, CCI lost its ability to anticipate and respond to market changes. Whatever Kutt's weaknesses may have been, he had been an effective leader and innovator, and after he resigned the company lost its focus and its competitive edge. Thereafter, CCI poured considerable sums of money into research and development, but failed to come up with products that addressed market needs. Furthermore, by 1975 the KEY-EDIT technology had been surpassed by competitors' products.[210] The equipment was still useful, and the company had many loyal clients; but it had fallen significantly behind the state of the art, necessitating price cuts to make KEY-EDIT systems attractive to new customers.

Three years of poor performance by CCI led to increased concern by the GAAB, which then commissioned Peat, Marwick and Mitchell to do another study. The study predicted that CCI would lose between $2 and $3 million in 1975 (it actually lost $12 million) and concluded that the company would not become viable on its own and that additional financing would be required as long as the present ownership and organizational structure remained.[211] The study argued that the company "has always lacked strong financial management and control. Departments and costs continually seemed to escalate out of control."[212] The GAAB had had enough and proposed to Alastair Gillespie, the minister of ITC, a deadline of September 30, 1975 to either sell the company or place it in receivership. The ODC also concurred.[213]

However, senior officials of ITC moved more slowly. They established an ad hoc committee involving the electrical and electronics branch of ITC, the GAAB, and the ODC to evaluate alternatives and to report by September 30. At approximately this time, the GAAB reversed its decision to restrict CCI's activities to production and OEM sales. The GAAB, together with CCI, Thorne Riddell and their lawyers McCarthy and McCarthy, set up two leasing companies, Financeco and Finecomp, to purchase and then lease CCI's equipment. Financeco and Finecomp were both legally separate from CCI and became the cushion between CCI and the government. Whereas the GAAB's original intent was to hire Thorne Riddell to manage the leasing companies, Thorne Riddell was unwilling to accept this responsibility, with the result that the GAAB and representatives from CCI also took part in the management of the companies. In practice, CCI did the leasing companies' paperwork and dominated the joint CCI-GAAB investment committee, which was to decide which CCI products the leasing companies would buy. The leasing companies also gave CCI unrealistically favourable terms. The price they paid for the equipment was 41 times the monthly leasing cost. Because they borrowed all their capital from banks, supported by 99-percent loan guarantees, it would take six years before the loans were paid off and the leasing companies were in a position to make a profit. By late 1975, however, there was reason to doubt that most systems would stay out on lease for six years before being returned.[214] Another way the agreements between CCI and the leasing companies were skewed in CCI's favour was that CCI was not required to buy back equipment for which payments were in arrears. The leasing companies were clearly a means of providing short-term financing and improving the look of the company's financial statements in preparation for finding a more permanent solution.

The ITC ad hoc committee on CCI was more optimistic than the GAAB's consultants and decided to recommend to Cabinet that the firm's debt to the Crown be converted into capital stock which, in addition to the stock already held by the federal and Ontario governments, would constitute majority ownership. The Crown's shares could then be sold to two companies which seemed interested, Fujitsu and Central Dynamics Ltd., a Montreal-based computer software and time-sharing company. Their interest was stimulated by the GAAB's willingness to issue a 99-percent guarantee for up to $30 million for lease financing.[215]

This proposal was then presented in Cabinet committee in February 1976. Opposition emerged from the ministers who sat on the Treasury Board. They felt that the ITC proposal contained insufficient information to evaluate the potential success of the CCI restructuring. However, ITC was able quickly to produce some of the data needed. The Treasury Board then recommended that the restructuring proposal be approved in principle, subject to further data being prepared by the department aimed at demonstrating that CCI would be financially viable. On February 26, the Cabinet endorsed the ITC proposal with the proviso that ITC had to prepare a Treasury Board submission on the financial viability of CCI.[216] In endorsing the proposal, Cabinet wanted to avoid the $52 million loss (split 2/3 to Ottawa and 1/3 to Ontario) which would be involved if the company were liquidated. It was also felt that the best option would be to keep alive the only Canadian-owned computer hardware manufacturer and improve its performance with the assistance of Fujitsu's technological and Central Dynamics' managerial skills.[217]

In April 1976, ITC established an ad hoc committee to investigate CCI's financial situation, consisting of six ITC representatives, three from the GAAB, three from CCI, two from the Ontario Development Corporation, and only two junior officers from Finance and one from Treasury Board. Shortly after this committee began its work, the final part of the Peat Marwick study commissioned by the GAAB was submitted: it reported significant problems with the sales projections and financial records of CCI and in essence questioned the information ITC had presented to Cabinet two months previously. It also concluded that "the exposure of the government under its guarantees of lease financing may be considerable." However, the electrical and electronics branch of ITC disagreed with the Peat Marwick study, arguing that the relationship with Fujitsu and the new management brought in from Central Dynamics would provide the company with the strength it needed. Fujitsu, like CCI, had fallen behind its competitors with its new products, and it was hoped that by combining CCI's excellent software team and Fujitsu's hardware team, the two companies could come up with the right product for the North American market. Fujitsu hoped to make CCI its point of entry into North America, a situation which could provide CCI with significant long-term benefits. In addition, by April 1976, CCI chairman Donald Early and president William Hutchison had been replaced respectively by Earle Wallick, the president of Central Dynamics, and Leslie Sellmeyer, a vice-president of Central Dynamics. The electrical and electronics branch believed that "with Fujitsu there is a reasonable chance that CCI can survive and prosper"; "the marketing/product development strategy is considered well-conceived and attainable"; and "the new management has the combination to be successful."[218]

The ITC proposal went to Treasury Board in June 1976. Peter Quinn, then director of the transportation, communication and science branch, argued against the proposed restructuring. However, even though ministers felt the ITC proposal lacked good financial data, they were satisfied with the assurances given by ITC that any increased federal government exposure would be matched proportionately by Ontario, and that Fujitsu would give CCI exclusive North American marketing rights for some of its products as well as access to some of its technology.[219]

The reorganization was put in some jeopardy when Central Dynamics backed out in October 1976, because they wished to merge CCI directly with their company rather than run it at arm's length, and because they themselves were having financial problems. The management team from Central Dynamics was split, with Sellmeyer and some others staying with CCI, and Wallick and some financial people returning to Central Dynamics. Nevertheless, ITC remained optimistic. The electrical and electronics branch told the GAAB that CCI's new management was making better progress than anticipated, and they were thus "convinced CCI can survive without Central Dynamics. In fact CCI does not need another partner outside of its Fujitsu relationship."[220] In December, an agreement was signed whereby Fujitsu agreed to provide CCI with "technological, manufacturing, financial, and marketing assistance and manufacturing and distribution rights and a reduction in royalties payable" in exchange for 3.3 million shares, or a 15-percent interest in CCI.[221] The GAAB and the ODC together continued to hold 60 percent of the company's equity, rather than the 33 percent that had been envisioned while Central Dynamics was still involved.[222] The GAAB, now renamed the Enterprise Development Board (EDB), agreed to insure 99 percent of CCI's borrowing for lease financing, up to an aggregate of $30 million.[223] On 17 March 1977, the Treasury Board agreed to approve ITC's submission regarding CCI, provided CCI submitted annual reports commencing in 1978. In addition, ITC was to submit semi-annual reports regarding loan guarantees and contributions under the Enterprise Development Program (the successor to the General Adjustment Assistance Program) and produce a complete evaluation of the program by 31 March 1979.[224]

Table 2 shows CCI's financial performance after its second restructuring. The first thing to notice is that the leasing companies sustained

Table 2. FINANCIAL PERFORMANCE OF CCI AND ITS LEASING COMPANIES, 1976 TO 1981

	1976	1977	1978	1979	1980	1981 (9 mos.)
			($ × 10³)			
CCI Revenues	25,299	18,812	23,047	22,698	11,924	N.A.
Cost of Sales	15,541	11,062	12,537	19,335	13,256	N.A.
Marketing and Administration	6,647	5,627	7,635	9,512	6,969	N.A.
Research & Development	2,087	1,876	1,674	2,444	3,279	N.A.
Government Grants	(700)	(1,193)	(807)	(1,530)	(1,698)	N.A.
Interest Expense	1,700	1,022	1,394	2,935	3,592	N.A.
Profit or (Loss)	24	418	614	(9,997)	(13,475)	(11,317)
Leasing Company (Losses)	(1,297)	(3,667)	(4,176)	(4,818)	(7,081)	(5,463)
Consolidated (Loss)	(1,273)	(3,249)	(3,562)	(14,815)	(20,556)	(16,780)

Source: CCI Annual Reports, Anderson Report, p. 29.

substantial losses in all years. However, CCI reported only its own performance to the government, which was clearly misleading, particularly from 1976 to 1978. This was recognized by Sellmeyer, the CEO, who at a CCI directors' meeting in October 1976, noted that the leasing companies' purchases from CCI "masked the current operations" of CCI.[225] One of the ways it did so was by disguising the fact that CCI was beginning to have customer service problems. Systems were returned by lessees because of obsolescence, malfunctioning or lack of maintenance. However, because CCI was not required to buy back this equipment, the leasing companies were left holding titles to equipment that was not producing revenue.[226] In addition, 1976 revenues rose dramatically because CCI included as sales $10 million worth of equipment that had been leased in previous years.[227] The company also had financial tricks up its sleeve in 1977: it adopted the policy of recognizing equipment sales to the leasing companies at the time equipment was shipped, rather than when documentation for the transfer and sale to the leasing company was complete, as it had done in the past. This increased 1977 revenues by $1.7 million and profits by $860,000.[228]

Whereas marketing and administration costs in 1976 and 1977 were dramatically reduced relative to the 1975 level of $8.2 million, by 1978, they began to rise substantially. Tight management control at CCI proved to be a temporary phenomenon. Indeed, a consultant who became CCI's vice-president of finance for a short while in 1980 observed that the company's bookkeeping was in a decrepit state and its accounting system did not produce accurate information. At the same time, CCI's auditors noted problems in the billing, collection, financial, and inventory systems.[229] In addition, the company's U.S. leasing operations rapidly became a millstone. The company had systems in so many widely dispersed places that the cost of sales support and service was extremely burdensome. The company's lack of money, however, did not prevent the board of directors from paying Sellmeyer well. His annual salary at the end of the year was $60,000 for 1976 and $80,000 for 1977, 1978, and 1979. In addition, Mr. Sellmeyer collected bonuses of $14,600 in 1978 and $20,400 in 1979, presumably based on the previous year's performance, and at all times had a company car. A few other executives also received bonuses during 1977–79, although not as bounteous, and it was customary for CCI's executives to have company cars throughout the period 1974–79.[230]

Sellmeyer's term as president was marked by other problems as well. He did not have Fujitsu's confidence, and CCI's continuing problems became a source of embarrassment to the managers at Fujitsu who had been responsible for the association. Eventually, out of frustration with the relationship with CCI, Fujitsu formed a joint venture with the American conglomerate, TRW. In addition, although CCI continued to spend considerable amounts of its own and grant money on research and development, it was still not achieving the hoped-for results. Fujitsu did spend some millions of dollars to help CCI develop a computer, but no marketable product resulted.[231] Eventually, Fujitsu lost interest in selling its products in Canada and established its own sales organization in the United States, with the result that CCI never became Fujitsu's North American marketing arm. In short, the relationship with Fujitsu never produced the tangible benefits the government expected.

By 1979, CCI's KEY-EDIT system was quite obsolete in comparison with the intelligent terminals, minicomputers, and microcomputers that the competition was producing. CCI's weakening competitive position explains the drastic narrowing of the margin between revenues and cost of sales in 1979: the company was trying to stay in business by slashing its prices. Indeed, two prospective purchasers of CCI noted that a major contract it had just then signed to supply equipment to ICL was so unfavourable that it would lose money on every unit sold.[232] CCI's only real strength at this time was that it had entered the lottery terminal business, where its equipment was accepted very well. In 1980, however, CCI's marketing strategy proved to be a failure, as sales simply collapsed. Finally, interest expenses rose dramatically over the period, as a result of increased borrowing to cover the company's deficits and rising interest rates.

In short, the story the numbers tell over the entire period is one of failure. The question we shall deal with is how the government came to realize it, and what action was taken.

By October 1979, it became evident to even the electrical and electronics branch of ITC that CCI's survival was in doubt, and the branch suggested to the EDB that the government attempt to merge CCI with another firm, or sell its interest in CCI to a firm that would attempt to maintain it as an ongoing business. ITC prepared a memorandum to the Clark government's Cabinet Committee on Economy in Government, suggesting that the Treasury Board Secretariat privatization unit find a buyer or merger partner for CCI. A report by the consulting firm of Crosbie, Armitage endorsed this approach and advised against liquidation on the grounds that it would involve substantial losses and have adverse public implications. By the time the Cabinet memorandum was discussed and the report received, the Clark government had been defeated in the House of Commons, and so had no opportunity to implement a policy of privatizing CCI.[233]

CCI's problems came to the attention of the new Liberal government very quickly. In May 1980, CCI's auditors, now Peat, Marwick and Mitchell, informed the EDB that they were concerned by the company's $10 million loss and intended to qualify their audit report, indicating that they were unable to assure themselves that CCI would remain in operation and thus that the balance sheet represented fairly the company's financial position. Such a statement would have made it more difficult, if not impossible, for the government to divest itself of the company. Ultimately, the EDB was able to avert this statement by providing an additional $12 million in loan guarantees to cover the period from November 1979 to the end of 1980. The EDB appointed John McDonald Brown, an EDB director and a vociferous critic of CCI, as president of CCI. Brown was an accountant, businessman, and computer consultant who had been an executive of the Nova Scotia Liberal party. His mandate was to determine whether the company could be turned around, what the cost of a turnaround would be, and, if a turnaround were not possible, to develop a plan to allow the government to minimize its losses.[234]

At this point, CCI's situation began to receive substantial Cabinet attention, in particular that of ITC Minister Herb Gray and Treasury Board President Donald Johnston. The next chapter will discuss how the government decided to disinvest in CCI.

Monitoring CCI

The main source of our discussion of the monitoring of CCI is a 1982 report to the Treasury Board by Lieutenant-General W.A.B. Anderson, a former secretary to the Ontario government's Management Board. The report has never been made public. There were three mechanisms for monitoring CCI and, after 1976, its affiliated leasing companies: the companies' boards of directors; the GAAB (EDB after 1977) and its parent department, ITC; and the Treasury Board, acting in its capacity as monitor of government spending.

During most of the period between 1972 and 1980, the board included representatives of CCI management, the business community, and the GAAB (EDB). Anderson finds that the board members did not really carry out their responsibilities in managing the company: they came to feel that responsibility rested with the GAAB (EDB). As a consequence, the CCI directors were something of a rubber stamp, agreeing to whatever the GAAB decided. The same was the case for the leasing companies, whose directors were two public servants and two partners of the accounting firm of Thorne, Riddell. The auditors told Anderson that they interpreted their role strictly as administrators for the leasing companies, with no management functions or responsibilities. Although Anderson found nothing in writing that expressly limited their activities in this way, it is clear that the realpolitik of this situation, like that of CCI itself, left it to the GAAB, not the private-sector representatives, to monitor the leasing companies.[235]

Although the information is sketchy, it appears that the the GAAB devoted a reasonable amount of attention to CCI between 1972 and 1975. William Hutchison, the CEO, produced semi-annual reports which, although lacking hard data, dealt with managerial issues and the company's performance relative to its budget. The annual reports were also prefaced with a statement by management. During that period, accounting practices were more conservative than they would be subsequently: without leasing companies, CCI could report only its actual revenues. Thus, after two years of poor performance (1973 and 1974), the GAAB felt sufficiently concerned that it commissioned the Peat Marwick consulting report, which concluded that CCI was not viable.

Anderson concentrated his attention on the monitoring of CCI by the EDB and ITC in the period after the 1976 restructuring, and he was very critical. The only monitoring means EDB initially requested were the year-end audited and quarterly unaudited financial statements for CCI. After authorizing another $30 million in loan guarantees in 1977, the EDB asked for statistical and analytical information four times a year regarding the leasing companies, but received it only sporadically. Not only was the quality of information poor, but between 1976 and 1978, the period of Sellmeyer's presidency, CCI management did not provide the required information. However, even that which was provided, such as the 1977 and 1978 annual reports of CCI and the leasing companies, was not analysed by the EDB, even though it would have revealed the difficulties CCI was facing.[236] The quality of monitoring of the CCI loan guarantee by the EDB was not unusual. Anderson cites a 1980 ITC audit of the EDB that found deficiencies in all aspects of the program's management. The program lacked a clear statement of objectives, documented criteria for project approval and termination, efficient delivery systems, a reliable program information system, and procedures for program monitoring and reporting. CCI was unusual only in that the amount of money that the government had at risk was much greater than that involved in other loans (which itself should have suggested closer monitoring).[237] The Enterprise Development Program was eventually shut down in 1983 amid suspicions of conflicts of interest.

Anderson was also critical of the individuals most closely associated with the GAAB loan guarantee. Harold Melanson, the EDB's secretary, was its representative on the investment committee of the leasing companies: until 1979, when he moved to CCI as a vice-president, he indicated that the leasing companies were in good shape. Anderson expressed amazement that Melanson could have made this report when the prices the leasing companies were paying CCI for equipment were 41 times the monthly rental fees. To recoup all production, administration, and interest costs — and thus allow the leasing companies to repay their bank loans — the equipment had to stay on lease for six years.[238]

EDB chairman Douglas Kendall sat on the CCI board between 1977 and 1979, and John McDonald Brown, an EDB member, was CEO of CCI from mid-1980. In both instances Anderson found that EDB deferred to the judgement of these individuals. The board was always presented with summary verbal reports rather than written analyses; often decisions were made by a telephone poll of the members. Anderson found

this informal decision-making process unsatisfactory,[239] and when combined with the CCI board's deference to the EDB, it meant that the only
people who had any real responsibility for CCI were Melanson, Kendall,
and later Brown. Kendall, an aging gentleman whose abilities are well
respected in government circles, apparently was having health problems at this time, suggesting that he played a less spirited role in EDB
matters than he once had.

Anderson was also concerned about the EDB's position within ITC.
Although its analytical capabilities were to be supported by staff within
several ITC branches (electrical and electronics branch, corporate analysis
branch, program branch), the staff who provided this advice were not
clearly accountable to the EDB. And although the EDB was formally
responsible to the minister of ITC, it appears that accountability for
management of the program was shared, in an undefined way, with the
deputy minister and the department. Anderson's ultimate concern was
that shared and vague accountability amounted to no accountability at
all.[240]

Anderson's account of the EDB's management of CCI during Brown's
presidency in 1980 and 1981 is particularly scathing:

> While the quantity of available information improved when the EDB put
> in its own management in 1980, the quality remained poor. There was
> often conflicting information and advice from within ITC and between
> CCI and ITC. There were consistent, gross errors in funding projections
> which necessitated repeated calls for further guarantees. For example,
> there were *17 guarantees provided between January 1, 1980 and Novem-
> ber 30, 1981 for a total of $30.9 million.* Each of these decisions was taken
> without any meaningful look at the total CCI project. The EDB mem-
> bers have noted that, at no time, were they provided with the type of
> overview that would have given them a perspective on the total CCI involve-
> ment —past, present, and future. Many of the decisions in this period
> were taken on an emergency basis, often through the use of a telephone
> poll, and dealt with an immediate requirement for a specific amount of
> money to keep the company afloat. [emphasis added]
>
> During the last two years, there was a growing number of officials rec-
> ommending the termination of the CCI project. The reports, with a few
> important exceptions, were almost all bad. However, there were still a
> few individuals in key positions who were somewhat 'bullish' on the future of
> the company. The EDB, on a number of occasions, postponed a final
> decision on the project. There always seemed to be some new event which
> indicated that the company could be turned around or sold or that the
> government liability could be reduced. The events included a renewed
> interest by Fujitsu, a major contract with ICL, various potential buyers,
> new management, and a new business plan. Each of these events required
> time to 'investigate,' 'negotiate' or 'develop.'[241]

The Treasury Board Secretariat's monitoring of the CCI investment
was not much better than ITC's. As a condition for approval of the 1976

restructuring, Treasury Board requested that ITC submit annual reports on CCI commencing in 1978. However, in a rapidly changing high-tech industry, two years is virtually a century and so such monitoring would clearly be inadequate. ITC provided CCI's 1978 and 1979 annual reports — without any analysis — but not those of the leasing companies. The secretariat did no analysis of its own. Treasury Board ministers were not advised of the existence, status, and role of the leasing companies until 1980. Members of the secretariat were close enough to the 1976 restructuring to know of the potential existence of the leasing companies. However, they did not dig deeply enough into the case to find out about the companies, and ITC was hardly willing to volunteer information that would be so damaging to its interests.[242]

Anderson finally dealt with the briefing of the most closely involved ministers. Between 1972 and 1976, ITC ministers were briefed six times, and the result was a mood of modest optimism that the company would overcome its current problems. In 1976, the conclusion was the same: that the government should maintain its relationship to CCI, as the situation was viable. Thus the pessimistic assessment of Peat, Marwick was not communicated upward by the bureaucracy. The predominant message of the frequent briefings of the minister in the Clark government was that the company was still viable and thus a candidate for privatization. Only in June 1980 did the minister in the Trudeau government, Herb Gray, begin to receive frequent and pessimistic briefings.[243]

The president of the Treasury Board was briefed by his officials regarding CCI's problems for the first time in 1976, when they recommended immediate sale. He was not briefed at all regarding the deteriorating situation between 1976 and 1979. Sinclair Stevens, the Treasury Board president in the Clark government, was told by his officials that CCI was not viable and should be sold. At the same time, Finance Minister Crosbie was told by his officials that it was viable and should be kept. In June 1980, the Treasury Board president in the Trudeau government was informed of CCI's difficulties by Herb Gray, and from then on his briefings became more frequent.[244]

The overall conclusion that Anderson drew on the basis of thorough interviews and perusal of all records was that, for much of the period, the closest monitors of the CCI investment were its advocates. Therefore, the hard questions that might have brought an earlier termination of this project were never raised.

SUMMARY

This chapter has focused on why, in every case we examined, investment turned into a failure: external challenges or problems out of management's control, errors by management, bad political decisions, and weaknesses in the monitoring system that held management accountable to the government, which, either through loans or equity investments, supported the project. Table 3 summarizes the problems.

Perhaps the most surprising thing about the external problems is how few there were; it does not appear that they were the critical factors leading to the failure of the five projects. Deuterium of Canada suffered increased construction costs because the winter of 1966–67 was abnormally severe. However, the project failed mainly because of the inexperience of the engineers designing the plant, its ongoing labour relations difficulties, and the mistake of allowing salt water to sit in the equipment for several months. Bricklin and Churchill Forest Industries did not really suffer from external difficulties. Bricklin chose a niche in the automobile market that was growing and could have been profitable. The ability of the Japanese and Europeans to overcome entry barriers to

Table 3. COMPARING THE PROBLEMS

Problems	DCL	BC	C'Air	CFI	CCI
External Problems					
weather	X				
recession hurts sales			X		
rising interest rates			X		X
adverse changes in regulatory framework			X		
strong competition					X
Managerial Problems					
technology-based					
lack of experience in product/process design	X		X		X
difficulty in developing or using a new technology	X	X	X		X
secretiveness about technology	X				
other					
excessive centralization		X			
excessive geographic decentralization		X		X	X
marketing dominates organization		X	X		X
poor labour relations	X	X		X	
subcontracting problems:					
– prices too high				X	X
– delays in delivery	X	X	X		
staff too large		X	X		X
nepotism		X			
project too large				X	

Problems	DCL	BC	C'Air	CFI	CCI
Monitoring problems					
managers mislead monitors		X	X	X	X
managers' secretiveness re:					
proprietary information	X				
re: information-system					
misleading accounting system			X		X
poor information systems		X		X	X
re: board of directors					
excessively passive			X		X
members lack expertise	X		X		X
re: government monitors					
monitors don't have enough					
information or right information		X		X	
monitors fail to analyse information			X		X
monitors lack expertise		X	X	X	X
monitors identify with or are					
"captured" by management			X	X	X
multiple monitors dissipate					
responsibility			X	X	X
loan guarantees reduce public,					
media monitoring			X		X
Political Problems					
political attachment undermines					
initial assessment of project		X		X	
weak initial contract				X	
monitoring undermined by					
politicians		X	X		X
politicians appoint directors					
lacking expertise	X		X		X
politicians give directors unclear					
mandate			X		

Legend: DCL = Deuterium of Canada Ltd.
         BC   = Bricklin
         C'Air = Canadair
         CFI   = Churchill Forest Industries
         CCI   = Consolidated Computer Inc.

the North American market indicates that entry was possible. Churchill Forest Industries suffered from a locational disadvantage: however, the federal and provincial governments were quite willing to provide subsidies that would have overcome the disadvantage. The real problem here, as will be discussed below, was the difficulty the provincial government experienced in attempting to monitor managers who were intent on and skilful at defrauding the government.

Of all the cases, probably Canadair had the heaviest burden of external problems: the 1982 recession, rising interest rates, and adverse changes in the regulatory framework, in particular the changed certification standards the Challenger had to meet and the airline deregulation which contributed to its losing its contract with Federal Express. Nevertheless, we do not think these factors were decisive. Only 24 percent of the Challenger project's cost was interest, whereas the rest was mainly attributable to the physical production of the aircraft.[245] Even though the weak 1982 market hurt sales, it was clear by then that the company would never sell enough aircraft to break even.[246] Although certification slowed the date at which the aircraft could be delivered, production was slowed as much by management's inability to produce the aircraft it had promised the market. Even though the loss of the Federal Express order shortened the Challenger's order book, it could have been used to advantage by allowing the company to switch over to the more dependable General Electric engines. Perhaps the last word on the significance of Canadair's various problems should go to former CDIC vice-president David Crane, who told us, "We figured out one day that it cost roughly $1.5 billion to develop the Challenger: $500 million was due to management mistakes, $500 million was due to the method of financing, and $500 million is probably what it should have cost."[247]

Consolidated Computer was also hurt by rising interest rates. However, interest payments in total constituted the following percentages of the consolidated losses of the company and its leasing subsidiaries: 34 percent in 1977, 39 percent in 1978, 20 percent in 1979, and 17 percent in 1980.[248] The final factor, strong competition, is external in the sense that it was a key characteristic of the market in which Consolidated was competing. In order to survive, management had to respond to that challenge. The fact that there is a substantial number of hardware manufacturers who broke into this market, some of which (particularly Apple) started from a base as small as Consolidated Computer, indicates that entry was by no means impossible.

The second set of problems we consider are managerial. In four of the five cases, management was involved in modifying existing technology or developing new technology, and in each case it failed. The engineers designing the Glace Bay heavy-water plant, the firm of Burns and Roe, had no experience in this area. Because of design problems, management error, or possibly sabotage, salt water was allowed to sit in the plant's tubing for several months, which led to the need for an almost total reconstruction of the plant commencing in 1971. The automobile design and engineering people Malcolm Bricklin hired appear to have been competent professionals; certainly they were knowledgeable about the state of the art in Detroit. The difficulties they faced were Bricklin's demands to develop, in very short order, a car using gull-wing doors and a body of acrylic bonded to fibreglass, both substantial technological advances. In the case of Canadair, an inexperienced engineering staff was attempting to design a new plane, working with an engine manufacturer attempting to design a new engine. After the departure of Mers Kutt, Consolidated Computer never appears to have regained its technological edge, and its research and development staff, despite substantial expenditures, were unable to keep up with the competition. Of the five, CFI was the only venture where technology was not an important problem: Kasser and his associates were as skilled in forest product technology as they were in raiding the Manitoba treasury.

The projects shared a number of other common problems. Canadair, Consolidated Computer, and Bricklin were all dominated by the marketing function, with the result that the marketers were promising the market a product that the company could not produce at the price, on the date, or with the specifications at which the product was promised. In all three, as well, the sales staff was much too large. The operations of Bricklin, Consolidated Computer, and CFI were too spread out geographically, which contributed to high overhead costs. CFI's geographic dispersal also exacerbated the problem of monitoring its management. Bricklin had the added problem of Malcolm Bricklin wanting to retain tight personal control over the organization, a situation which led to delay and poorly informed decisions. In three cases (Deuterium, Bricklin, and CFI) there were labour relations problems. Management was faced with a workforce that did not have the necessary skills, and it appears that in all three management handled this challenge poorly. Bricklin's nepotism exacerbated this problem.

In every case, relations with subcontractors turned out to be a serious problem. Deuterium suffered from late delivery of equipment. Bricklin was unable to plan its production schedule, with the result that parts could never be ordered on time or in sufficient quantities to receive volume discounts. Canadair chose the wrong company to design the engines. In addition, poor production planning caused many of the parts that were ordered to be scrapped. There is some evidence that Consolidated Computer's management were not diligent enough in keeping component costs down. One might want to suggest that the problems were caused by the negligence of parts suppliers. For instance, Canadair sued Avco Lycoming: at the time of writing, the case is still pending. However, the magnitude of the suit ($110 million) is still only a small part of the cost of developing the Challenger, and much less than the $500 million of development cost that Crane attributed to management error. In all cases, management must bear the responsibility for choosing the contractor and for formulating the production schedules that led to a great deal of suboptimal contracting. The subcontracting problem in the case of CFI was quite different, since the subcontractors were not operating at arm's length from the general contractor, and indeed were being used to overcharge the government.

The overall impression that someone with a background in management education might draw from all these undertakings is that they include a wide range of errors, perhaps even most that are possible to make: product development errors, inability to coordinate functional areas, poor organizational design, poor labour relations, and errors in subcontracting and parts acquisition. Not at all a cheerful record!

The third set of causes for failure focus on the monitoring system. There is a theoretical literature which suggests that, in the private sector, owners of capital have a strong incentive to monitor the performance of management and either improve it or replace management. Some of the mechanisms cited are the board of directors; the stock market, which acts as a daily indicator of corporate performance and as the arena for a takeover bid; the power of banks to investigate the performance of borrowers, and the executive labour market, in particular its use of stock options as a form of compensation.[249] The question of concern to us here is whether our firms established monitoring systems that could have performed the functions that monitoring systems in private-sector firms, in theory, should perform.

To begin with, it should be noted that in all five cases there was a definite monitoring problem. Jerome Spevack jealously guarded his patents for heavy-water technology. Malcolm Bricklin and his associates attempted to mislead the New Brunswick government regarding the extent of their investment, the amount of development work they actually had done, and their ongoing expenditures. Canadair management was less than candid with the government about Challenger's prospects. Consolidated Computer's management was not forthright about the company's financial problems or its competitive position. Finally, Alexander Kasser deliberately misled the Manitoba government about where the money it invested was going and what it was being used for.

In four of the five cases, the management information systems, including accounting, were faulty. Canadair's management made aggressive use of program accounting, which made the company's performance look better than it really was. For three years, Consolidated Computer was able to hide its losses by means of its leasing companies. The overall management information and control systems for Bricklin, Churchill Forest Industries, and Consolidated Computer performed poorly, which complicated the task of monitoring.

The boards of directors of several of the projects were weak. The Nova Scotia government appointees who dominated the Deuterium Board admitted that they lacked expertise in the nuclear energy area. (This, however, did not stop them from making a number of unwise decisions, such as the hiring of the firm of Brown and Root as the principal contractor in the construction of the heavy-water plant.) Canadair's directors also lacked aviation industry expertise. Some instances of appointments to the boards of directors were the result of political patronage, and the individuals involved did not have the expertise or the inclination to play an active role in the management of the company.

In addition to monitoring by the board of directors, in four of the five cases, management had some responsibility to report directly to a public servant or committee of public servants who served as monitors. These relationships broke down for a number of reasons. In CFI's initial contract with Monoca, disclosure of the company's principals or that of its subcontractors was not required. With regard to Bricklin, Premier Hatfield's strong political attachment to the project undermined the monitoring. In two cases, Canadair and Consolidated Computer, we feel that the monitors whom the government appointed were often unduly sympathetic to the company and were not sufficiently skeptical. With CFI, we would go further: the two principal monitors, Rex Grose and James Zeigler, were "captured" by Kasser, so that their effectiveness was totally compromised.

A monitor must receive information and then have the time and expertise to process it. But the monitors in Bricklin, Canadair, CFI, and Consolidated Computer lacked expertise about the very industry in which the firm was competing. The monitors in Bricklin and CFI were not given either enough information or the right information. Those monitoring Canadair and Consolidated Computer failed to use what limited expertise they had and did not analyse the information. The inadequacy of the monitors in their use of information is very disturbing to us.

In two situations, we find evidence of the "after you, Alphonse; no, after you, Gaston" syndrome. The existence of multiple monitors, rather than improving monitoring, led to each set of monitors assuming that the other had done its job, with the consequence that no monitoring was done at all. At the outset of the CFI project, the Manitoba Cabinet under Premier Roblin assumed that the Manitoba Development Fund had reviewed the initial loan and the Fund assumed that Cabinet had reviewed the loan. In the case of CCI, the Enterprise Development Board assumed that CCI was being monitored by one of its members who also sat on the CCI board; however, the other members of the CCI board assumed that the EDB was monitoring the company.

The final monitoring issue we wish to mention is loan guarantees. They were issued in all projects except for CFI. In two (Canadair and Consolidated Computer) the guarantees served to reduce the visibility of the project to the media, the opposition, and the public, because they could be approved by order-in-council and therefore did not require legislative debate, as would have been the case had the money been appropriated through the budgetary process. (In contrast, Deuterium and Bricklin were highly visible in the small polities in which they were located, and they were a source of ongoing media, political, and public interest.)

The overall conclusion we can draw is that the monitoring process was deficient in every project. We suggest that it was least deficient in

Deuterium, because the government board members had control over the company: lacking expertise, they made bad decisions. In the case of Bricklin, the monitors had a reasonable amount of information about the car's technical problems and the company's managerial problems, but gave management relatively free rein for quite some time. In the cases of Canadair and Consolidated Computer, there were mechanisms in place, but advocates of the projects often controlled the monitoring process; more objective parties did not get enough information, or did not have the expertise or inclination to monitor it. Finally, the process was least effective for CFI, where it was completely subverted by the company; the only true monitors were the media. If weak monitoring systems can contribute to the sort of failures we have seen, we believe that public enterprises (whether Crown corporations, mixed enterprises, or recipients of large government loans) need strong monitoring systems.

The fourth possible cause of these failures was bad political decision-making. The choice of Deuterium over the other bidders was a political decision, one that was opposed by the bureaucracy; subsequent problems were due mainly to managerial errors and poor decisions by the members of the DCL board, to whom the politicians had delegated authority. However, federal and provincial Nova Scotia politicians compounded DCL's problems by convincing the federal government to increase the size of the project in 1966, which increased government's exposure. In the case of Bricklin, the decision to invest was clearly Premier Hatfield's, and his attachment to the project weakened the bureaucracy's monitoring of it for quite a while. In addition, he chose to ignore the bad news he was receiving about the project. Similarly, politicians had a large role to play in CFI; the desire of the Roblin government to have a forestry megaproject for the 1966 election campaign contributed to the one-sidedness of the original contract, which in turn contributed to the difficulty of monitoring CFI. Certainly the politicians should have been more cautious about signing contracts without legal advice and about dealing with companies that would not disclose information about their principals. Once this structure was established, the key players were free to interact within it. Thus, Kasser's cleverness, Grose's duplicity, and Zeigler's slow-wittedness led to the ultimate outcome. In the case of Canadair, the strong commitment of the Quebec Liberal caucus and of Jean Chrétien to the Challenger probably undermined monitoring by the public service. Also, the appointment of directors with little or no aviation industry expertise and the board's lack of a clear mandate also weakened the monitoring regime. Finally, the evidence concerning CCI suggests that the primary responsibility for CCI's problems was bureaucratic, rather than political. Until the mid-1970s, decisions about CCI were made entirely at the bureaucratic level. Ministers of ITC and presidents of the Treasury Board were infrequently briefed about CCI (except in 1976), and the bureaucrats' briefings were excessively optimistic. The strongest hypothesis of political responsibility we could make would be that the Cabinet's willingness to support the company in 1976 may have undermined the monitoring regime in the following three years. To summarize, the evidence suggests that the politicians must bear a major share of the responsibility for the failures in four of the five projects we have examined.

As we have seen above, because of weak monitoring systems and politicians' attachment to the projects, news of their difficulties was slow in arriving at the highest levels of government. However, the news ultimately arrived, sometimes with the media as messenger. Table 4 demonstrates that, when this happened, the monitoring regime was always dramatically strengthened. This involved such actions as the hiring of consultants, government task forces, government participation on the board of directors, increased briefing of ministers, hands-on management of the project by public servants, replacement of management, changes in ownership by converting debt to equity or converting the public enterprise to a Crown corporation, and in one case, setting up a commission of inquiry to do a post mortem.

The increased monitoring appears to have taken three main forms. First, each government, upon recognizing that it lacked specific industry information, attempted to increase its knowledge about the firms, their technologies, and their position relative to competition by hiring consultants. In some cases (Bricklin, Canadair, CFI) consultants were also hired to establish information systems, which management had failed to do. In two cases (the interdepartmental task force on Canadair and Alistair Stewart's inquiry regarding CFI), this data-gathering function was supplemented by task forces within government. The second form of increased monitoring, which usually followed once the first had been completed, was closer management of the project. This sometimes (Deuterium, Bricklin, Canadair) involved public servants making many

Table 4. ESCALATION OF MONITORING

Action	DCL	BC	C'Air	CFI	CCI
Hiring consultants	X	X	X	X	X
Government task force			X	X	
Active participation on board of directors			X		
Increased briefing of ministers	X	X	X	X	X
Hands-on management	X	X	X		
Replacement of management	X	X	X	X	X
Conversion of debt to equity	X	X	X	X	X
Conversion to a Crown corporation	X		X	X	
Commission of inquiry "post mortem"				X	

strategic and even operating decisions for the company. However, given the workload that senior public servants already faced, this could not be a sustainable long-run approach. Thus, in each case it was followed by the appointment of new management. The new managers sometimes came from outside the company (Deuterium, Bricklin, CFI) and sometimes from inside (Canadair, CCI). In each case, it was hoped that they would have the skills necessary to solve the problems the firm was facing. In some cases, most notably CCI, several new managers were not able to turn the company around. A result of this second phase of closer monitoring was increased briefing of ministers, and this occurred in all five projects.

The third phase of increased monitoring is the institutionalization of a closer relationship between the government and the enterprise. This involved both the replacement of debt with equity, when the government's initial support was in the form of loans, and, in three cases, the conversion of the public enterprise to a Crown corporation. It could then be subjected to the normal monitoring regime for a Crown corporation. For Bricklin and Consolidated Computer, no Crown corporation was established because, as will be discussed in the following chapter, the government chose to divest itself of the company.

To one project, Churchill Forest Industries, a commission of inquiry was appointed to study what went wrong. We suggest that it was done in this case because the government that appointed the commission came to power so late in the history of the project that it knew that most of the blame would fall on its political predecessor. In three other cases (Bricklin, CCI, Canadair) the government that was responsible for the problems remained in power and could scarcely have been expected to have established a commission that would have condemned it. With regard to Deuterium, Gerald Regan's government, which took power in 1970, was probably not inclined to establish a commission because of the role the federal Liberal party (of which Regan himself had been an M.P.) also played in the project. Thus, in four cases, the politicians somehow summoned up the fortitude to resist public demands for unnecessary commissions.

This, then, concludes our look at the errors that contributed to the failure of these five enterprises. In the next chapter we look at the decisions the governments made about whether or not to divest themselves of these projects once their problems had become clear.

4

To Divest or Not to Divest

INTRODUCTION

The previous chapter concluded that in each of the five cases, the government drastically increased its monitoring so as to obtain the information necessary for making a decision with regard to what ultimately should be done with the respective enterprises. This chapter concludes our narrative by attempting to explain, and hence compare, the various decisions.

This chapter is, in a sense, the obverse of chapter 2, which attempted to explain the original investment decisions. There, we used those decisions to test the vote maximization hypothesis. Here, we will continue to use vote maximization as well as two other possible explanations for the decisions. On the one hand, the vote maximization hypothesis would predict a political preference for keeping the projects in operation if they provided jobs to workers who would otherwise be unemployed. On the other hand, because the public had become aware that the projects were commercial failures, they had become a source of embarrassment to the government. The question politicians would have had to consider was whether the blow to a government's image of admitting that it made a bad decision in the past is worse than the damage done by perpetuating a bad project. The vote maximization hypothesis may also be of some help in explaining the timing of decisions on the basis of the political cycle. The hypothesis would predict that it is more likely that a government would admit its errors immediately after, rather than immediately before, an election.

A second factor that might be of use in explaining these decisions is political ideology. We would expect NDP governments to prefer public ownership and Conservative governments to prefer privatization. In addition, the ideology of nation- or province-building, which seems to be embraced by all segments of the political spectrum, might also explain decisions to keep a project in operation.

A third explanation is budgetary. The politicians who were deciding whether to keep the projects in operation recognized that there were sunk costs which could not be recovered. They had to decide whether the marginal costs of continuing the projects, assuming they could be better managed and monitored, were worth bearing. Such a decision would be strongly influenced by the government's budgetary position: if

117

the government was operating in a period of constraint, because of a large deficit, little revenue growth, or a reluctance to increase taxes, then it is less likely that politicians would decide to keep such projects in operation.

Deuterium of Canada

The Nova Scotia Conservative government, headed by G.I. Smith, considered four options after receiving Dupont's report in August 1969 predicting that it would cost $30 million and take two years to make the Glace Bay heavy-water plant operational: investing the money itself; attempting to persuade the federal government, through Atomic Energy of Canada (AECL), to provide additional support; attempting to find another investor, such as Canadian General Electric, to buy the plant; or simply scrapping the plant.[1]

Since an election was planned in 1970, scrapping the plant would be a disastrous admission of failure, and General Electric was not interested in buying the plant. Of the two remaining options, assistance from the federal government was preferable to spending more of the province's money. In addition, it was clear that the federal government had an interest in supporting the rehabilitation of the plant. AECL was expecting that, by 1972, there would be a shortage of heavy water to supply export and domestic demands. Indeed, by mid-1969 it had taken options on all available American heavy water (which still appeared to be insufficient to meet the demand) at the high price of US $28.50 per pound.[2] If the Glace Bay plant could be made to deliver in two years for another $30 million, this would be less expensive than starting construction on a new plant or buying more American heavy water. However, the federal government was attempting to hold back on expenditures in order to fight the inflation Canada was then experiencing. Premier Smith initially raised the subject with Prime Minister Trudeau that fall, but Trudeau was noncommittal. Negotiations began between Deuterium Canada and AECL.

While the negotiations were going on, the Smith government established a special legislative committee to hold hearings regarding the plant's problems. Jerome Spevack, one of the first witnesses, blamed the government-appointed directors of DCL for many bad decisions; he said he found it incredible that a year could have been wasted on third-party engineering studies and offered to put the plant into production in short order for $10 million. Spevack's testimony was sufficiently embarrassing to the government that it had the committee postpone its hearings indefinitely. At this time, DCL also initiated lawsuits against the four companies involved in the construction of the plant.[3]

Ultimately, DCL and AECL reached an agreement on additional assistance in April 1970. By then, AECL and DCL had satisfied themselves that the plant could be rehabilitated in accordance with the Dupont study. AECL agreed (1) to prepay the first year's purchase of heavy water, a sum of $16.4 million; (2) to increase the price it would pay for heavy water from $18.50 to $20.50 per pound, an increment worth $20 million over the life of the contract; and (3) to speed up the payment of $5 million of ADA grants to the province for DCL. Adding up these three types of assistance, Prime Minister Trudeau announced a package valued at $41.4 million. In return for this support, DCL gave AECL the right to review its decisions regarding a new plant operator, the plant's management structure, the rehabilitation plan, and the arrangements which DCL was making to terminate its secrecy obligations to Spevack. Although the agreement with AECL helped Nova Scotia financially, the province would still have to bear a shortfall on capital and interest recovery then estimated at $5 to $6 million per annum during the life of the contract. Trudeau's announcement of the deal in the House of Commons met with immediate expressions of support from all the opposition parties.[4]

Deuterium invited Canadian General Electric, whose Port Hawkesbury heavy-water plant was nearing completion, to inspect and report on the condition of the Glace Bay plant. The report, delivered in August 1970, did not estimate costs, but concluded that the rehabilitation required would be much more extensive than the Dupont report had predicted.[5] Canadian General Electric was also approached to provide the new management for Deuterium, but they were too busy completing their own plant to take on Glace Bay as well.[6] The government then decided to build a management team, hiring the president of Sydney Steel as vice-president of Deuterium, the president of a Calgary engineering firm as general manager, and the project manager of the CGE Port Hawkesbury plant as president.[7]

The Deuterium project became an issue in the provincial election held on 11 October 1970. Gerald Regan, the Liberal leader, criticized the Conservative government for its mismanagement of the project and promised that he would succeed in getting the plant completed and into production. Smith's government had announced its new management appointments just before the election to show the voters that it had the project under control. Federal government House leader Allan MacEachen also took part in the election campaign, criticizing Premier Smith for the failures of the Glace Bay plant.[8]

The Liberals were elected on October 11. Premier Regan, aware of the escalating cost estimates for rehabilitating the Glace Bay plant, did not want another Conservative leader to do unto him as he had done unto the hapless Smith. Shortly after his election, he went to Ottawa to tell J.J. Greene, the minister of Energy, Mines and Resources, that the province no longer wanted the responsibility for the plant, and that AECL should either find an operator for the plant or take it over itself. On 29

January 1971, Greene announced that AECL would spend $300,000 for an engineering assessment to determine the feasibility and probable cost of bringing the Glace Bay plant into production.[9] The study, delivered in May, indicated that rehabilitation of the Glace Bay plant would be even more expensive than previously thought, but that it would still be cheaper and faster to rehabilitate the plant than to build a new one of equivalent capacity.

In October 1971, Prime Minister Trudeau announced in Halifax that AECL would lease the plant from Nova Scotia for $1 per annum and that it would take responsibility for its reconstruction (now estimated to cost $95 million and take three years) and its operation. In the supplementary estimates shortly thereafter, AECL received a loan from the federal government to pay for the rehabilitation: revenues from the plant were expected to repay the loan over a period of sixteen years, at which point the lease would end and the plant revert to the province.[10]

Our explanation of the federal government's decision to take on the Glace Bay plant is based on a number of factors in addition to the financial analysis: the strength of the government's commitment to the development and international marketing of the CANDU nuclear reactor; MacEachen's powerful role in the federal cabinet as advocate for the chronically high unemployment region of Cape Breton; the desire of the federal Liberals to provide support for their provincial cousins; and the approaching 1972 federal election.

Shortly after AECL was given the mandate to rebuild the Glace Bay plant, it approached six major process industry companies (Polymer, CGE, Canadian Industries Limited, Dow Chemical, Union Carbide, and Imperial Oil) to see if any was interested in operating the plant. None was, and so AECL established a heavy-water products division to run the plant itself.[11]

AECL's rehabilitation of the plant turned out to be a continuing tale of woe. The three towers for processing were re-usable: however, rather than use the original processing method designed by Burns and Roe, AECL chose a new one which would result in higher production, but at an additional capital cost of $7 million. As well, the new process would be more complicated to operate than the original. AECL also decided to make as much use of the existing equipment as possible. However, cleaning and testing the equipment, as well as providing new spare parts, were expensive and time-consuming. In addition, the attempt to adapt the old equipment to a new process created great difficulty and also increased the cost more than had been expected. Indeed, using old parts was ultimately more expensive than buying new ones. The labour problems that had plagued the construction of the original plant continued: skilled labour was in short supply, labour productivity was poor, and there were four major strikes between June 1973 and July 1975. In order to avoid the use of sea water, a dam and reservoir had to be constructed.

Finally, the Glace Bay generating station had to be upgraded at a cost of $10 million, of which AECL paid about half.[12]

In 1976, the plant was at last brought into operation but closed again in 1977 for extensive modifications and replacement of some of the original parts. Production began again in 1978, but full capacity has never been achieved. The rehabilitation ended up costing the federal government $225 million, far more than the $95 million originally planned. In addition, the federal government bought the plant from the Nova Scotia government in 1973 for $66 million.[13]

The General Electric plant at Port Hawkesbury, while much more successful than the Glace Bay plant, had problems of its own. Production began in 1971, but for the first few years it operated at only 60 percent of capacity. The increase in the price of oil, the plant's major energy source, combined with its fixed-price contract with AECL, made it uneconomical. Rather than renegotiate the contract, AECL, whose own heavy-water products division was already planning to operate the Glace Bay plant, sought and received government approval to buy the Port Hawkesbury plant, for which it paid $93 million in 1975.[14]

Since the mid-1970s, the demand for all forms of energy has decreased, and far fewer CANDU reactors have been sold at home or abroad than anticipated by AECL in the heady early days of the program. Nevertheless, the two heavy-water plants continued to produce heavy water that was simply being stockpiled. At present, the stockpile is large enough to last for ten years even according to the most optimistic assumptions about the nuclear energy market. By the mid-1980s, the annual operating costs for the two plants, which employ 700 people, were $125 million dollars, or $179,000 per worker! In addition, there were the hidden costs of the subsidies for imported oil and Cape Breton coal, which were used to fuel the plants.[15]

In 1982, the Liberal-appointed board of directors of AECL and the Department of Energy, Mines and Resources proposed to Cabinet that the government shut down the two plants, but the government refused, in part because of the high unemployment rate in Cape Breton and in part due to the influence of then Deputy Prime Minister Allan MacEachen.

After the election of a Conservative government, whose commitment to reducing public spending is somewhat stronger than the Liberals', and MacEachen's departure to the Senate, AECL management again proposed shutting down the two plants. By spring 1985, Cape Bretoners came to expect the inevitability that the Conservative government would close the plants. In his budget speech of May 23, Finance Minister Michael Wilson made the expected announcement.

As compensation for the closing, and in order to induce the private sector to support the weakened Cape Breton economy, Wilson also announced a 60-percent tax credit, chargeable against income earned anywhere in Canada, on new investments in Cape Breton. As a result of this incentive, as well as a federal government investment of $64.2 million, Magna International, a Toronto-based auto-parts maker, agreed to invest $64.4 million to build two auto-parts plants in Cape Breton. The two plants, to be located in Port Hawkesbury and North Sydney, would employ a total of 270 people.[16] Should the government not recover its investment, an event we consider quite probable, the subsidy per job created would amount to approximately $240,000.

BRICKLIN

The information that the New Brunswick government received from the Clarkson Gordon management consultants in September 1975 regarding Bricklin was fatal to the project. The consultants doubted the company's management capabilities, reminded the government that the technology still had not been perfected, and predicted that the government would be required to invest up to $14 million more in the next fiscal year. Bricklin departed from its strategy of incremental funding requests and asked for a loan of $10 million. By this point, New Brunswick had already invested over $25 million in the Bricklin project: given its small population and resource base and its 1975 deficit of $50 million on revenues of $800 million, another 10-to-15 million dollars invested in a project that was creating only 600 jobs and which had dubious prospects looked most unappealing.

The consultants' report went directly to Economic Growth Minister Lawrence Garvie, who throughout 1975 had monitored the project more closely than his predecessor. The report and the $10-million loan request led Garvie to recommend that Premier Hatfield and his Cabinet refuse to lend any more money to Bricklin, which would mean putting the company into receivership. Throughout the previous year, the bad news Premier Hatfield had received about Bricklin so overwhelmed any hopeful news that he really had no choice but to go along with the recommendation. The timing, less than a year into his mandate, was optimal: by the next election Bricklin could be a dead issue. On 24 September 1975, Garvie and Hatfield arrived at a Bricklin board meeting and announced that the province would advance no more money. The board voted to put the company into receivership.[17]

Two days later, Hatfield gave a press conference about the Bricklin failure. In a prepared statement, he talked about how the new government financing provided the previous January, combined with management changes, had given rise to some optimism. He went on to say, "By April, the prospects had improved even further. Some consolidation in the management and facilities had been realized, and, more importantly, production had increased significantly. Our analysis in May gave reason for cautious optimism in the project." Despite the "real but marginal improvement" that occurred in the spring, production costs and "general economic conditions" continued to hurt the company through-out the summer. In August, the government had asked the company to prepare a realistic operating plan by September 8 and to raise some outside capital. When the company did neither, and instead asked the government for more money, the government decided to refuse. As Hatfield put it,

> Although the government had always believed that the potential advan-tages of the project were worth the financial risk taken, we have also known from the beginning that there was a point beyond which the government should not, on its own, risk additional government funds on this one project. That point has been reached.[18]

Hatfield went on to promise that the government would seek opportuni-ties to find a buyer or operator for the Bricklin plants and would cover the last week of salaries for Bricklin workers. The premier looked to the future: "It is more important than ever to devote ourselves to economic growth and job creation in our province and this remains the top prior-ity of our government." For that reason, he decided to keep a commit-ment to visit Japan to meet with government and industry officials. Because the company was then in the hands of receivers, Hatfield could avoid any detailed questions about it. He expressed no intention of resign-ing or appointing a royal commission.[19]

Clearly, Hatfield's tactics in handling the problem — shifting the blame, doing something to satisfy the claims of New Brunswick Bricklin workers, looking to the future, avoiding detailed questions, and then leaving town for a while — were most effective.

The economic growth ministry attempted to find another manufac-turer interested in the Bricklin plants and products, but without success. The receivers recovered only about $450,000 for the assets, which was $100,000 less than the cost of the receivership itself. Thus, Bricklin's creditors received nothing, and by the end of 1976 the receivership was terminated.[20] A total of only 2880 cars had been produced.

Today, Malcolm Bricklin operates a New York-based car-importing business, Yugo of America, which sells a line of vehicles manufactured in Yugoslavia.

CANADAIR

Throughout 1982, it was becoming clear to senior officials in the De-partment of Regional Industrial Expansion that it would be impossi-ble for them to monitor and manage Canadair on an ongoing basis. Moreover, they lacked confidence in the ability of the company's board of directors to monitor and its staff to manage. They began to favour the creation of a managerial structure with greater expertise to monitor Canadair as well as various other government enterprises for which the department was also responsible.

In addition, in the Cabinet and at the most senior level in the Privy Council Office, it was felt that such a structure could be used as a vehicle for pursuing nationalist and interventionist economic policies. Certainly, these people had always been disappointed with the Canada Development Corporation, whose president, Anthony Hampson, had skilfully preserved the corporation's autonomy and prevented it from becoming a vehicle of government policy.[21] Therefore, the Canada Development Investment Corporation (CDIC) was established in November 1982, with Maurice Strong as chairman and Joel Bell as CEO. It was to report directly to the minister of State for Social Development, rather than to a line department. CDIC's initial portfolio consisted of Canadair, de Havilland, Teleglobe Canada, and Eldorado Nuclear Limited. Joel Bell, president of CDIC, described its role as a holding company in the following way:

> The essential role of a holding company is to carry out the most thorough-going analysis of all aspects of the business: financial, operational, technical, marketing. Really there is no aspect that does not fall within the purview and responsibility of an investor, representing his shareholder interests vis-à-vis those companies. It is in the essence of what we do as a holding company that we carry out the most probing kind of review.[22]

For several months, the government was able to keep Canadair's problems out of public view. For example, in October 1982, the government asked Parliament to approve a $200-million equity infusion for Canadair, stating merely that it would be used to retire debt and improve the company's debt-equity ratio. In November, Canadair Vice-President P.J. Aird told the House Finance Committee that Canadair would have an after-tax profit of $1.5 million in 1982.

All of this cover-up came to an end on 13 April 1983 with CBC's airing of an exposé on *The Fifth Estate*, which began the Canadair scandal in earnest. The program estimated that the cost to taxpayers of developing the Challenger could reach $2.3 billion and revealed that only 76 of the originally scheduled 255 Challengers had been built to date. The show also uncovered the disastrous Federal Express deal and the fact that three Pepsico Venezuela executives had purchased a Challenger jet which they were leasing back to Canadair. In addition, the Challenger was portrayed as unsafe.[23]

The Fifth Estate episode sparked a flurry of critical commentary in the Commons and in the press. Revenue Minister Pierre Bussières promised that an internal inquiry would take place, but resisted a full public inquiry. Prime Minister Trudeau told opposition M.P.s demanding immediate access to Canadair's financial records that they would have to wait until the government sought Parliament's approval for a further infusion of cash.[24]

A few days later, a resurgence of controversy occurred over the 1981 conviction of Alaska Senator George Hohman, whom the courts decided had accepted a bribe from a Canadair salesman to vote in favour of the purchase of two CL-215 water bombers.[25] At the same time, the federal government announced it was contemplating purchasing up to twenty water bombers, a project expected to insure 500 Canadair jobs for two years.[26] The company received unfavourable press in both instances, and the public's perception of Canadair as an expensive pet project of the Trudeau government increased.

On May 18, the government announced it would put another $240 million in equity into Canadair. Little rationale was given for the additional spending, except that most aviation firms worldwide were in difficulty.[27] A few days before this announcement, it was revealed that Canadair's board of directors had asked President Fred Kearns to take an early retirement, effective June 10.[28]

On June 7, Senator Jack Austin, the minister reponsible for Canadair, gave a lengthy statement to the Standing Committee on Public Accounts and the Standing Committee on Finance, Trade and Economic Affairs. Austin not only discussed Canadair's request for a further $240 million to meet its cash requirements to the end of the year, but he also revealed that the company had shown a record-breaking $1.4 billion loss in 1982. Most of the loss was due to a write-off of $1.054 billion in soft costs, which had been capitalized when they were incurred because their recovery seemed probable, but were expensed in 1982 because of the Challenger's dimmer prospects.[29] Kearns' retirement was not nearly enough to dampen the criticism that ensued; Liberal backbenchers joined with Conservative and NDP M.P.s in demanding the dismissal of the rest of Canadair's upper management. Senator Austin replied that witchhunts were not fashionable in contemporary politics.[30] As the controversy continued over the next several days, Trudeau took the stance that the loss was unfortunate, but that Canadair must be kept alive if Canada was to maintain a presence in the aeronautics industry.[31] In addition, on the day Kearns' retirement became effective, CDIC Vice-President Gil Bennett was named interim president of Canadair.[32]

In late May, Canadair launched a $109.6 million lawsuit against U.S. engine manufacturer Avco Lycoming, claiming that delivery delays and mechanical problems hampered the development of the Challenger and raised production costs.[33] Avco said it was willing to fight Canadair, and two months later launched a US $100 million (Can. $123 million) countersuit for cancelling the remainder of the contract.[34]

Efforts to counteract the effects of the bad publicity about Canadair became noticeable. In the wake of layoff announcements in June and July came further news about which provinces were to receive the twenty water bombers whose proposed purchase had been announced several months earlier. A potential sale of six Challengers to the West German air reserve was also announced. The public relations efforts suffered a set-back, however, when on September 1, CDIC revealed that Canadair had lost another $107 million in the first six months of 1983.[35]

In October, Canadair president Gil Bennett announced that the company's management team would undergo a major reorganization, but that the Challenger program would not be abandoned. The expected cost of cancelling the program was $450 million over five years, whereas he predicted Canadair would need no further infusions if, as had been proposed, its debts were handed over to the CDIC. The company's vice-presidents were reduced from twenty-two to twelve, although six of these were simply assigned the title of director, one step down from vice-president status. A company spokesman declined to say if the demoted vice-presidents would also take salary cuts. Of the four who left the company, two unnamed vice-presidents were fired and two others, Harry Halton and Peter Aird, took early retirement.[36] As might be expected, the Public Accounts Committee's findings, released approximately a month after the purge, were sharply critical of the departed managers.[37]

Up to this time, Senator Austin and the CDIC still had not given Parliament detailed recommendations on what should be done with Canadair, nor had the Shieldings report been released to Parliament and the public. This situation was rectified in part on 20 December 1983, when Austin announced that interested M.P.s and reporters could obtain copies of an expurgated version of the Shieldings report. A considerable amount of financial, production and sales data was withheld to avoid creating any further problems in the market for the company. However, the text of the report was uncensored and included Shieldings' gloomy assessment of Challenger's worth. The *Globe and Mail* pointed out:

> Release of the Shieldings study . . . is considered to be one more step in getting all of Canadair's linen out on the laundry table. It is also giving CDIC a chance to defuse Shieldings' controversial assessment of the Challenger and to respond to the comment about the Government's involvement in the executive-jet business — before these points are raised by someone else with access to the consultant's study.[38]

If averting controversy was indeed one of CDIC's goals, their timing was propitious; so close to Christmas, newspaper coverage of the report's release was perfunctory.

On 7 March 1984, still before CDIC had announced its detailed game plan for Canadair, the company increased its claim against Avco Lycoming from $109.6 million to $480 million. Just two days before, the Supplementary Estimates indicated Ottawa's plans to inject a further $310 million of equity into the company.[39] As Gil Bennett had hinted five months before, CDIC intended to create a new Canadair to take over the existing company's assets, while old Canadair would be a corporate shell which would retain the company's $1.35 billion in long-term debt. CDIC would then ask the government for $150 million to $200 million per year to pay off old Canadair's debts. Most of the additional $310 million requirement would be used for this purpose, as well as for accomplishing the reorganization.[40]

Austin called the decision "a business decision made for business reasons." The world market for large corporate aircraft was estimated at 100 to 150 sales per year. The Challenger could bring Canadair a profit with annual sales of just fifteen aircraft per year, or 10 to 15 percent of the total market. It was believed Canadair could make at least this many sales. The reason for the renewed optimism about the Challenger's market prospects was that the aircraft's major handicap at that point was the uncertainty surrounding Canadair's future. For as long as the company showed a negative net worth, the possibility of bankruptcy was ever-present. The closure of Canadair would mean parts and service for the Challenger would no longer be available, and without parts and service, the value of an aircraft, whether for continued use or for resale, drops dramatically. With the fate of the Challenger program hanging in the balance, potential customers could not be persuaded to lay down $11 million or more for a jet whose value might suddenly plummet. The company's sales for 1983 supported this assessment, as only six orders for Challengers were obtained. Once the company's financial health was restored, Bennett believed there would be no difficulty in selling the Challenger.[41]

Also contributing to the decision to reorganize Canadair was the fact that Austin and CDIC had long since rejected Shieldings' opinion that the Challenger added little of significance to Canadian technological capabilities. Canadair had developed expertise in the design of advanced-technology airfoils, state-of-the-art hydraulic, electrical, and avionic systems, and composite materials. The Challenger was the first aircraft to pass the American Federal Aviation Administration's new, more stringent airworthiness requirements, giving Canadair the lead in certification expertise. The Challenger was also considerably quieter and cleaner than other executive aircraft; in fact, it was so quiet that it was the only large business jet permitted to take off and land during curfew hours at several major airports.[42]

Canadair's recorded loss for 1983 was $334 million, of which only $83.8 million was an operating loss, despite the extreme slump in Challenger sales. The remainder consisted of $155.3 million in interest expenses and an additional $95 million of unrecoverable Challenger development costs. Since the government had guaranteed Canadair's $1.35 billion in long-term loans, this amount would have to have been paid out no matter what the Challenger's fate. Over and above this amount, the cost of shutting down the program would have been $400 million to $420 million, approximately half of which would have been an immediate expense. In addition, about 1200 jobs in Montreal would be lost if Challenger production were discontinued.[43] With unemployment in Quebec still running about 2 percent above the national average, the decision to relieve Canadair of its debt burden and revitalize the company was therefore attractive to government not only from a financial, but also from a political standpoint.

For perhaps the first time since the inception of the Challenger program, Canadair's performance began to live up to its promises. With the purchase of seven Challengers by the West German air reserve late in 1984, the company succeeded in selling seventeen Challengers and recorded an estimated $1.7 million profit on sales of $407 million in 1984. At year-end, 4500 people were employed at Canadair, a figure that held more or less constant since August of 1983.[44]

Soon after the Conservatives took power in September of 1984, they began initiatives to sell Canadair and certain other Crown investments. To increase the company's attractiveness to potential purchasers, the federal government bought up Canadair's remaining inventory of nine Challenger 600s for use by the Defence Department. The mission for which seven of the nine are being used, training Canadian Forces personnel in ways of coping with jamming and other forms of electronic warfare, is somewhat dubious, since presumably a less expensive aircraft would do the job just as well. In addition, the government bought four 601s for use in its jet fleet, and Crown corporations bought two. Another ten Challenger 601s were purchased in 1985, seven by American corporations and three by the Chinese government.[45]

Unlike the case with De Havilland Aircraft, which was sold to Boeing in December 1985, the government has not yet received an acceptable offer for Canadair, and so its goal of privatization remains unrealized.

CHURCHILL FOREST INDUSTRIES

After the government seized the CFI project on 8 January 1971, Stothert Engineering was given the responsibility of bringing the pulp mill, the paper mill and the sawmills into production. Stothert had estimated that the pulp and paper mill would take about $1.25 million to complete and the sawmill $1.5 million. As it happened, however, they found it necessary to spend another $12 million to bring the complex into operation. In addition, the operating loss for 1971 was nearly $8 million and for 1972, $5 million.

In February 1973, Stothert hired an experienced general manager, Fred Moden, on a three-year contract. Told to operate the plant as if it were his own, he provided the strong leadership that had been lacking until that time and quickly gained the confidence and support of the labour force. He recognized that the plant's technological advances would permit him to reduce substantially the cooking time of the wood pulp and still produce a superior product. The decreased cooking time allowed him to increase the plant's daily production by 30 percent. During the nine-month period ending 30 September 1973, the complex generated a profit of $1.48 million before interest and depreciation.[46] According to Stothert:

Charts are available for almost every pulp and paper mill start-up in Canada showing the percent of rated capacity achieved each year after start-up. The start-up at The Pas was average, neither being the best nor the worst of numerous start-ups across Canada. This says a great deal for the quality of the majority of local residents who were hired and trained to operate these mills at The Pas. Their experience and capabilities grew each year with the year by year increase in production over the start-up curve.[47]

In March 1973, the Crown corporation Manitoba Forestry Resources Ltd. (Manfor) was formed to take over the complex on October 1.[48] Leif Hallgrimson, who had been appointed receiver and general manager in 1971, stayed on as president and chairman. Leon Mitchell, the former law partner of minister Sidney Green and a member of the Commission of Inquiry, was appointed to the board, as was former Attorney-General Al Mackling after he suffered an election defeat. Charles Hunt, an NDP M.P.P. who had assisted Alistair Stewart in his inquiry, was also named. Of the eight directors (excluding the chairman), five were active or retired civil servants, two were politicians, and one was a retired trucker.[49]

Between 1 October 1973 and 30 September 1974, the complex produced an average of 370 tons per day and earned a cash profit of $9 million. The following year, an average production of 430 tons per day was achieved. Unfortunately, the recession in both Canada and the United States drastically reduced the demand for both paper and lumber. With profitability so adversely affected, Moden turned to the problem of the inadequate pulp-making capacity relative to the sawmill capacity. For both the sawmill and the pulp and paper mill to operate efficiently, the pulp and paper capacity needed to be increased to 800 tons per day. Moden estimated the additional cost would be $60 million, and that the expanded plant would show an overall profit of 16 percent. However, in this estimate, Moden had considered mostly the higher labour productivity that could be achieved in a larger mill; Stothert's feasibility study showed that the additional wood required would have to be brought in from such great distances that any savings made would be completely offset by the cost of transporting the wood. The estimated return on investment for the expansion was a mere 1 percent, and the proposal was thus turned down.[50] When Moden's contract ended in September 1975, the board of directors declined to renew it.[51]

The government had appointed the Commission of Inquiry a few weeks after taking control of the project in January 1971.[52] It was composed of chairman Charles Rhodes Smith, who had recently retired as Chief Justice of Manitoba at the age of 75, Leon Mitchell, and Dr. Murray Donnelly, head of the political science department at the University of Manitoba. Their 2000-page report, released in August 1974, downplayed the NDP's adverse impact on the project, but in other respects was fair, thorough, and, with a few exceptions, accurate.

The capital expenditures for the entire project up to 30 September 1974 were calculated to be $154.7 million. The estimated value of the complex at that date was $73 million. The difference was shown as a capital deficit on Manfor's balance sheet. In the following ten years of operations, Manfor's financial performance was poor, consistently losing money; however, it provided an employment level of one thousand jobs. Table 5 details Manfor's performance.

In 1982, Murray Harvey became chairman of Manfor. Harvey had been a civil servant for nineteen years and was the owner of the successful local paper, *The Opasquia Times*, but he had no experience in the pulp and paper industry. In an interview, which appeared in the *Pulp and Paper Journal*, Harvey stated that Manfor would aim for both profitability and maintaining employment. This statement has proven somewhat ironic, in that recent developments in the pulp and paper industry have made increased mechanization and reductions in labour requirements necessary conditions for continued profitability.[53]

Charges of theft, fraud, and conspiracy to defraud were brought against Kasser, Reiser, and several others, but all had fled to European countries with which Canada has no extradiction treaties. No charges were laid against Grose, who cooperated fully with the government in their case against Kasser. Kasser was tried by an Austrian court in 1980 and cleared of any wrongdoing. Certain irregularities surrounded Kasser's hastily acquired Austrian citizenship (he had been an American citizen since 1955), and the suggestion has been made that the verdict of innocence was purchased. There may be some truth in this claim in view of the fact that Reiser and two others were found guilty by a Swiss court in 1983. Even so, they were ordered to pay a mere $100,000 to cover the costs of the investigation. The pursuit of Kasser, Reiser, and four others cost the Manitoba government $4 million. The *Pulp and Paper Journal* article that reported this added: "Kasser still corresponds with the Manitoba government, most recently offering them his now-patented process for turning the mill into a viable operation."[54]

More recently, an article on Manitoba's money-losing Crown corporations appeared in the *Globe and Mail*. One of those discussed was Manfor:

[Manfor] is a persistent and heavy money loser, going through $10-million last year and $24-million in the two previous years, according to president John B. Sweeney and Jerry Storie, Manitoba's Minister of Business Development and Tourism, who is responsible for Manfor. . . .

Manitoba recently spent $50-million modernizing the operation, which Mr. Sweeney says has had annual sales of $60 to $70-million, but no profits. Mr. Sweeney says the company is worth $400-million and he expects it to lose only $2- or $3-million next year. He predicts "close to spectacular" profits after the soft markets of the next few years — enough profits to pay off its debts over the next decade.[55]

Table 5. MANFOR'S PERFORMANCE, 1974 TO 1983

Year	Operating Profit* ($ × 10⁶)	Net Income ($ × 10⁶)	Capital Expenditures ($ × 10⁶)	Book Value of Assets ($ × 10⁶)	Employment
1974	10.9	3.6	5.7	110.2	1084
1975	3.5	(4.4)	8.2	108.1	1100
1976	(3.0)	(11.7)	4.2	106.5	950
1977	(3.7)	(3.4)	1.2	103.9	N.A.
1978	(.7)	(10.4)	2.5	101.1	1000
1979	8.0	0	4.2	99.8	N.A.
1980	11.9	2.7	3.2	95.6	1000
1981	9.5	.7	2.8	99.1	N.A.
1982	(3.9)	(13.8)	3.9	97.2	1000
1983	(16.1)	(24.7)	2.7	89.3	N.A.
1984 (approximate)	(2.5)	(9.0)	N.A.	N.A.	900

* before depreciation and interest
Source: Manfor *Annual Reports*.

Manfor was in a profit position for 1984 until a sudden unexpected softening of markets in the fourth quarter, resulting in a cash loss of $2.5 million for 1984 and a total loss (including depreciation) of about $9 million. The modernized plant is now state-of-the-art, and requires less labour, but it is hoped that the increased capacity of the mill will allow the corporation to maintain employment at approximately its current level. The 1985 financial results, which were not available at the time of writing, were expected to be much worse than 1984's. However, it should be noted that the same factors which are confounding Manfor's efforts — worldwide overcapacity, a drop in pulp and paper prices, and lack of demand — are also creating problems for the rest of Canada's pulp and paper producers.[56] Nevertheless, the company remains handicapped compared to its competitors because it is unable to diversify (recently a vital strategy for other major pulp and paper manufacturers) and must respond to more social and political pressures (such as maintaining employment despite the trend toward increased automation and smaller workforces) simply because it is a Crown corporation. Manfor's management team and the government are still looking to improve the company's performance, however, and it is expected that 1986 will be a better year as a result of the modernizing which was done in 1985.

CONSOLIDATED COMPUTER INCORPORATED

The appointment of John McDonald Brown as president of CCI in 1980 marked the beginning of the third phase of CCI's history. The company had begun as a troubled but promising private enterprise, and had gradually metamorphosed into a quasi-governmental body by virtue of being controlled by the GAAB (later EDB) and ODC. Far from being weaned from its dependence on government money, CCI was more dependent than ever. The 1972 reorganization had cost the government a mere $7 million; the 1976 reorganization cost the federal and Ontario governments together $21 million. Despite the fact that both restructurings ostensibly took place to try to attract a buyer or major investor for the company, our evidence suggests that no ongoing effort was made toward this end in the periods between the restructurings. After 1976, the leasing companies' need for loan insurance accelerated, the loan insurance itself increased from 90 percent to 99 percent of the value of the loan, and CCI itself continued to require direct cash infusions from its government sponsors. Once Sellmeyer was replaced by Brown, the company became a virtual stretcher case; in the 1980 and 1981 fiscal years, the company received seventeen loan guarantees totalling $30.9 million to keep it propped up long enough so it could be sold.

The members of the EDB were sufficiently concerned about CCI's prospects in June 1980 that they requested that Treasury Board President Donald Johnston be informed about the situation and the action they had taken in guaranteeing additional loans and appointing Brown as the new president of CCI.[57] In addition, given the growing probability that the government would be required to make good on its loan guarantees, Herb Gray, minister of ITC, asked the Cabinet Committee on Economic Development to hold $60 million of the economic development policy reserve for that purpose.[58]

In response to the new situation at CCI, the Treasury Board Secretariat, which had long been skeptical about CCI's prospects, hired CCI's accountants to study alternative ways to wind down the operations of CCI and its leasing subsidiaries. The accountants' report, completed in January 1981, calculated the loss to the government of an immediate liquidation at $65 to $70 million in loan insurance that would have to be paid out. If the company were wound down slowly, the government would have to pay out approximately the same amount between 1981 and 1983. The accountants recommended the immediate liquidation alternative.[59] During this time, John McDonald Brown was preparing an optimistic new business plan for CCI, which envisaged a three-year turnaround. The plan called for cost-cutting, obtaining subcontracts to manufacture computer hardware, a more aggressive marketing campaign, and taking better advantage of the Fujitsu connection.[60]

After hearing Brown's new business plan, ITC regained its traditional optimism about CCI's prospects and on 23 March 1981 submitted a memorandum to Cabinet rejecting the accountants' recommendation to liquidate in favour of keeping the company in business. Their preferred option would involve the payment of $48 million in loan guarantees, another $6 million in new funding for CCI's ongoing operations, and up to $6 million in research and development support over the next three years. Even though EDB members were not unanimous in their support for this proposal, EDB chairman Douglas Kendall wrote to ITC deputy minister Robert Johnstone urging all parties to support it, because "it is cheaper [than the liquidation options] and I believe there is a business worth saving which can be viable once it has its debt load removed. As to management, this has a good chance of being effective."[61]

Peter Quinn, who had returned to ITC as senior assistant deputy minister of finance and programs, surprisingly came out in favour of the continuation option. He had been critical of the company during his tenure as GAAB secretary and during the 1976 restructuring when he was with Treasury Board. In the memorandum to Cabinet he now stated: "I am convinced it can work with Brown."[62]

The ITC memorandum went first to the Ministry of State for Economic Development for an assessment note. The note argued that there were two main options, liquidation or continuation of the company as proposed by ITC: "CCI presents ministers with a classic investment decision . . . the options presented are to accept the sure loss of something less than $70 million, or to gamble that a further investment could lower the loss . . . outcomes between the two extremes are unlikely: the company will either succeed or it will fail."[63] The writers of the note canvassed departmental opinion: both ITC and the Department of Finance believed that CCI's prospects were good, whereas the Treasury Board Secretariat expressed concern that CCI's debt load had accelerated to $70 million without previous notification of ministers and argued against a third bail-out of CCI.

The Cabinet Committee on Economic Development considered the ITC proposal on 14 April 1981. Ministers decided not to accept either alternative but rather to ask ITC to investigate a third option; namely, paying out $76 million to cover all of CCI's loan insurance claims and then seeking a private sector purchaser for the now-debt-free company.[64] In the discussion of the proposal, several ministers shared Johnston's surprise and concern that CCI's losses had not been brought to their attention earlier.[65] Within this context, it is understandable that the ministers were more impressed by Johnston's skepticism than Gray's optimism. Yet, the ministers must have felt that selling the company would avoid the political embarrassment of letting it go bankrupt.

A month after the meeting, ITC prepared an addendum to its memorandum to Cabinet indicating that it had received preliminary expressions of interest in CCI from a number of Canadian-owned computer companies and was asking for funding to pay off the insured loans, to insure additional loans until the company was sold, and to support additional product development. ITC proposed a deadline of 31 December 1981 to make the sale.[66] This proposal went back to the Economic

Development Committee on May 26 and Cabinet on June 4. Treasury Board President Donald Johnston was still concerned about how much it would cost to restructure CCI for sale to the private sector.[67] The Cabinet accepted the ITC proposal to restructure and sell CCI, but with two provisos: (1) that the president of Treasury Board and the minister of ITC be jointly authorized to oversee the restructuring and sale in such a way as to minimize the total cost to the Crown, and (2) that Treasury Board approval be required for additional ITC spending on, or loan guarantees for, CCI.[68]

In July, the Treasury Board approved ITC's proposals regarding restructuring of the firm and payments to it, but required ITC to seek Treasury Board approval regarding the selection and terms of reference of a consultant to advise on the CCI divestiture.[69] The consultant chosen was Shieldings Investments, which, while complimenting Brown on his efforts to improve CCI's operations, made it very clear that the company had virtually no future.[70] For example, the report said that CCI should not be viewed as a "stand-alone" business because "CCI's balance sheet is shadowed by an indigestible amount of bad will."[71]

An article in the *Globe and Mail* at this time mirrors Shieldings's view of the company.[72] On one hand, the article quotes Elmer Strong, the director of ITC's electrical and electronics division, ("we are convinced there is a capability there") and John Brown ("the equipment CCI produces is not dead and useless"). Strong's division was responsible for trying to find a buyer for CCI and was going to great lengths to do so. On the other hand, the article quoted an Ottawa technology analyst, who said:

> The company is technically bankrupt and the only way it can re-establish itself in the marketplace is to develop new products in which the buyers will have confidence. To turn it around, they would need to invest a good $2 million a year. But it has no position in the marketplace. It's been outstripped by its competitors.

The article also noted that three companies — Gandalf, Mitel, and Systemhouse — all were not interested in acquiring CCI.[73] Several companies, among them Mitel and Fujitsu, had entered into negotiations to purchase CCI once it became debt-free, but each of the deals had fallen through after meetings were held between the prospective buyer and the company.

In October, the Cabinet gave ITC and Treasury Board Secretariat a mandate to form a task force to implement the CCI divestiture.[74] The task force had three objectives: (1) to find a buyer as soon as possible, so as to minimize the ongoing cash drain of $50,000 per day on the government; (2) to negotiate the sale in such a way that the government would have neither a legal nor a "moral commitment" to provide further financial assistance to CCI; and (3) to "eliminate any further danger that an employee or agent of the Crown might be seen to have benefited from the divestiture." The task force operationalized the second objective by trying to ensure that CCI would survive for at least two years independent of the government.[75] The third objective ruled out an offer by Brown and some associates he had brought into the company. Several months later, the Anderson report described the offer as having at least the potential appearance of a conflict of interest.[76]

In soliciting offers, the task force indicated that the federal and Ontario governments would sell all their shares in CCI and the leasing subsidiaries for one dollar. The government would also pay approximately $45 million to the insured lenders of CCI and $46 million to those of the leasing companies. The task force calculated that CCI was suffering an annual operating loss, exclusive of interest, of $6.4 million. However, the leasing companies had an annual cash flow of $9 million in 1982 — which the task force projected would decline to approximately $1.5 million in 1986. Thus, with its debt burden removed, CCI, together with its leasing companies, would probably be profitable for a year or two. In order to keep purchasers from increasing the profitability of the transaction by immediately bankrupting CCI and then liquidating the leases, the government would pay off CCI's creditors and continue to hold the purchaser responsible for the leasing companies' debts. After two years, the government would begin to forgive these debts. Similarly, although the government would sell CCI's promissory notes for $1, it would prevent the buyer from paying any interest or principal on the notes for three years unless it maintained CCI as a going concern.[77] The government also wanted the purchaser to renounce any claim to a tax loss carry-forward from the purchase and to agree to use the leasing companies' cash flow only to support CCI.

Ultimately, two offers were received, one from Nabu Manufacturing and the other from Comterm Inc., both manufacturers of computer terminals and related electronics products. Nabu's interest was in the company's manufacturing facilities, some of its employees, and in the revenue from the remaining leases. Nabu was judged the stronger company in terms of profitability, breadth of product line, and managerial skills. In addition, it offered the government $100,000 for the company and a share of the lease revenue estimated at between $6 and $8 million over five years.[78] Nabu's offer was accepted, and the transaction was made on 20 November 1981. Industry Minister Herb Gray announced the divestiture, admitting that the government had to pay out $91 million to cover the loan guarantees, but at the same time, pointing out Nabu's commitment to keep the company operating for at least two years, which would therefore maintain "virtually all" of CCI's 475 jobs.[79] This payout, added to the $7 million in loan guarantees paid by the

GAAB in 1971 and the $21 million in government loans to CCI which had been converted to equity in 1976, meant that the government's total loss on CCI was close to $120 million. Of this amount, more than $45 million comprised the combined interest costs of CCI and the two leasing companies over their total life.[80]

In February 1982, the Anderson report was leaked to the *Globe and Mail*.[81] Despite this airing of Anderson's criticisms of the government, there were only a few stories in the press about CCI.[82] Several months later, the Conservatives called for a full investigation of the affair by the commercial crime division of the RCMP. This was rejected by the government. In doing so, Justice Minister Chrétien informed the opposition that the Justice Department, acting on Anderson's recommendation that the government attempt to determine whether the directors and officers of the leasing companies had conscientiously discharged their responsibilities, hired an outside lawyer who concluded that the government had no grounds for legal proceedings against anyone associated with CCI and that there was no evidence indicating a need for criminal investigation or a commission of inquiry.[83] Nevertheless, disciplinary action was taken within the Department of Regional Industrial Expansion against the officers of the leasing corporations, and the careers of the most enthusiastic advocates of CCI have not flourished. For example, Peter Quinn, while retaining his assistant deputy minister's rank, lost all operational responsibilities and soon left Ottawa to become director of external review and evaluation at the Inter-American Bank in Washington. Anderson made a number of other recommendations regarding the monitoring of government enterprise, which will be discussed in our final chapter.

Nabu ran Consolidated Computer until March 1984, two-and-a-half years after acquiring it, and then put it into receivership.[84] Nabu was having problems of its own, and in November 1984, closed down Nabu Network, the wholly owned subsidiary that had absorbed CCI. CCI is presently held by a new subsidiary, Computer Innovations. Although CCI has ceased to exist, there is some cash flow being derived from the equipment still on lease, and Computer Innovations estimates that to date the government has recovered at least the $6 million that was projected at the time of the divestiture.[85]

Summary

Table 6 summarizes the information concerning the choices governments made between the alternatives of divestment and continued support. The table is organized on the basis of the factors discussed in the introduction to this chapter as possible influences on the divestment decision. In addition, it records the timing of the decision in terms of the political cycle and the tactics used by politicians when implementing the decision.

Table 6. TO DIVEST OR NOT TO DIVEST

Factors Affecting Decisions	Deuterium of Canada Decisions			
	i) 1970 — province seeks federal assistance	ii) 1971 — fed. gov't. decides to rebuild DCL	iii) 1982 — fed. gov't. keeps heavy-water plants open	iv) fed. gov't. closes heavy-water plants
Outcome	i) 1970 — province seeks federal assistance	ii) 1971 — fed. gov't. decides to rebuild DCL	iii) 1982 — fed. gov't. keeps heavy-water plants open	iv) fed. gov't. closes heavy-water plants
Firm's financial situation	– estimated new plant cost > estimated rehabilitation cost – predicted heavy-water shortage		– annual operating cost $125 million – no demand for heavy water	
Firm's employment level	700 construction jobs in a region of high structural unemployment		– 700 jobs in a region of high structural unemployment (14%)	
Government's budgetary situation	N.S. a "have not" province	national economy strong, no federal budget stringency	serious recession, growing deficit	economic recovery, $35 billion deficit
Government's ideological position	province-building	desire to develop CANDU technology	more efficient but not smaller public sector, economic recovery	privatization, efficiency, deficit reduction
Public Opinion	support for "province-building" and job creation in N.S.		N.S. wants to retain jobs	N.S. wants to retain jobs, national support for gov't. ideology
Advocates/Opponents	MacEachen, Smith, Regan	MacEachen, Regan	MacEachen, Regan	Carney, Macdonald, Stevens, de Cotret, Buchanan
Political Timing	6 months before N.S. election	1 year before federal election	2 years before election	year after fed. election, 3½ years after prov. election
Implementation tactics	– AECL increases control over DCL – new management hired during election campaign	– announcement in Halifax – AECL takes over construction	—	– 60% tax credit for new investment in Cape Breton – task force on Cape Breton's economic prospects

Table 6. TO DIVEST OR NOT TO DIVEST cont'd.

Factors Affecting Decisions	Bricklin	CFI
Outcome	province puts Bricklin into receivership	government operates plant in 1971, '72; Crown corporation (Manfor) est'd. in 1973.
Firm's financial situation	consultants predict $14 million loss in 1975–76; poor management, technical problems	– CFI in poor financial, managerial condition at takeover – $12 million invested in 1971–72 to complete plant – operating losses of $8 million in 1971, $5 million in 1972, profit of $1.5 million in 1973.
Firm's employment level	650 jobs in Saint John and Minto	1000 jobs in The Pas
Government's budgetary situation	"have not" province already spent $25 million on Bricklin; 1975 deficit of $50 million	surplus of $34 million on budget of $840 million
Government's ideological position	province-building	democratic socialism — support for gov't ownership, province-building
Public Opinion	support for province-building, concern over losses	concern re. losses, support for public ownership, province-building
Advocates/Opponents	Hatfield, Garvie	NDP government
Political Timing	10 months after election	Crown corporation announced 3 months before 1973 election
Implementation tactics	– shift the blame – trip to Japan – no inquiry – provide documents to archives	– commission of inquiry – hired an experienced plant manager – "political" board of directors

Table 6. TO DIVEST OR NOT TO DIVEST cont'd.

Factors Affecting Decisions	Canadair	
	Decisions	
	i) 1982 — fed. gov't. eliminates Canadair debt, gives company to CDIC	ii) 1984 — fed. gov't. decides to privatize company
Outcome		
Firm's financial situation	– massive debt load ($1.5 billion) – development of Challenger 601 completed – variable cost breakeven = 15 aircraft/year – cost of terminating Challenger = $400 million	– Challenger sales: 1983, 6; 1984, 17; 1985, 23 – Canadair: 1983 loss of $334 million; 1984 profit of $1.7 million
Firm's employment level	6000 jobs in Montreal during a serious recession (13% local unemployment rate)	4500 jobs in Montreal
Government's budgetary situation	serious recession, rapidly growing deficit	economic recovery, $35 billion deficit
Government's ideological position	more efficient but not smaller public sector, economic recovery	privatization, efficiency, deficit reduction
Public Opinion	Quebec wants to retain jobs	Quebec wants to retain jobs, national support for government ideology
Advocates/Opponents	Quebec Liberal caucus	Stevens, Conservative Quebec caucus
Political Timing	– 2½ years after federal election	2 months after election
Implementation tactics	– closer monitoring by CDIC – change in management	– gov't. purchase of 13 Challengers

Table 6. TO DIVEST OR NOT TO DIVEST cont'd.

CCI

Factors Affecting Decisions	Decisions
Outcome	April-June, 1981 — federal government decides to sell CCI to private sector
Firm's financial situation	– debt > $90 million, operating loss > $6 million per year, consultants (Peat Marwick, Shieldings) pessimistic about firm's prospects
Firm's employment level	470 skilled jobs in a high employment industry and region
Government's budgetary situation	loan guarantees charged to policy reserve of economic development
Government's ideological position	more efficient but not smaller public sector
Public Opinion	critical of ongoing support for unprofitable companies
Advocates/Opponents	Gray (ITC)/Johnston (TBS), other economic dev't committee ministers
Political Timing	one year after election
Implementation tactics	– sale terms: guarantee company will stay in operation for at least 2 years; sever all links with government – no inquiry

Consider the factors explaining the decisions. In almost every undertaking, the decision made was consistent with the results of the analysis
of the firm's financial situation. (It should be noted that we are speak-
ing of the firm's balance sheet as seen by a public-sector owner; as will
be discussed below, its balance sheets might look quite different to a
private sector owner.) In the case of Deuterium, both the 1970 and 1971
consulting studies estimated the cost of rehabilitation of the plant as less
than the cost of building a new plant. (We have not seen these studies,
but we are assuming that they were done "honestly," rather than as an
attempt to justify a political decision.) At that time, it was still reasonable to speculate that there would be a heavy-water shortage. Bricklin
was losing money and had not solved its managerial and technical
problems. The cost of terminating the Challenger project was substantial,
and by 1982, the company had developed a viable product (the Challenger 601) and needed to sell only fifteen units per year to cover its
variable costs. Marketing studies argued that such a sales level was defi-
nitely feasible. At the time the Manitoba government took over the CFI
forestry complex, private management was in a sad state. Furthermore,
the government recognized that it had a state-of-the-art facility very
near completion and would soon prove capable of covering its operating costs. Consolidated Computer, in contrast, was failing to cover its
operating costs and thus falling more deeply into debt, with little prospect of recovery.

In most cases, the broader political influences upon the government
decision served to complement the financial factor. The two decisions
to rehabilitate the Deuterium plant were affected by the desire of both
the provincial and federal governments to create jobs in a region of high
unemployment and by the skill of federal and provincial politicians,
particularly Allan MacEachen, in advancing their regional interests.
Whereas divestment from Bricklin involved a loss of jobs in two cities,
public opinion throughout the province had so turned against the project that it became a political liability; in addition, it was impossible for
Hatfield to ignore the growing power base of Lawrence Garvie, whose
department was closely monitoring the investment. The federal government was unwilling to shut down the Challenger program during the
recession, thereby increasing unemployment and adding the project's
termination costs to the growing deficit; furthermore, the Liberals' Quebec caucus provided strong support. The federal government's decision
to divest itself of CCI was made in mid-1981, before the recession. The
ministers on the Cabinet Committee on Economic Development were
willing to take the loss resulting from the loan guarantees in 1981, a
year in which they had a $250-million policy reserve in their economic
development envelope, a sum sufficient to cover the loss. In addition,
Treasury Board president Donald Johnston articulated their common
concern that they had not been informed about CCI's mounting losses.

In a situation where ministers are to be collectively responsible for managing the envelope, this sense of having been betrayed contributed to their unwillingness to keep supporting CCI.

In one case, the financial and political factors appear to be completely at odds. The federal government's decision to reject AECL's financially oriented advice and keep the two heavy-water plants open in 1982 was the result of its unwillingness to compound structural unemployment at a time of macroeconomic crisis and of the continued influence of Allan MacEachen and Gerald Regan. The two factors that changed when the Conservatives took power in 1984 were the government's ideological position, which was strongly supportive of reduction in the deficit and more efficient public management, and the departure from the government benches of MacEachen and Regan, the project's two strongest partisans. Although the Cape Breton unemployment problem remained, and became more acute because of fires in a major colliery and fish plant,[86] the balance of political forces by then had shifted in favour of closing the heavy-water plants.

The ideology of the party in power seems to have played a major role in the ultimate decision in CFI and Canadair, also. After the forestry complex at The Pas was completed and in operation, it might have been possible to sell it as a going concern to a private-sector operator, but instead the NDP government's commitment to public ownership (reinforced, to be sure, by the Kasser experience) led to the establishment of a Crown corporation. The opposite occurred with the new Canadair. With its debt wiped off the books, it was making money and selling enough Challengers to cover the project's variable costs; in addition, the company seems to have developed a workable management structure. However, because the Conservative government does not see airframe manufacturing as a strategic industry, Canadair is destined for privatization. The purchase of thirteen Canadair Challengers by the government can be seen as an attempt to clean up the company's balance sheet and make it more attractive to prospective purchasers.

One of the major motivations for all of these projects was job creation, and it is possible to assess their efficiency by estimating the unrecovered government expenditures (or subsidy) per job for each project. This is done in Table 7 below. The calculations, expressed in terms of the common denominator of jobs per year, are approximate; for example, we used current, rather than constant, dollars. Since the Challenger operation appears to be breaking even, the subsidy per job would be quite small, and we did not attempt to calculate it. Although Manfor has not recovered all of Manitoba's original investment in CFI, it has recovered some. We were unable to determine from the Manfor statements just how much has been recovered and so we have counted Manfor's losses, including capital recovery, as a subsidy for the current operating phase.

The greatest losses were incurred in heavy-water production (until its termination in 1986) and in the development of the Challenger. Look-ing at the decisions made, we may conclude that Manitoba is willing to keep Manfor in business at a subsidy of $7000 per job per year, whereas New Brunswick was unwilling to support Bricklin when the subsidy per job reached almost $20,000 per job per year. The Trudeau government appears to have been financially inconsistent: while it was willing to produce heavy water at a subsidy of $179,000 per worker per year, it closed down Consolidated Computer, which required a much smaller subsidy of $20,000 per job per year. Of course, financial inconsistency is not necessarily political inconsistency: MacEachen carried more clout in Cabinet than did Herb Gray.

One factor common to all five cases is political timing. Decisions to keep facilities operating (Deuterium rehabilitation, rejection of AECL's proposal to close the two heavy-water plants, Canadair restructuring, CFI operation by the Manitoba government, and establishment of CFI as a Crown corporation) were all taken either in mid-term or shortly before an election. Divestment decisions (Bricklin, CCI, Canadair privatization, shutting down the two heavy-water plants) all came soon after elections. In short, governments are willing to admit mistakes and directly increase the unemployment rolls only when voters will have a long time to forget about these decisions and to observe other govern-ment actions that will favourably influence their voting in the next election. Thus, timing decisions certainly were consistent with the vote maximization hypothesis.

Table 7. UNRECOVERED GOVERNMENT EXPENDITURES (SUBSIDY) PER ANNUAL JOB CREATED

Project	Project Development Phase	Operating Phase
Deuterium of Canada	$300 million for 700 jobs from 1965 to 1976 = $35,700/job/year	$125 million for 700 jobs = $179,000/job/year
Bricklin	—	$25 million for 650 jobs in 1974 and 1975 = $19,200/job/year
Canadair	$1.4 billion for 3000 jobs from 1977 to 1982 = $78,000/job/year	—
Churchill Forest Industries	—	$71.4 million loss for 1000 jobs from 1974 to 1983 = $7000/job/year
Consolidated Computer	—	$120 million for 500 jobs from 1970 to 1981 = $20,000/job/year

It is interesting to compare the public sector's timing of divestment decisions with that of the private sector. To begin with, there is no election cycle in the private sector, so that divestment can occur at any time, rather than in one to two of every four to five years. Private-sector firms are most likely to cut out their weak operations during a recession: the public sector is more likely to support its weak operations during a recession if, as certainly is the case in Canada, it adopts a contra-cyclical fiscal policy. The difference between public and private sector budgeting systems also has implications for the divestment decision. Public-sector budgeting, with the possible exception of the federal government's policy and expenditure management system, or PEMS, is usually done on a one-year basis. With such a short time horizon, the option of maintaining a weak operation is favoured, because the one-year costs will be less than the cost of shutting it down, most of which will also be incurred in that year. This will certainly be the case if the project has been financed by loan guarantees, which the government must pay off when it terminates the operation. In contrast, the private sector presumably would make such decisions on a profitability basis which, if operationalized as discounted cash flow, would give greater weight to expected future losses than would the government's budgeting system.

We might ask ourselves whether the private sector would have kept the five enterprises in operation as long as the public sector did. Consider each of them as though it were owned by a hypothetical multidivisional corporation, which can underwrite divisional losses, but which has internal review mechanisms and a capital budgeting process.[87] There are a number of quite famous instances of multidivisional firms that have divested themselves of large and unprofitable divisions, such as Inco selling its electronic storage battery division, Ford stopping production of the Edsel, and RCA leaving the computer industry.

Undoubtedly, a hypothetical multidivisional firm would have shut down operations at the two Cape Breton heavy-water plants when the market for CANDU nuclear reactors soured in the late seventies. Canadair's unorthodox use of program accounting hid the real costs of the Challenger program from the government for longer than the costs would have been hidden from corporate management; the recession of 1982 would probably have been the last straw, bringing the owner to terminate the program. Although Manfor has sometimes been able to cover its operating costs, its few profitable years have seen a low return on equity; a multidivisional firm would probably have closed it down when additional capital expenditures became necessary to keep it in operation. Consolidated Computer might have been a success, because the multidivisional firm would have been more likely to impose managerial discipline and provide leasing capital at the outset. The multidivisional owner, however, would have likely liquidated it after its losses in 1973 and 1974. In any event, the multidivisional firm would not have allowed the masking of CCI's unprofitability through leasing companies to go undetected for three years (1977–79), as did the government. It is unlikely that a multidivisional firm would have managed Bricklin the way the New Brunswick government did, although it is hard to say whether it would have closed it down much faster, given that after the November 1974 election the government acted quickly to assess the situation and terminate the project.

The final issue we consider, the tactics used in implementing the politicians' decisions, provides evidence of politicians' normal behaviour in terms of shifting the blame for, and diverting public attention away from, failures and, conversely, taking the credit for successes. When the New Brunswick government put Bricklin into receivership, Premier Hatfield attempted to lay the blame for the company's problems on the company and on general economic conditions. Hatfield himself took advantage of a visit to Japan to let the issue cool. No inquiry was established, though the government eventually released its copious documents to the provincial archives. We surmise that the government assumed that the volume of documents itself would deter the press (as opposed to researchers with less pressing deadlines) from further investigation.

The federal government's sale of CCI was handled with similar concern for distancing itself from failure. The sale was arranged so that the company would stay in operation for at least two years, so as to preclude any moral commitment the government might have to ensure its operations. Care was also taken that no one who had been involved in the management of CCI when it was government-owned would appear to have benefited from the divestiture. No inquiry was held.

The Trudeau government initially (1982 and early 1983) attempted to keep Canadair's problems under wraps, but the investigative reporting by the CBC and newspapers made this impossible. When the government finally admitted the nature of the Challenger project's problems and Canadair's $1.4-billion loss in 1982, it nonetheless attempted to shift part of the blame to the recession and Canadair's managers. Furthermore, the government tried to mitigate the impact of the "bad news" with "good news" about Canadair's financial and managerial restructuring.

With the projects that were continued, we see the opposite political tendency, namely the scramble to take credit and maximize visibility. Premier Smith took credit for the federal government's $41-million program in 1970 to assist Deuterium and hired new management during the election campaign to show he was actively managing the project. Trudeau made sure to announce AECL's takeover of the Glace Bay plant so as to maximize its beneficial political impact. The Manitoba NDP government established a commission of inquiry concerning CFI to make sure the Conservatives' role in its failure was understood by the public. After running the company for two years, the government announced that it would become a Crown corporation shortly before the 1973 election. The government then hired a professional manager, but used the board of directors for political appointments.

In conclusion, this chapter has shown that the factors having the greatest influence over government decisions about whether or not to divest themselves of these projects were the projects' financial prospects and the governments' budgetary situations and ideologies, as opposed to the simplistic notion of keeping the projects in operation in order to win votes in areas of high unemployment. However, the timing of the decisions and the politicians' tactics of shifting the blame and taking the credit are consistent with the vote maximization hypothesis.

5

Conclusions
and Recommendations

Let us summarize the patterns observed in previous chapters concerning the origins, problems, and termination of the five projects. Most of the projects began because they had political support; their timing and location were often intended to win the support of voters — sometimes marginal groups and sometimes the entire electorate. Although the projects were not without some economic justification, the investment analyses underlying the original decisions were often superficial or biased. Government support was usually given by means of loans, loan guarantees, or letters of comfort. A variety of monitoring systems were established: government representatives on the board of directors, direct reporting to government departments, or monitoring by government lending programs.

The projects ran into difficulty primarily because of management errors, bad political decisions, and poor monitoring systems, rather than adverse environmental changes. The management errors often included the inability to develop new technology; domination of the organization by the marketing function, resulting in the company's promising the market more than it could deliver; excessive geographic decentralization; poor labour relations; and poor choice of and performance by subcontractors.

The bad political decisions were usually made at the project's inception, but their impacts would be felt throughout the life of the project. They included contracts that made it hard to monitor the entrepreneurs; the appointment of directors on the basis of political patronage rather than expertise; the failure to give boards of directors or public service monitors any clear direction; and uncritical commitment to the project, which tended to undermine monitoring by public servants. As a consequence, the monitoring systems proved to be inadequate in dealing with managers who were often less than forthright and sometimes dishonest in their reporting. Management information systems were often inadequate. Public servants monitoring the companies lacked expertise and often were co-opted into becoming company advocates. The use of multiple monitors diffused responsibility, so that each passed the buck to the other. Finally, loan guarantees or letters of comfort often served to mask the government's increasing financial commitments to the companies — without the monitors, Parliament, or the public realizing what was happening.

147

Despite the ineffective monitoring systems, government eventually realized that something was wrong and responded by intensifying monitoring activity. This involved (1) the hiring of consultants to provide expertise about the industry and/or improve management information systems; (2) increasing the financial commitment by converting loans into equity and private into mixed enterprise and then Crown corporations; and (3) "hands on" management by ministers and public servants.

When it came to decisions about divestment or retention of the enterprises, government usually did what its analysis of the financial impact on government finances would dictate, though it was clear that these decisions were also motivated by political considerations, such as responding to public opinion, or budgetary considerations, such as the competition for scarce resources. The timing of these decisions had a political component as well: governments were more likely to divest or liquidate earlier than later in their mandates. Finally, the tactics by which these decisions were implemented showed the normal tendency of politicians to shift the blame for, and distance themselves from, what the public perceived as failure and to take credit for what was seen as success.

The strongest overall conclusion that emerges from this clearly nonrandom sample of five cases of investment failure is that Canadian governments have performed very ineffectively as bankers or venture capitalists. In terms of the responsibilities of private-sector bankers, the governments did poorly in appraising loans; their monitoring systems were weak, and their criteria for terminating loans were excessively softhearted, with the result that failing ventures were kept in operation long past the point when the private sector would have liquidated them. Because of these case studies, it is hard to avoid telling government to get out of the banking or venture-capital business and leave it to the private sector, which (notwithstanding the recent failures of the Canadian Commercial Bank and Northlands Bank) can usually do it better.

However, we are not claiming that it is impossible for any government anywhere ever to play successfully the role of banker. The Japanese government, in particular through its Ministry of International Trade and Industry (MITI), is an example of a government that has been actively and successfully involved in the allocation of capital. It has been able to do this both because of the way its bureaucracy works and, more broadly, because of the nature of Japanese culture. The Japanese bureaucracy makes a policy of recruiting the best and the brightest to be its senior officials by means of competitive exams taken right after college. In a typical year, 35,000 graduates will take the senior public service exam, but only 1000 will be offered positions of lifetime employment within the various departments. The young senior bureaucrats spend their first ten years in organizational learning. This program includes working in a department's various bureaus; an assignment overseas, such as taking an MBA or working as an attaché at a Japanese embassy or the Japanese External Trade Organization; an assignment in a local office of a particular department; and assignments on loan to other departments. By the end of ten years of organizational learning, the senior public servants are thoroughly knowledgeable about their department and its environment. Then they become actively involved in policy making, rising to the highest positions within the department that recruited them and where they will spend the rest of their career.

A strong argument can be made that Japanese senior bureaucrats who spend their first ten years in broad organizational learning and the rest of their career in one department have much more expertise than their Canadian counterparts. Indeed, in recent years the Canadian bureaucracy has moved its senior personnel from department to department with great frequency, with the consequence that they have become generalists who have little knowledge of any particular policy sector.[1]

The implications of this in the area of industrial policy are quite clear. The Japanese bureaucrats in MITI have much more industry expertise and knowledge than their Canadian counterparts, with the result that they are much more capable of making intelligent investment decisions.[2] Of course, MITI's success is not only a consequence of its organizational structure, but also a result of the postwar Japanese ideology, according to which market-oriented and export-led economic growth was seen by the entire society as a desirable goal, and business/ government cooperation — including the sharing of information — as an important means of achieving that goal.

In their book about Canada's industry policy, *Canada Can Compete!*, D'Cruz and Fleck, though generally proposing market-oriented policies, make an exception in that they advocate a strong role for government in managing the commodity sector. It is interesting to note that the organizational structure they suggest for implementing this policy is a near carbon-copy of MITI's, in that it would be composed of industry bureaus, whose senior staff would be required to remain in their position for long periods of time in order to build up expertise.[3] Although it is unlikely that Canada will restructure its senior public service on the Japanese model, the model has a particularly valuable point to make about the importance of expertise in policy formulation, particularly if our government is to play the role of banker.

The government's record as a banker should sound a note of caution for the private sector. Private firms that are in difficulty often approach government as a lender of last resort. They should be wary of doing this because government is in the business of maintaining political power, and enterprises supported by the government will be expected to carry out policy mandates and to curry public favour, rather than make sound business decisions. Once a firm has accepted a government loan, it may be difficult to escape the political embrace. Our investigation shows that, in every case, the original entrepreneurs or managers had their business taken away from them by the government. Simply put, private-sector entrepreneurs should not assume that they can get something for nothing, that is, without becoming a political pawn.

It is also worth remembering that each highly publicized failure of a government-assisted enterprise contributes to the growing perception that any company in which the government is involved is inherently unsound, and that this perception affects the company's ability to compete. The difficulties experienced by all five companies in obtaining credit through normal channels once they had begun to receive government support suggests that mixed enterprises are viewed by suppliers, customers, and banks as different from private enterprises, and that their image is rather tarnished. Clairtone, a government-assisted company not mentioned in this book, was lured to Nova Scotia by IEL in the early 1960s and met its demise for precisely this reason. The company received additional bank credit to cover emergency expenses time and time again while it was still privately owned, but after the government invested in it, Clairtone was told to go to the government when it needed a loan of $2 million. One of the two entrepreneurs who formed the company claims:

> The bank's whole attitude changed because they believed there was a daddy in there who could bail us out anytime and who had to bail us out. The banks had held a very responsible attitude toward us, they had really helped us, guided us, supported us. But with the government in there for [$9 million], they abdicated their responsibility to the government . . . Before, they would have taken the risk because the thought of the Bank of Commerce having to pull the rug out from under Clairtone would have been inconceivable. It would be a very unpleasant thing to do to a popular, creative Canadian company. But . . . after the government had pumped in $10 million and there were 1,000 jobs at stake in Nova Scotia, they knew that I or the government of Nova Scotia would find ways to finance it, so why should they expose themselves.[4]

The above illustrates one of the reasons why it is so difficult for a company to get out from under the government's wing once it has taken refuge there.

We will not be surprised if our warnings are heeded by neither government nor business. Governments will continue to bail out troubled corporations and troubled corporations will continue to ask for bailouts. Governments will probably want an ongoing involvement in some new ventures in strategic policy areas. Even governments whose ideologies favour a greater use of the market will probably continue to operate direct-lending or loan-guarantee programs to support small business and exports. Governments may privatize some of their activities, but they will still retain many Crown corporations, and these Crown corporations will have ongoing capital needs and still have to be monitored.

Given that government will continue to play the role of banker, how can we ensure that it does so in a more effective and efficient way? The two types of government-banker involvement of most concern to us are the overseeing of the capital expenditures of Crown corporations and the provision of loan guarantees or letters of comfort to private-sector firms. The latter has often occurred on an ad hoc basis with departments of industry guaranteeing loans to specific firms, rather than as part of some ongoing lending or loan-guarantee program. Our recommendations are addressed primarily to Crown corporations and ad-hoc loan guarantees, taking into account the difference in ownership structures where necessary. It should be remembered that the cases discussed in this book generally started as loan guarantees or letters of comfort which were converted to government equity and Crown corporations as the firms' problems worsened. Our hope is that our recommendations will help to prevent this process of failure from occurring. In general, we recommend improvements to the monitoring systems for Crown corporations and loan guarantees, so that government can make more informed decisions concerning whether or not to invest, can oversee management more effectively when it does invest, and can terminate involvement in unsuccessful projects more rapidly. Furthermore, we would like to see effective monitoring systems established on an ongoing basis, rather than installed as panic responses to crisis situations. We see these recommendations as being consistent with the provisions of Bill C-24, which in 1984 amended the sections of the Financial Administration Act dealing with Crown corporations. We also wish to see similar improvements in the monitoring regime for loan guarantees.

The reader might feel that there is something of a contradiction between our approach to writing history, which emphasizes the role played by individuals in determining outcomes, and our recommendations, which suggest the implementation of better monitoring systems. We recognize that there will always be clever individuals who will attempt to thwart management systems in order to produce personal gains at the expense of the public's welfare. Clearly, no system will be able to catch all conceiveable abuses. Nevertheless, the monitoring systems in our cases were so ineffective that they gave characters such as Alexander Kasser, Malcolm Bricklin, and Rex Grose far too much freedom. Better monitoring systems could have limited their scope of operations and thereby prevented abuses.

Our suggestions concerning monitoring deal with four areas: the role of boards of directors, the use of government directives to Crown corporations or loan-guarantee recipients, monitoring by government of Crown corporations and loan guarantee recipients, and monitoring by auditors.

ROLE OF BOARDS OF DIRECTORS

This study, as well as other studies such as the Lambert report, demonstrate that the board of directors of Crown corporations, even though it includes senior public servants as members, often lacks clear directives from government concerning the corporation's mission. Furthermore, the board lacks expertise, primarily because many of the directors owe their position to political patronage. When government guarantees loans, it often attempts to monitor a corporation's performance by appointing public servants to its board of directors. Our study has shown that this has often failed because the public servants find themselves in a conflict-of-interest situation between their departmental responsibilities and their duty to manage the company in the best interest of the shareholders. In some cases, the non-government board members assumed that the public servants were acting in their departmental capacity and therefore deferred to the government directors.

Boards of directors have two major functions: to advise management on how best to run the business and to hold management accountable for the running of the business. In the cases we looked at, they performed neither role effectively. How can they do better? The Public Accounts Committee, in its report on Canadair, recommends the appointment of people with more expertise to the boards of Crown corporations and the communication by the government of clear policy mandates to Crown corporation boards. Bill C-24 specifies that the government, after consulting with a Crown corporation's board of directors, can give it binding written directives.[5] Both the Public Accounts Committee and the Anderson report recommend that public servants with day-to-day program responsibilities that can affect a Crown corporation not be appointed to its board.[6]

Boards of Crown corporations and the "mixed" boards of loan-guarantee recipients fail because their members lack the expertise to serve as advisers and the knowledge of government policy to hold the corporations accountable. We feel it would be possible to achieve both the advising and monitoring objectives, but not in the context of one institution. Ministers and public servants would rather communicate directly with the managers of Crown corporations or firms receiving loan guarantees than through a board of directors. Thus, boards of directors would be more useful as advisers to management, and management should be directly monitored by the government.

We recommend that government not appoint any directors to the board of a company to which it has given a loan guarantee. Such a firm should be monitored directly by the government, as discussed below.

The board of directors of Crown corporations should conceive of themselves primarily as advisers to management. If this is to occur, the major criterion for appointment to the board of directors must be expertise. Certainly "political" appointments — choosing inexpert people on the basis of political rewards — should be discouraged. We recognize that this runs counter to the practice of the current government, as most of its Crown corporation appointments appear to be made on the basis of patronage, rather than expertise. We wonder if there is any way this practice can be changed, both for the present government and for future governments.

The board of directors of Crown corporations should include people appointed by management and people appointed by government, perhaps half and half. If directors of Crown corporations are to function as advisers to management, it would obviously be in the self-interest of management to choose people who have sufficient expertise to give useful advice. **To ensure a higher calibre of expertise, these appointments could be made by Parliament, rather than by Order-in-Council, with members' votes not constrained by party discipline.** This would make the appointments process similar to Congressional ratification of political appointees in the United States, which does appear to be successful in preventing appointments of unqualified people on the basis of patronage.

THE USE OF DIRECTIVES

The board of directors should be given as clear a statement as possible of the government's objectives for the Crown corporation or for the loan-guarantee recipient. This would make the directors more effective advisers to management. We recognize that, if politicians wish to use Crown corporations or loan guarantees to maximize political support, they may be unwilling to provide such statements. Nevertheless, it is our hope that the public, having come to recognize the waste that has often occurred in such cases, will demand more honesty from politicians.

The proposals recommended above mean that government would not exercise its powers as shareholder in Crown corporations or as guarantor through the board of directors. **In both cases, if government wishes to influence management's policies or replace individual managers, it should do so through written directives.** With regard to Crown corporations, the directives would be binding because the government is the sole shareholder; in the case of firms receiving loan guarantees, if necessary, the directives could be accompanied by the sanction of refusing to guarantee current or future borrowing. In effect, we are proposing that the provision for directives for Crown corporations in Bill C-24 be extended to loan-guarantee recipients as well.

We would expect these directives to be communicated at first verbally to management, and then in writing if necessary. More than likely the board of directors would want to know the reasons underlying government directives. **In addition to explanations of government's directives by management, we feel it would be desirable to have occasional meetings between the board and the public servants and ministers responsible for the monitoring of Crown corporations or loan-guarantee recipients.** Such meetings could be held both on a regular basis, perhaps once a year, to review the corporation's overall progress, and on an ad hoc basis when strategic decisions must be taken, or when disagreements arise between the board and the government as to the course the corporation should take.

IMPROVING GOVERNMENT MONITORING

We have seen a number of cases where government monitoring failed because the individuals given the task lacked expertise, time or energy, or became "captured." The frequent hiring of management consultants was a strong indication of these failures. We think that effective monitoring can be sufficiently institutionalized to avoid the panic hiring of management consultants. In order for monitoring to be effective, the monitors must receive a clear mandate from the politicians, and they must have expertise.

Crown Corporations

In recent years, governments have made some useful efforts to improve their monitoring of Crown corporations. A number of them have established holding companies to oversee their portfolio of Crown corporations. It is crucial that the staffs of such holding companies have people with expertise in financial and industry analysis. The government will have to compete with the private sector to hire accountants, MBAs, stock market analysts, and others who have this expertise. This will entail a greater expense, but the cost of inexpert monitoring, as we have seen, is far greater.

Multidivisional Crown holding companies should be established wherever possible. Given the size of the federal government, it would not be possible to make all federal Crown corporations subsidiaries of the CDIC, for example. However, the creation of several corporations based on the CDIC model by the federal government, as well as their establishment in the provinces would be useful. Provincial holding corporations should be required to make annual reports to the legislature on the performance of the corporations they oversee, just as Bill C-24 requires such reporting for federal corporations.

We believe that these multidivisional holding companies would behave differently from the inadequate bureaucratic monitors of the past because (1) they would have a more distant relationship with the government, (2) they would recruit staff with financial and industry expertise who prefer the more autonomous setting, and (3) they would have to report publicly on corporate performance, which should create some pressure for efficiency. If companies on the CDIC model are not established, special monitoring units within the bureaucracy would be preferable to the current arrangements, which often involve part-time monitoring by public servants with little understanding of the business aspects of the mission of Crown corporations. Once again, the people in these units should be experts in financial and industry analysis.

Management should report to their government monitors in writing and in person at frequent intervals, probably quarterly. Reports should discuss the firm's past performance and future plans in detail. The requirements of Bill C-24 that the corporation's CEO produce annual corporate plans as well as report to his directors, his minister, and the Treasury Board Secretariat on developments "likely to have a material effect on the performance of the Crown corporation" are useful and should be followed at the provincial level as well.[7]

Government Loan Guarantees

Loan guarantees and letters of comfort have proved to be a serious problem in the management of government enterprise, because they have allowed government departments to escape the scrutiny of both the government's internal financial controls and the legislature and because their incremental nature has allowed commitments to grow without any re-examination of their rationale or of the recipient's performance. The cases have also shown that, if loans are totally guaranteed, private-sector lenders do not monitor the performance of the borrower as they would loans for which they themselves are ultimately responsible. In addition, as Lessard, Baldwin, and Mason have argued theoretically, loan guarantees give borrowers an incentive to take excessive risk.[8]

On the other hand, the virtue of loan guarantees, as compared with government infusions of equity or government loans at subsidized interest rates, is that private-sector lenders charge guaranteed borrowers an interest rate commensurate with the risk involved. Thus, recipients are forced to pay the social opportunity cost of capital which, from the point of view of efficient resource allocation, is clearly desirable.

One way to improve the scrutiny of government enterprise's borrowing while retaining the social-opportunity cost for capital would be to forbid the government to use loan guarantees, thus forcing it to lend directly and requiring it to do so at the social-opportunity cost of capital. One simple way to do this would be to charge the prime rate. This procedure would have the advantage of the initial loan being subjected to the scrutiny of the budgetary process and parliamentary review. However, there would still be the problem of borrowers believing that interest payments to the government could be deferred, reduced, or just forgiven, all of which the government has frequently done in the past.

Another approach would be to retain loan guarantees but increase their monitoring. For instance, all recipients of loan guarantees could be monitored in the same way that federal Crown corporations are monitored, both by the Treasury Board and by holding companies or the departments through whose ministers they report to Parliament. Once again, this monitoring must be done by people who have expertise in financial and industry analysis. In addition, loan guarantees could be brought into the budgetary process, as the federal government has already begun to do. Departments should be required to report their outstanding loan guarantees to the budgetary agency, to report on the condition of their loans, and to seek approval to increase loan guarantees.

In addition to making loan guarantees part of the budgetary process, information about them should be made available to the public. Loan guarantees should become part of the Estimates, thereby becoming subject to parliamentary scrutiny. Just as the government is presently publishing information about tax expenditures, it should be required to produce an annual report about loan guarantees, listing them by the department responsible for the guarantee, by the company receiving it, the location of the activity being supported, and the total financial commitment.

If the government ultimately decides to bankrupt a company that has received guarantees, all or at least a substantial part of the funds required to do so should be taken from the budget of the department or envelope responsible for the loans. The result might be that departments would be less inclined to give loan guarantees in the first place, if they realized that they have an opportunity cost in terms of other activities that would have to be foregone if the guarantees had to be paid out.

To summarize, although government should continue to have the power to give loan guarantees, they should be more closely monitored by being incorporated into the regular budgetary expenditure process and by producing an annual report to Parliament.

We think that an argument could even be made for requiring all Crown corporations to finance their capital investments through loan guarantees, rather than through direct government investment. This would force the government to take into account the opportunity cost of capital when making investment decisions for the Crown corporation sector, which in turn could have the salutary effects of reducing the volume of such investment and the use of excessively capital-intensive technology. Furthermore, annually reported loan-guarantee financing would make the subsidies received by Crown corporations more visible to the public, which would improve the process of policy formulation.

In addition to loan guarantees for specific enterprises, there are ongoing government loan-guarantee or lending programs. Two of the cases discussed in this report, Churchill Forest Industries and Consolidated Computer, dealt with large ad hoc departmental lending (CFI) or loan guarantees (CCI) which were poorly handled by programs intended to provide smaller loans (Manitoba Development Fund) or loan guarantees (Enterprise Development Board). The Commission of Inquiry into

The Pas Forestry and Industrial Complex made numerous recommendations for improving the Manitoba Development Fund's lending procedures, such as requiring that the identity of borrowers be disclosed to the Fund and preventing the Fund from lending to companies domiciled in countries not having tax treaties with Canada.[9] Similarly, the Anderson report recommended the establishment of clearer lines of accountability between the Enterprise Development Board and DRIE, greater accountability of the EDB to the Treasury Board for loan guarantees beyond a critical size, and more precise criteria for giving and terminating EDB loan guarantees.[10] These recommendations were made moot with the termination of the EDB in 1983. **Nevertheless, the monitoring processes of all other ongoing government lending or loan-guarantee programs should be as rigorous as those that these two reports have recommended.**

THE ROLE OF AUDITORS

Our cases have shown that private sector auditors often went along with "aggressive" accounting policies on the part of management, behaviour that served to disguise managerial problems from government monitors. How can Crown corporations or loan-guarantee recipients be audited more effectively? The first institution to look to is the Auditor General, whose staff undoubtedly has unique expertise in understanding the finances of government enterprise. The Public Accounts Committee report recommends that the Auditor General be entitled to participate on the audit committees of Crown and government-controlled corporations that he does not audit; that, when the auditors of the corporation inform the Auditor General of matters they feel should be brought to the attention of Parliament, the Auditor General have a right to examine the corporation's books and records; and finally that the Auditor General establish standards for the auditing of these corporations and assure Parliament that they are being followed.[11] In addition, Bill C-24 has given the Auditor General the right (unless waived) to audit all Schedule C Crown corporations after 1 January 1989.[12] Regardless of whether the Auditor General and his staff take on this increased work load, or whether they just develop auditing standards for Crown corporations, the result will be more effective auditing.

In addition, we feel that the Auditor General should have a role to play in the auditing of firms that receive loan guarantees. **While loan-guarantee recipients have the right to choose their own auditors, the Auditor General should develop standards for the auditing of loan-guarantee recipients. If the Auditor General is not satisfied with the auditing of any loan-guarantee recipient, he should have the right to review the auditor's work and, if he thinks it necessary, conduct his own audit.** This recommendation might make the owners of firms that ask for government loan guarantees uncomfortable. We are not troubled by this, since accepting a loan guarantee should obligate the recipient to undergo an increased level of monitoring.

One accounting rule that should be established for recipients of loan guarantees is that their financial statements should be presented on both a disaggregated and consolidated basis, with the latter making sure to include all their subsidiaries and any relevant related companies. Bill C-24 now requires federal Crown corporations to include all subsidiary companies.[13] In the CCI case, however, the enterprise's true financial condition was disguised because the status of two related companies was not required to be reported by virtue of their being legally separate entities, not subsidiaries. It is imperative that such a situation not be allowed to occur again.

*   *   *

To conclude, our analysis of the five cases indicates that governments ended up losing a great deal of money for the following reasons: investments were often undertaken to satisfy political objectives and without serious analysis of their commercial prospects; they were poorly managed and monitored; and they were carried on long after their failure became obvious. We do not think it would suffice simply to exhort politicians to be more responsible with public money; the temptation to use public money to buy political power seems almost impossible to overcome. Our hope is that the establishment of stronger monitoring regimes and publicizing the performance of Crown corporations and loan-guarantee recipients will make politicians, bureaucrats, and the public more aware of the consequences of public-sector investments. If politicians and bureaucrats were forced by the budgetary process to compare these investments with other forms of expenditure, they might not look as attractive. If the ongoing performance of Crown corporations and loan-guarantee recipients is monitored by the Auditor General, by Parliament, and thus by the media and the public, waste and inefficiency will generate an unpopularity that may constrain the political impulse to throw money at marginal voters.

If the evidence from these case studies contributes to the establishment of better monitoring systems, then it has been of some use to the Canadian public.

NOTES

CHAPTER 1

1. Sandford F. Borins, *The Language of the Skies: the Bilingual Air Traffic Control Conflict in Canada* (Montreal, 1983), pp. 237-43.

CHAPTER 2

1. M.J. Trebilcock and J.R.S. Prichard, "Crown Corporations: The Calculus of Instrument Choice," pp. 1-98 in J.R.S. Prichard, ed., *Crown Corporations in Canada* (Toronto, 1983); M.J. Trebilcock, R.S. Prichard, D.G. Hartle, and D.N. Dewees, *The Choice of Governing Instrument* (Ottawa, 1982).
2. Trebilcock et al., "Crown Corporations," p. 16.
3. The background history to Deuterium of Canada is described in P. Mathias, *Forced Growth* (Toronto, 1971), pp. 103-123 and in G. Sims, "The Evolution of AECL" (M.A. thesis, Carleton University, 1979), pp. 150-158.
4. Sims, "The Evolution of AECL," p. 167.
5. Sims, "The Evolution of AECL," p. 168.
6. Sims, "The Evolution of AECL," pp. 153, 169.
7. L. MacIntyre, "Heavy water story climax nearing," *Halifax Chronicle-Herald*, 13 April 1971.
8. Sims, "The Evolution of AECL," p. 172.
9. See note 7.
10. R. George, *The Life and Times of Industrial Estates Limited* (Halifax, 1974), pp. 93-98.
11. See note 7.
12. "N.S. clears all legal hurdles for heavy water," *Halifax Chronicle-Herald*, 14 April 1971.
13. Ibid.
14. Sims, "The Evolution of AECL," pp. 160, 161, 173, 174.
15. See note 7.
16. See note 7.
17. House of Commons *Debates*, 2 Dec. 1963, p. 5314.
18. House of Commons *Debates*, 25 May 1972, p. 2563.
19. Sims, "The Evolution of AECL," p. 161.
20. H.A. Fredericks with A. Chambers, *Bricklin* (Fredericton, 1977), pp. 6-11.
21. Fredericks and Chambers, *Bricklin*, pp. 11-16.
22. Fredericks and Chambers, *Bricklin*, pp. 16-17.
23. Multiplex Corporation, "Bricklin Canada Ltd.: A Submission to the Department of Regional Economic Expansion," 6 April 1973; Fredericks, *Bricklin*, pp. 20-21.
24. Fredericks and Chambers, *Bricklin*, pp. 21-22; interview with Harry Nason, former deputy minister of Economic Growth, Province of New Brunswick, 9 Oct. 1985.
25. Nason interview; Nason testimony to the Public Accounts Committee, New Brunswick Legislature, 24 May 1975, pp. 1-4.
26. Hal Quinn, "Working without a net," *Maclean's*, 18 February 1985, p. 17.
27. Nason interview.
28. Nason interview.

29. "Quebec laisse échapper un projet qui aurait pu ressusciter SOMA," *Le Devoir*, 21 June 1973.

30. Fredericks and Chambers, *Bricklin*, pp. 25–27; Nason interview; "Auto Plant Announced for Saint John," *Fredericton Daily Gleaner*, 23 June 1973.

31. Agreement between Bricklin Canada Ltd., General Vehicle, Inc., Bricklin Vehicle Corporation, Provincial Holdings Ltd., and Her Majesty the Queen in right of the Province of New Brunswick, 26 June 1973.

32. House of Commons *Debates*, 22 Oct. 1975, p. 8450.

33. Interview with David Crane, vice-president, corporate relations, Canada Development Investment Corporation, 22 May 1984.

34. House of Commons *Debates*, 19 Dec. 1975, p. 10198; *The Fifth Estate*, 13 April 1983.

35. Interview with Charles Rathgeb, director, Canadair, 21 June 1984.

36. Neither the management team nor the non-government members of the board of directors were privy to this report, and they were even unaware of its existence until much later (Public Accounts Committee Hearings, 9 June 1983, 86:22).

37. Jean Chrétien, *Straight From The Heart* (Toronto, 1985), p. 90.

38. "Canadair: big league at last," *Montreal Gazette*, 18 Aug. 1980; House of Commons Public Accounts Committee, *Minutes*, 7 June 1983, p. 85:12.

39. Public Accounts Committee, *Minutes*, 21 June 1985, p. 89:23.

40. Report of the Commission of Inquiry Into The Pas Forestry and Industrial Complex at The Pas, Manitoba, August 1974 (hereafter called CI Report), p. 92.

41. CI Report, p. 99. Taken from the Business Development Act, Section 9(2).

42. CI Report, p. 100–01.

43. CI Report, p. 108. From the commentary by deputy provincial treasurer R.M. Burns, pp. 18–19.

44. CI Report, p. 111. From Grose's comments on Burns' commentary, p. 6.

45. Ultimately the Conservatives were unable to find an investor before the election they called for 14 December 1962. Despite the absence of any concrete proposal for forestry development in the north, they won handily, taking 33 seats in the 57-seat legislature, a loss of three seats from the previous election ("Conservatives Re-elected: Liberals Gain 2," *Winnipeg Free Press*, 15 December 1962).

46. W.C. Newman, *What Happened When Dr. Kasser Came To Northern Manitoba*, (Winnipeg, 1976) pp. 10–11.

47. CI Report, p. 129. From the report of the Committee on Manitoba's Economic Future, March, 1963.

48. CI Report, p. 126.

49. The Commission of Inquiry reviewed expert testimony on the subject of wood costs from Albert E. Penney. Mr. Penney worked for 30 years in the pulp and paper industry between 1937 and 1967. He commented: "Even with the help of the proposed Government incentives, there was no way that figure [$14.80 per cord] would have been credible . . . I go back to my records in 1965 in which . . . under a very favourable situation, where the stumpage charge was remarkably low . . . and where the growth per acre was over 35 cords per acre, three times that which it was at The Pas . . . the log cost in those days was $18.00 a cord, and that was a very, very favourable situation . . . In fact, I think that Delahey . . . estimated $25.00 a cord at The Pas . . . Even if you took a cost of logs of $20.00 a cord, which is still optimistic . . . the results would have been to add something like 2½ million dollars to what they [Arthur D. Little] estimated . . . If you went to any major pulp and paper company in Canada with the information that Arthur D. Little had, it would not have been credible. They would not have believed it." (CI Report, pp. 135–36).

50. The CI Report adds: "A check by Penney indicated the Sandwell figures of 1961

were realistic, and we therefore conclude that the figures of 1964 were artificial and probably concocted for promotional purposes" (p. 137).

51. CI Report, p. 157.
52. CI Report, p. 164.
53. CI Report, p. 166-68. Also, Newman, *What Happened*, p. 20-21.
54. CI Report, p. 170; letter from W.D. Stothert, chairman, Stothert Group Inc., 26 Nov. 1985.
55. Mathias, *Forced Growth*, p. 132.
56. Stothert letter.
57. CI Report, pp. 358-59.
58. CI Report, p. 275.
59. CI Report, p. 257.
60. CI Report, pp. 263-65.
61. CI Report, pp. 277-78.
62. Newman, *What Happened*, p. 23.
63. CI Report, p. 271.
64. Mathias, *Forced Growth*, p. 29.
65. CI Report, p. 279.
66. "Manitoba May Vote June 6," *Winnipeg Free Press*, 13 April 1966.
67. "Constituency Maps Show Final Results", *Winnipeg Free Press*, 24 June 1966.
68. Consolidated Computer Limited, "Summary of Consolidated Computer Limited's lease financing with the Canadian government" (unpublished memorandum, 1971).
69. "Upstart shakes computer world," *Ottawa Citizen*, 19 Oct. 1970.
70. Ibid.; interview with Mers Kutt, former president, Consolidated Computer, 17 May 1984.
71. Kutt interview.
72. Department of Industry, Trade and Commerce Act, "General Adjustment Assistance Regulations," Consolidated Regulations of Canada, chapter 971, (Ottawa, 1978), pp. 7603-12; Interview with Anthony Hampson, former chairperson, General Adjustment Assistance Board, 31 July 1984.
73. Burns Brothers and Denton, "Institutional Report on Consolidated Computers Ltd.," February 1970.
74. Shearson, Hammill, Inc., "Preliminary Prospectus: 600,000 Common Shares (without par value) Consolidated Computer Limited," 20 July 1971, p. 18.
75. Consolidated Computer Limited memorandum; Kutt interview.

CHAPTER 3

1. See C.W. Hofer and D. Schendel, *Strategy Formulation: Analytical Concepts* (St. Paul, 1978); and M.E. Porter, *Competitive Strategy: Techniques for Analyzing Industries and Competitors* (New York, 1980).
2. L. MacIntyre, "Seven attempts made to sell Deuterium," *Halifax Chronicle-Herald*, 15 April 1971.
3. Ibid.
4. Ibid.
5. G. Sims, "The Evolution of AECL," M.A. thesis, Carleton University, 1979, p. 179.
6. MacIntyre, "Seven attempts."
7. Sims, "The Evolution of AECL," pp. 175-77.
8. Ibid., 177-78.
9. P. Mathias, *Forced Growth* (Toronto, 1971), pp. 114-15.
10. L. MacIntyre, "Cape Breton workers had minor role," *Halifax Chronicle-Herald*, 16 April 1971.

11. Ibid.; R.E. George, *The Life and Times of Industrial Estates Limited* (Halifax, 1974), p. 82; I.M. MacKeigan, "Report of Industrial Inquiry Commission respecting Deuterium construction projects" (Halifax, Government of Nova Scotia, 1967).
12. MacIntyre, "Cape Breton workers."
13. Mathias, *Forced Growth*, pp. 116-17.
14. Ibid., 118.
15. Ibid.; Sims, "The Evolution of AECL," p. 182; "Deteriorated remains of deuterium plant called a diabolical waste of $120 million," *Globe and Mail*, 25 August 1972.
16. Mathias, *Forced Growth*, p. 119; MacIntyre, "Cape Breton workers."
17. Mathias, *Forced Growth*, p. 121; Terry Allan, Nova Scotia publicity officer for AECL, interview, 4 Jan. 1985.
18. H.A. Fredericks with Allan Chambers, *Bricklin* (Fredericton, 1977), pp. 31-37.
19. Ibid., 39-41, 48-50, 52.
20. Ibid., 1-3,30-31, 50,51, 104.
21. Ibid., 29-30.
22. Ibid., 41-42.
23. Ibid., 29-30.
24. Ibid., 37-38.
25. Letter from Harry Nason, former deputy minister of Economic Growth, Province of New Brunswick, 1 Nov. 1985.
26. Fredericks and Chambers, *Bricklin*, p. 54.
27. Ibid., 34, 51, 85.
28. Ibid., 10, 11, 14, 84, 92-93.
29. Ibid., 56.
30. Ibid., 59.
31. Ibid., 60.
32. Nason testimony to the Public Accounts Committee of the New Brunswick Legislature, 29 May 1985, p. 3.
33. Nason testimony, p. 43; Interview with G.S. Wheatley, Executive Director, Financial Programs, Department of Commerce and Development, New Brunswick, 27 Jan. 1984.
34. Memorandum, 15 March 1978, Bricklin project files, New Brunswick archives.
35. Balance sheet, Bricklin Canada Ltd., January 1974, Bricklin project files.
36. R.K. Fletcher (General Manager, New Brunswick Multiplex Corporation), letter to Premier Hatfield, 20 Dec. 1973, Bricklin project files.
37. Fredericks and Chambers, *Bricklin*, p. 34.
38. Ibid., 44-45; letter from Harry Nason, 1 November 1985.
39. Fredericks and Chambers, *Bricklin*, p. 55.
40. Provincial Holdings Ltd., letter to Bricklin Canada Ltd., 10 October 1974, Bricklin project files.
41. Fredericks and Chambers, *Bricklin*, p. 61.
42. Ibid., 62-63; J.I.M. Whitcomb, letter to Peter MacNutt, 27 Nov. 1974, Bricklin project files.
43. Fredericks and Chambers, *Bricklin*, pp. 64-66.
44. G.S. Wheatley, letter to Joseph Rose, 4 Dec. 1974; C.E. Sawyer, letter to H.A. Nason, 6 December 1974, Bricklin project files.
45. Fredericks and Chambers, *Bricklin*, p. 67.
46. Ibid., 70.
47. Ibid., 80-81.
48. H.A. Nason, letter to Malcolm Bricklin, 6 Jan. 1975, Bricklin project files.
49. Fredericks and Chambers, *Bricklin*, pp. 86-87.
50. Malcolm Bricklin, letter to Provincial Holdings Ltd., 15 Jan. 1975, Bricklin project files.

51. Fredericks and Chambers, *Bricklin*, pp. 91–92.
52. Provincial Holdings Ltd., letter to Malcolm Bricklin, 13 Feb. 1975, Bricklin project files.
53. G.S. Wheatley, letter to Joseph Rose, 22 Jan. 1975, Bricklin project files.
54. Fredericks and Chambers, *Bricklin*, p. 105.
55. Clarkson, Gordon and Company, letters to H.A. Nason, 18 April 1975 and 7 August 1975, Bricklin project files.
56. Clarkson, Gordon and Company, letters to Malcolm Bricklin, Sept. 8 and 23, 1975, Bricklin project files; Fredericks and Chambers, *Bricklin*, pp. 111–16.
57. Fredericks and Chambers, *Bricklin*, p. 112.
58. Bricklin Canada Ltd., "Financial Proposal," 17 Sept. 1975, Bricklin project files.
59. House of Commons Public Accounts Committee (henceforth PAC), *Minutes*, 21 June 1983, 89:39.
60. "Canadair: Big league at last," *Montreal Gazette*, 18 Aug. 1980.
61. Ibid.
62. Patrick Finn, "Challenger set to confound prophets," *Montreal Star*, 23 July 1977.
63. PAC *Minutes*, 7 June 1983, 85:12.
64. Interview with Charles Rathgeb, Director, Canadair, 21 June 1984.
65. PAC *Minutes*, 14 June 1983, 87:19.
66. PAC *Minutes*, 7 June 1983, 85:13.
67. "Canadair: Big league at last," *Montreal Gazette*, 18 Aug. 1980.
68. PAC *Minutes*, 14 June 1983, 87:9–10.
69. PAC *Minutes*, 7 June 1983, 85:12.
70. Ibid., 13.
71. Ibid.
72. Crane interview.
73. "Canadair buyer cancels deal gets free plane," *Toronto Star*, 13 April 1983.
74. PAC *Minutes*, 7 June 1983, 85:14.
75. PAC *Minutes*, 7 June 1983, 85:15; 9 June 1983, 86:17.
76. PAC *Minutes*, 7 June 1983, 85:15.
77. PAC *Minutes*, 9 June 1983, 86:17.
78. "Pilot is killed in test of Challenger plane," *Globe and Mail*, 4 April 1980.
79. PAC *Minutes*, 7 June 1983, 85:14.
80. Ibid., 35.
81. PAC *Minutes*, 23 June 1983, 90:32.
82. PAC *Minutes*, 7 June 1983, 85:31; House of Commons Committee on Finance, Trade, and Economic Affairs *Minutes*, 13 March 1984, 85:18.
83. See H.I. Ansoff and J.M. Stewart, "Strategies for a technology-based business," *Harvard Business Review* (Nov.-Dec. 1967), pp. 71–83; and T.J. Peters and R. Waterman Jr., *In Search of Excellence: Lessons from America's Best-Run Companies* (New York, 1982), pp. 156–99.
84. PAC *Minutes*, 7 June 1983, 85:18–19.
85. Ibid.
86. PAC *Minutes*, 7 June 1983, 85:33; 16 June 1983, 88:8–13.
87. Letter from Gordon Ritchie, Federal Economic Development Coordinator, Department of Regional Industrial Expansion, 2 Dec. 1985.
88. PAC *Minutes*, 21 June 1983, 89:5, 28–29.
89. Ibid., 29.
90. Ibid., 24.
91. Ibid., 52.
92. Ibid., 30.
93. PAC *Minutes*, 16 June 1983, 88:37, 42; 21 June 1983, 89:23–25.
94. PAC *Minutes*, 21 June 1983, 89:52.
95. Ibid., 19–20.

96. Ibid., 31.
97. Ibid.
98. Telephone interview with Jean-Pierre Goyer, former Canadair director, 8 Oct. 1985; Rathgeb interview.
99. Telephone interview with Antoine Guérin, 22 Oct. 1985.
100. Rathgeb interview.
101. Goyer interview.
102. Letter from Gordon Ritchie, 2 Dec. 1985: "The Board was further diluted by the addition of a number of political patronage appointees whose sole qualification was political affiliation."
103. PAC *Minutes*, November 1, 15, 17, 1983, 93:4, 6.
104. PAC *Minutes*, 23 June 1983, 90:44-45.
105. Letter from Gordon Ritchie, 2 Dec. 1985: "These problems [the lack of technical competence and financial expertise] were clearly accentuated by the rather curious conception of his role held by the government director for much of this period, Mr. Antoine Guérin. Guérin was responsible for strongly advancing the government shareholder's interests on the board of directors, for closely monitoring the corporation's activities through his departmental staff, and for keeping his minister closely informed. The record will reveal whether he performed any of these functions adequately."
106. PAC *Minutes*, 21 June 1983, 89:10.
107. Ibid., 25-26.
108. Ibid., 10, 52.
109. Guérin interview.
110. PAC *Minutes*, 21 June 1983, 89:59.
111. PAC *Minutes*, 21 June 1983, 89:59.
112. PAC *Minutes*, 7 June 1983, 85:25; 21 June 1983, 89:12-13.
113. PAC *Minutes*, 21 June 1983, 89:14,44.
114. Goyer interview; "Former director points finger as Canadair silence shatters", *Globe and Mail*, 10 Sept. 1985.
115. Memorandum from Jean-Pierre Goyer to Michael Pitfield, 9 June 1981.
116. PAC *Minutes*, 21 June 1983, 89:11.
117. Ibid., 13-14.
118. The Hon. Herb Gray, letter to Frederick Kearns, 6 April 1982.
119. PAC *Minutes*, 21 June 1983, 89:46.
120. The Hon. Ed Lumley, letter to Frederick Kearns, 5 Nov. 1982.
121. Shieldings Investments Ltd., *Canadair Analysis, Report Two*, November 1982, p. 4.
122. Report of the Commission of Inquiry into The Pas Forestry and Industrial Complex, Manitoba, August 1974, p. 262.
123. Mathias, *Forced Growth*, p. 81.
124. Exhibits 40 and 45 of the Commission of Inquiry Report.
125. W.C. Newman, *What Happened When Dr. Kasser Came to Northern Manitoba* (Winnipeg, 1976), p. 175. The quoted passage is taken from testimony of Edward Schreyer.
126. Testimony of Rex E. Grose, Vol. 29, 26 Oct. 1971, p. 134.
127. Commission of Inquiry Report (henceforth *CI Report*), p. 257.
128. *CI Report*, p. 372.
129. *CI Report*, p. 369.
130. *CI Report*, p. 368.
131. *CI Report*, p. 333.
132. *CI Report*, p. 337.
133. *CI Report*, p. 338.
134. *CI Report*, p. 421.

135. *CI Report*, p. 422.
136. *Winnipeg Free Press*, 1 Sept. 1967; *CI Report*, p. 430.
137. Philip Mathias, "Citizen Sindona," *Financial Post*, 12 April 1986.
138. *CI Report*, 1862; also, Newman, *What Happened*, p. 19.
139. Newman, *What Happened*, p. 49.
140. Stothert letter, p. 3.
141. Newman, *What Happened*, p. 49.
142. *CI Report*, pp. 800–02.
143. Ibid., 805–06.
144. Ibid., 807.
145. Ibid., 811.
146. Ibid., 846.
147. Ibid., 972.
148. Ibid., 969.
149. Ibid., 995–1001.
150. Ibid., 1030.
151. Ibid., 1142–54.
152. Testimony of Albert Bissonnette, Vol. 237, 22 Nov. 1972.
153. *CI Report*, pp. 1190–91.
154. Ibid., 1900.
155. Ibid., 1896–97.
156. Newman, *What Happened*, p. 120.
157. Telephone interview with Supt. D.A. Docker, RCMP, August, 1984.
158. *CI Report*, p. 1906.
159. Newman, *What Happened*, p. 33.
160. *CI Report*, pp. 1535–36.
161. *CI Report*, p. 484.
162. Testimony of David Rodgers, Vol. 81, 25 Jan. 1972, pp. 102–104.
163. *CI Report*, p. 857.
164. Ibid., 1701–03.
165. Ibid., 1668.
166. Ibid., 1686–1703.
167. Newman, *What Happened*, p. 51.
168. Mathias interview.
169. Testimony of David Rodgers, Vol. 82, 26 Jan. 1972, pp. 44–45.
170. Newman, *What Happened*, p. 83.
171. Ibid., 85.
172. "Forest Complex: A New Deal", *Winnipeg Free Press*, 31 July 1969.
173. Newman, *What Happened*, p. 85.
174. Ibid., *Report*, pp. 1440–44.
175. Mathias interview.
176. Newman, *What Happened*, p. 87.
177. Ibid., 88.
178. Mathias interview.
179. *CI Report*, p. 1454.
180. Ibid., 1459.
181. Newman, *What Happened*, p. 92.
182. Stothert letter, pp. 4–5.
183. Newman, *What Happened*, p. 98.
184. *CI Report*, pp. 1485–87.
185. Ibid., 1467–70.
186. Ibid., 1501.
187. Ibid., 1514.
188. Newman, *What Happened*, p. 104.

189. Newman, *What Happened*, p. 116.
190. Stothert letter, p. 6.
191. Shearson, Hammill, Inc., "Preliminary Prospectus: 600,000 Common Shares (without par value) Consolidated Computer Limited," July 1971, pp. 13-15, 20, 21; "Upstart shakes computer world," *Ottawa Citizen*, 19 Oct. 1970.
192. Gordon Cowperthwaite, interview, 28 Oct. 1985.
193. GAAB, letter to Consolidated Computer Ltd., 8 June 1971.
194. Mers Kutt, interview, 17 May 1984; Anthony Hampson, interview, 31 July 1984.
195. Shearson, Hammill, Inc., "Preliminary Prospectus," pp. 19-20.
196. Arthur D. Little, "Market and Product Analysis, Consolidated Computer Services, Ltd.," Report to Shearson, Hammill, June 1971, p. 2.
197. Kutt interview.
198. David Kilgour, letter to Mers Kutt, 26 Aug. 1971.
199. "The inside story of a $100-million high-tech failure," *Toronto Star*, 19 Sept. 1982.
200. Cowperthwaite interview.
201. Kutt, interview.
202. Mers Kutt "Purpose of Meeting", undated memo (probably October 1971); Mers Kutt, letters to Hon. Pierre E. Trudeau and Hon. William G. Davis, 1 Sept. 1971.
203. "Potential rescuers of computer firm given extra time," *Globe and Mail*, 25 Nov. 1971.
204. "ICL decision is expected soon on Consolidated Computer," *Globe and Mail*, 9 Dec. 1971.
205. W.A.B. Anderson, report to the president, Treasury Board, regarding Consolidated Computer Inc., 10 Feb. 1982 (hereafter called Anderson report), p. 50.
206. Treasury Board Secretariat, "Consolidated Computer Incorporated, Preliminary Chronology as at December 1, 1981" (hereafter called CCI Chronology), pp. 1, 2; "Kutt, Pamenter resign, CCL has new plan for creditors," *Canadian Datasystems*, January 1972, p. 48.
207. Kutt interview.
208. W.G. Hutchison, Half-Year Report, 11 Aug. 1972, pp. 7-8; CCI, 1974 *Annual Report*, p. 1.
209. Ibid.
210. Anderson report, p. 37.
211. CCI Chronology, p. 2.
212. Anderson report, p. 39.
213. CCI Chronology, p. 2.
214. Anderson report, pp. 43-44.
215. CCI Chronology, pp. 3-4.
216. Ibid., 4-6.
217. Don Jamieson, testimony to the House of Commons Committee on Finance, Trade and Economic Affairs, *Minutes*, 17 March 1976, 88:6.
218. CCI Chronology, pp. 6-7.
219. Ibid., 8.
220. Ibid., 11.
221. Principal agreement among her majesty the Queen in right of Canada, Ontario Development Corporation, Fujitsu Ltd, and Consolidated Computer Inc., 20 Dec. 1976, pp. 5-6.
222. CCI Chronology, p. 9; Restructuring Agreement (1976), pp. 5, 15.
223. Consolidated Computer Inc., Enterprise Development Regulations, *Consolidated Regulations of Canada* (Ottawa, 1978), p. 7577.
224. Anderson report, p. 38; CCI Chronology, p. 11.
225. Anderson report, p. 29.
226. Ibid., 44.
227. Ibid.

228. CCI, Consolidated financial statements for the year ended December 31, 1977, p. 5.
229. Anderson report, pp. 39–40.
230. Ibid., Appendix 3, p. 1.
231. Eleanor Boyle, "High hopes for high-tech firm go sour," *Toronto Star*, 6 Dec. 1981.
232. Anderson report, p. 40.
233. CCI Chronology, pp. 11–13.
234. Ibid., 14–15; interview with J. McDonald Brown, 4 April 1986.
235. Anderson report, pp. 31–32.
236. Ibid., 36–37.
237. Ibid., 34–36.
238. Ibid., 37, 43.
239. Ibid., 38.
240. Ibid., 48, 49.
241. Ibid., 51.
242. Ibid., 38–39.
243. Ibid., 46.
244. Ibid., 47.
245. PAC *Minutes*, 7 June 1983, 85:34.
246. Canadair reduced its forecast of total Challenger sales from 506 in June 1981 to 419 in December 1982. It increased its estimate of the break-even quantity from 349 to 389 in the same period, with the result that the break-even date for the program was pushed forward from 1986 to 1992. See PAC *Minutes*, 7 June 1983, 85:31.
247. David Crane, interview, 22 May 1984.
248. See Table 2 above.
249. See M.C. Jensen and W.H. Meckling, "Theory of the firm: managerial behaviour, agency costs, and ownership structure," *Journal of Financial Economics* 3 (1976), pp. 305–60.

CHAPTER 4

1. Philip Mathias, *Forced Growth*, (Toronto, 1971), p. 119.
2. Ibid.
3. Ibid., 121.
4. House of Commons *Debates*, 10 April 1970, pp. 5711–13.
5. G. Sims, "The Evolution of AECL" (M.A. thesis, Carleton University, 1979), p. 182.
6. Linden MacIntyre, "CGE may back out of Deuterium plant deal," *Halifax Chronicle-Herald*, 16 Sept. 1970.
7. Linden MacIntyre, "Plant rehabilitation may start this fall," *Halifax Chronicle-Herald*, 19 Sept. 1970.
8. "MacEachen makes surprise appearance," *Halifax Chronicle-Herald*, 23 Sept. 1970.
9. House of Commons *Debates*, 29 Jan. 1971, pp. 2887–88.
10. Sims, "The Evolution of AECL," p. 183.
11. Ibid., 184.
12. Ibid.
13. Ibid., 186.
14. Ibid., 190.
15. "Future is dim for two plants with no market," *Globe and Mail*, 14 Jan. 1985.
16. Ibid.; "AECL seeks to shut heavy water plants due to oversupply," *Globe and Mail*, 8 Feb. 1985; "Federal tax haven to ease cost cutting for Cape Bretoners," *Globe and Mail*, 24 May 1985; Chris Wood, "The high cost of jobs in Cape Breton," *Macleans*,

2 Dec. 1985; "Magna Plans to build two Cape Breton plants," *Globe and Mail*, 12 April 1986.

17. H.A. Fredericks and A. Chambers, *Bricklin* (Fredericton, 1977), pp. 116-19.

18. Ibid., 119-20.

19. Ibid., 120-21.

20. The Clarkson Company Ltd., letter to the Bank of Montreal, 13 Dec. 1976; and letter to the Royal Trust Company Ltd., 14 Dec. 1976.

21. Peter Foster, "Battle of the Sectors," *Saturday Night*, March 1983.

22. PAC *Minutes*, 14 June 1983, p. 87:27.

23. "Canadair buyer cancels deal, gets free plane," *Toronto Star*, 13 April 1983.

24. "Public probe of Canadair deal sought by NDP," *Toronto Star*, 14 April 1983.

25. "Canadair linked to bribery case," *Calgary Herald*, 19 April 1983.

26. "500 jobs expected from Canadair deal," *Montreal Gazette*, 25 April 1983.

27. "Canadair to receive $240 million from Ottawa," *Toronto Star*, 19 May 1983.

28. "Canadair asks more amid hints of big losses," *Toronto Star*, 17 May 1983.

29. Report by Senator Austin to the Standing Committee on Public Accounts and the Standing Committee on Finance, Trade and Economic Affairs, 7 June 1983, p. 36.

30. James Daw, "Fire Canadair bosses, Liberal MPs demand," *Toronto Star*, 8 June 1983; "Canadair loss largest ever," *Winnipeg Free Press*, 8 June 1983, p. 32.

31. "We must keep Canadair alive: Trudeau," *Toronto Star*, 9 June 1983.

32. "Canadair chief named," *Winnipeg Free Press*, 11 June 1983.

33. "Engine maker to fight Canadair suit," *Toronto Star*, 17 June 1983.

34. "Engine maker sues Canadair for $100 million," *Toronto Star*, 5 August 1983.

35. Eleanor Boyle, "Federal agency loses $173 million led by big deficit at Canadair Ltd.," *Montreal Gazette*, 1 Sept. 1983.

36. James Daw, "Challenger jet stays: Canadair chief," *Toronto Star*, 19 Oct. 1983; "Canadair to cut 'cumbersome' top brass," *Winnipeg Free Press*, 19 Oct. 1983.

37. "Canadair poorly run, report says," *Globe and Mail*, 18 Nov. 1983; Joel Ruimy, "Bungling led to Canadair loss, sharply worded report says," *Toronto Star*, 18 Nov. 1983.

38. Clifford Edward, "Ottawa releases study on Canadair structure," *Globe and Mail*, 21 Dec. 1983.

39. "Canadair claiming $480 million from U.S. firm," *Toronto Star*, 7 March 1984.

40. James Rusk, "Ottawa takes over debts of Canadair," *Globe and Mail*, 14 March 1984.

41. Ibid.

42. Press release from Senator Jack Austin, Minister of State Responsible for Canada Development Investment Corporation, 20 Dec. 1983, p. 7 and 8. This is the press release that accompanied the expurgated Shieldings Report.

43. Rusk, "Ottawa takes over debts of Canadair."

44. Telephone interview with Ron Pickler, Public Relations Director, Canadair, 11 March 1985.

45. David Stewart-Patterson, "Ottawa to buy unsold aircraft from Canadair," *Globe and Mail*, 6 March 1985; "Canadair makes China sale," *Financial Post*, 9 Nov. 1985.

46. W.C. Newman, *What Happened When Dr. Kasser Came to Northern Manitoba* (Winnipeg, 1976), p. 119.

47. Stothert letter, p. 9.

48. Newman, *What Happened*, p. 119.

49. Ibid., 136.

50. Stothert letter, p. 9.

51. Newman, *What Happened*, p. 120.

52. Ibid., 123.

53. "Manfor's new chairman bullish on mill's future," *Pulp and Paper Journal*, November, 1982, pp. 32-37.

54. "Manitoba loses CFI fraud case," *Pulp and Paper Journal*, March, 1983, p. 7.
55. Michael Tenszen, "Money-losing Crown firms haunt the NDP in Manitoba," *Globe and Mail*, 26 Feb. 1985.
56. Jim Lyon, "Forest industry must change to prosper," *Financial Post*, 9 Nov. 1985.
57. Treasury Board Secretariat, "Consolidated Computer Incorporated, preliminary chronology as at 1 December 1981, (henceforth CCI chronology)," p. 15; Herb Gray, letter to Donald Johnston, 23 June 1980.
58. Herb Gray, letter to Donald Johnston, 25 May 1981.
59. CCI chronology, p. 16.
60. Jonathan Chevreau, "Ottawa's computer loser is on the block," *Globe and Mail*, 13 July 1981.
61. CCI chronology, pp. 16–17.
62. Ibid.
63. Ibid., 18.
64. Herb Gray, letter to Donald Johnston, 25 May 1981.
65. Donald Johnston, letter to Herb Gray, 12 May 1981.
66. CCI chronology, pp. 18–19.
67. Donald Johnston, letter to Herb Gray, 12 May 1981.
68. CCI chronology, p. 19.
69. Ibid.
70. Interview with Conrad von Finkenstein, legal adviser to Department of Regional Industrial Expansion, 22 Feb. 1985; Anderson report, p. 51.
71. CCI chronology, p. 20.
72. J. Chevreau, "Ottawa's computer loser is on the block," *Globe and Mail*, 13 July 1981.
73. Ibid.
74. CCI chronology, p. 20.
75. CCI Divestiture Team, "Report to the Hon. Herb Gray, Minister of ITC, and the Hon. Donald Johnston, President of the Treasury Board," 16 Nov. 1981.
76. Anderson report, p. 47.
77. CCI Divestiture Team report, pp. 4–10.
78. Ibid., 11–29.
79. "Ottawa lost $91 million helping computer-maker," *Vancouver Sun*, 27 Nov. 1981.
80. Anderson report, p. 29.
81. James Rusk, "Report indicts Government over $125 million loss," *Globe and Mail*, 20 Feb. 1982.
82. Eleanor Boyle, "High hopes for high-tech firm go sour," *Toronto Star*, 6 Dec. 1981; Joan Cohen, "Ottawa's secret computer flop," *Winnipeg Free Press*, 17 Dec. 1981; Fred Lebolt, "The inside story of a $100-million high-tech failure," *Toronto Star*, 19 Sept. 1982.
83. Fred Lebolt, "Consolidated Computer probe rejected," *Toronto Star*, 7 July 1982.
84. "Consolidated Computer is kept alive," *Globe and Mail*, 13 March 1984.
85. Telephone interview with J. Groenwald, chief financial officer, Computer Innovations, 9 Jan. 1986.
86. Alan Story, "Hard times hit tiny Glace Bay," *Toronto Star*, 11 March 1985.
87. The classic treatment of the nature and implications of the multidivisional organizational form is Oliver Williamson, *Markets and Hierarchies: Analysis and Implications* (New York, 1975).

CHAPTER 5

1. Sandford Borins, "Public Management in Japan: Are There Lessons To Be Learned?", *Canadian Public Administration*, summer 1986.

2. For a thorough discussion of MITI's organizational history and role in Japanese economic management, see Chalmers Johnson, *MITI and the Japanese Miracle* (Berkeley, 1982).
3. J.R. D'Cruz and J.D. Fleck, *Canada Can Compete!* (Montreal, 1985), pp. 101–102.
4. Dean Walker, "Peter Munk plots a comeback (in Canada)," *Executive*, December 1978, p. 62.
5. House of Commons, Bill C-24, *An Act to Amend the Financial Administration Act in relation to Crown corporations and to amend other Acts in consequence thereof*, 28 June 1984, section 99.
6. PAC *Minutes*, 17 Nov. 1983, p. 93:8; Anderson report, p. 53.
7. Bill C-24, section 151.
8. D.R. Lessard, C.Y. Baldwin, S.P. Mason, "A methodology for evaluating financial incentives to create unemployment." Technical study #20 prepared for the Task Force on Labour Market Development (Ottawa, 1981), pp. 82–84.
9. Commission of Inquiry into the Pas Forestry and Industrial Complex, *Report*, vol. 5 (Winnipeg, 1974), pp. 1973–2001.
10. Anderson report, p. 53.
11. PAC *Minutes*, 17 Nov. 1983, p. 93:8.
12. Bill C-24, section 141.
13. Bill C-24, sections 129, 130, 131, 132, 134, and 138.

INDEX